CAPTAIN MIDNIGHT'S
Post-War Radio Years

Radio's
High-Tech
Adventure
Thrills!

by Leonard Zane

Captain Midnight's Post-War Radio Years
© 2012 Leonard Zane. All Rights Reserved.

No part of this book may be reproduced in any form or by any means, electronic, mechanical, digital, photocopying or recording, except for the inclusion in a review, without permission in writing from the publisher.

Published in the USA by:
BearManor Media
PO Box 1129
Duncan, Oklahoma 73534-1129
www.bearmanormedia.com

ISBN 978-1-59393-217-6

Printed in the United States of America.
Book design by Brian Pearce | Red Jacket Press.

To the memory of Jim Harmon

Acknowledgments

I am deeply grateful to Stephen A. Kallis, Jr. for his remarkable foresight and efforts in recovering the history of radio's Captain Midnight. His dedication and diligence in the 1970s gained access to The Wander Company's Ovaltine-sponsored program scripts. At the Ovaltine Foods facility in Villa Park, Illinois, Mr. Kallis made extensive audio recordings of daily script summaries and outlines. This effort kept the 1940–1949 history of Captain Midnight radio stories from vanishing into undeserved oblivion. Steve published the definitive history of Captain Midnight's radio years during World War II. Following that 2000 book, *Radio's Captain Midnight — The Wartime Biography*, he has since been gracious enough to allow me to transcribe his recorded notes for Captain Midnight's post-WWII radio shows, and those notes became the basis for the present book on the post-war adventures.

It's also been most fortunate and gratifying to receive editing assistance from author and Old Time Radio enthusiast Barbara Harmon, the widow of the late and legendary Jim Harmon.

Table of Contents

ACKNOWLEDGMENTS 5

PREFACE 11

1. **RAY OF REVENGE** 19

2. **DISAPPEARING SHIPS** 39

3. **DEADLY BIOLOGICAL WEAPON** 47

4. **PACIFIC CITY PERIL** 65

5. **THE HOLIDAY BEACH WEAPON** 73

6. **THE SLAVE SMUGGLERS** 85

7. **DEATH DEALS A DIAMOND** 103

8. **THE DEVIL'S SECRET** 115

9. **THE SNOW-WHITE PANTHER** 133

10. **FASTER THAN SOUND** 147

11. **THE JEWELS OF THE QUEEN OF SHEBA** 163

12. **PIRACY ON THE HIGH SEAS** 195

13. **THE SKY RUSTLER** 205

14. **DEATH HAS FOUR FACES** 213

15. **THE RETURN OF IVAN SHARK** 231

16. **THE DEVIL ON ICE** 257

17. **THE RETURN OF CAPTAIN MIDNIGHT** 283

APPENDIX 1:
ROBERT M. BURTT AND JIM HARMON 289

APPENDIX 2:
1946-1949 CODE-O-GRAPH DETAILS 295

APPENDIX 3:
CAPTAIN MIDNIGHT'S POCKET LOCATORS 305

APPENDIX 4:
SURVIVING POST-WAR RECORDINGS 313

APPENDIX 5:
"THE LAND THAT TIME FORGOT" 315

INDEX 321

Preface

ORIGINAL AUTHORS
OF RADIO'S CAPTAIN MIDNIGHT

The Captain Midnight radio series was created by Robert Morris ("Bob") Burtt and Wilfred Gibbs ("Bill") Moore, who were both retired WWI military pilots. Burtt had been a second lieutenant, and Moore a captain and former commander of the famous British Flying Corps 29th Squadron.

Wilfred Moore had collaborated with Robert Burtt on authoring the Captain Midnight radio episodes from 1938 until Moore's untimely death, on 14 July 1939, at the age of 43. Moore never co-wrote any Ovaltine-sponsored Captain Midnight programs during that show's run from 1940-1949. The Ovaltine radio scripts were solely the work of Robert Burtt. But there are serious questions on whether even he wrote the March through December 1949 radio programs, particularly the half-hour shows that were broadcast from 20 September to 15 December in the final year of 1949.

Robert M. Burtt did author at least 1,750 Captain Midnight radio episodes in the 1940s — plus all the Sky King radio episodes that ran from 1946-1954! Throughout the 1940s, Burtt's writing averaged nearly a million words per year.[1] Even other very industrious and prominent authors — such as The Lone Ranger's Fran Striker and The Shadow pulp magazine's Walter B. Gibson (under the pseudonym Maxwell Grant) — were no more prolific than that. Burtt's exciting radio work greatly inspired young and adult listeners alike: some twenty million radio listeners, and in about equal proportions, according to the late Ovaltine-Wander Company's marketing executive Lyle G. Bergmann.[2] One of Robert Burtt's own memories recalls the thrilling inspiration he created, and also some backlash:

> On the rare days when I've written a few sentences that please me, I like to think of the boy who gazed at me in awe and stammered, "Gee, you write Captain Midnight. You're my favorite author."
>
> However, there's the painful side to this memory for I can't forget the words of his mother a few moments later. "So you write the trash he'd rather listen to than eat," she said, eyeing me sternly. "Why, it makes him so excited he can't go to sleep. In my opinion you're just a miserable hack."
>
> Robert M. Burtt

The author of the present book is one of those highly enthusiastic kids, and is most grateful to Robert M. Burtt for how much he helped youths of the 1940s build greater moral fiber, courage, and love of adventure!

BACKGROUND INFORMATION ON RADIO'S CAPTAIN MIDNIGHT

Readers are referred to Stephen A. Kallis, Jr.'s book, *Radio's Captain Midnight — The Wartime Biography* ("RCMWB") for background information and WWII adventures of radio's Captain Midnight. The present book's author is deeply indebted to Mr. Kallis's work and great dedication in discovering and publishing the definitive work on radio's Captain Midnight from 1940-1945. Mr. Kallis is also a leading expert on Captain Midnight's "Code-O-Graph" ciphering devices. Because of this, Code-O-Graph explanations in the present book are largely taken from his writings, and with his permission, and a number of his Captain Midnight manual and aircraft photographs are also reproduced.

The present book picks up in late 1945 where the Kallis book left off. It continues utilizing aforementioned audio-recorded notes of the Captain Midnight radio adventures, which have been transcribed by the present writer. Other information comes from eleven post-war Ovaltine audio recordings that survive,[3] coupled with additional studies and surmises to supplement the source material.

OVALTINE-SPONSORED CAPTAIN MIDNIGHT STORY CHARACTERISTICS

There are some clear story-line characteristics in the Ovaltine-sponsored Captain Midnight radio series. Stephen Kallis' *RCMWB* summarizes the wartime exploits, portraying espionage and counter-espionage adventures that sometimes contained cutting-edge or quite plausible technologies during the 1940 to 1945 period. In the post-war years, radio's Captain Midnight incorporated much more science fiction and speculative fantasy — plus a bit more humor! So from the latter part of 1945 through 1949, the story patterns came to share more in common

Captain Midnight's Secret Squadron. PHOTOGRAPHS: STEPHEN A. KALLIS, JR.

with the fantasies of Edgar Rice Burroughs, and also those of Lester Dent's imaginative Doc Savage pulp magazine tales.

The 1945-1949 post-war Captain Midnight adventures include such bold things as intercontinental death-ray weaponry, prehistoric saurians, cavemen, and a mysterious gem that glows green during only one week out of the year — and only at a certain place in Africa — for nearly three millennia. Even these creations, however, sprang from research and certain plausible concepts in Robert Burtt's imagination.

CANONIC POST-WWII CAPTAIN MIDNIGHT BROADCASTS

The post-war Captain Midnight radio broadcasts averaged three serial stories per year, with each story-thread spanning about thirteen weeks. That's an average of 13 weeks times 5 days per week, times 3, which equals

195 serial episodes per year. There were no Captain Midnight broadcasts during thirteen summer weeks.

Unlike the consistently high standards of Ovaltine's WWII Captain Midnight broadcasts, the post-war radio programs manifested some serious quality variations. This was especially true near the end of the series in 1949, when the story caliber sharply deteriorated, and the serial episodes even started using organ music.

In September 1949, the radio show's format changed even more radically. It went from five-day-per-week serials (of mostly thirteen weeks for each story) to standalone, half-hour broadcasts twice a week that were greatly inferior to the better serials. The degraded quality of later serials and the standalones led Captain Midnight radio experts to establish three criteria to qualify broadcasts for admission into the legitimate Captain Midnight radio "canon." The criteria, essential for the canon, are:

(1) Ovaltine-sponsored, 15-minute serial format.
(2) Grand-scale adventures of international or national impact.
(3) Fully realistic technical effects. No organ or other background music.

"The Devil on Ice" serial, which ran from 14 January through 28 February 1949, is considered the last canonic Captain Midnight radio adventure. Later 1949 broadcasts are disqualified from the canon by authoritative Captain Midnight radio enthusiasts. Such later programs include: "The Shadow of the Black Opal" (a March-April serial about an opal mine); "The Phantom Rustlers" (an April-May serial about cattle rustling, using planes as abducting vehicles); "The Yellow Spider" (a May-June serial about young auto thieves); "The Flying Ruby" (a September, half-hour standalone show about a ruby theft using a model airplane); and all the other 1949 half-hour programs. While mentioning but not summarizing those stories, this history considers them less than authentic and reliable representations of the main characters and of Ovaltine's Captain Midnight radio saga.

DEDUCTIONS, SURMISES, SPECULATIONS, AND GUESSES!

The present book includes deductions and surmises of possible factual bases underlying various science-fiction and fantasy aspects of the post-war radio serials. Moreover, because the recorded notes of daily script summaries and general script outlining could not be exhaustive, numerous elements in this book are deduced, speculated, and even guessed at to fill in continuity within the story threads. While the notes contained key story points and activities, some speculative "dot-connecting" nonetheless had to be incorporated for smooth flow of actions.

In the final analysis, only the complete Captain Midnight radio scripts and broadcasts could tell the entire enormous saga. But even then, the radio broadcasts sometimes deviated from record-copy scripts, and so interpretation would still be required to determine the more valid source — if either. This is because even script and/or broadcast content was sometimes contradictory, or had to be obscured or misrepresented due to security, legal, available time, budget, and other reasons.

CAPTAIN MIDNIGHT'S IDENTITY

On 7 October 2007, Stephen A. Kallis, Jr. posted an Amazon.com review of the book *Illustrated Radio Premium Catalog and Price Guide*. This book was written by Tom Tumbusch and published in 1989. Kallis's review described it as "a superior reference work," and went on to say: "Tom Tumbusch has been a scholar of radio and cereal premiums for at least 30 years. He has published a number of *Tomart's Guides*, the latest being in 1991."

On page 33 of his 1989 book, Tom Tumbusch said: "Since readers of this book are privileged to know old radio's top secrets the true identity of Captain Midnight can be revealed. His name was Stuart 'Red' Albright." ('Red' was a nickname given Captain Albright in the Skelly Oil Company's sponsoring of the Captain Midnight radio program, from 1938-1940, and dropped by the 1940–1949 Ovaltine-sponsored programs.) Leonard Zane emailed Tom Tumbusch about his sources of the first name, "Stuart." On 8 October 2007, Mr. Tumbusch emailed back: "I wrote that Captain Midnight passage back in 1976 and had at least two references for whatever I included in the book. I used mainly old radio magazines for my research…I also used premium ads from the newspaper comic sections…I still have all my reference materials…"

Since October 2007, Stephen A. Kallis, Jr. accepted Tumbusch's findings; and Kallis's short story "The Case of the Disappearing Designer" begins with the words: "Stuart James ('Jim') Albright, who, under the code name, Captain Midnight, was the leader of the Secret Squadron." "Jim" appeared in the Captain Midnight television series that ran from 9 September 1954 to 21 January 1956. In 1958, the TV series was syndicated as "Jet Jackson, Flying Commando," after Ovaltine ceased its sponsorship.

Pages 8-19 of *RCMWB* contain speculations and fictionalizing about Captain Midnight's background. Some background in *RCMWB*'s "Genesis" chapter is patterned after Robert M. Burtt's WWI experiences; and in "The Hidden Years" chapter, some is purely made up about the inner circles of Captain Midnight and Ivan Shark. The true facts do remain "hidden;" that is, unknown, if ever imparted by the radio scripts and broadcasts. Historical basis simply does not exist. The present book acknowledges fictional musings, but confines speculations more to "dot connecting," where source notes are clearly incomplete or problematical, as explained above in "the final analysis."

Jim Harmon. PHOTOGRAPH: LEONARD ZANE

JIM HARMON

Finally, this book probably never would have happened had it not been for inspiration throughout the years by author and Old Time Radio expert, Jim Harmon. Ever since the 1970s, Jim had encouraged me to help rekindle the memory and thrill of radio's Captain Midnight and to keep that spirit alive.

So climb aboard now and hold on for high-tech adventure!

Leonard Zane
Sierra Madre, California

ENDNOTES

1 Burtt, Robert M. "28 Exciting Years," *Writers' Digest*, November 1961, pp. 1 and 3. See also Appendix 1 for background information on Robert M. Burtt.

2 SS-11, Agent William Kelly, was re-christened Lyle William Kelly by author Stephen A. Kallis, Jr. This was in honor of Lyle G. Bergmann, who graciously provided author Kallis with extensive access to Ovaltine's huge trove of Captain Midnight radio scripts in the 1970s. That generous access enabled Mr. Kallis to tape-record detailed notes of the daily Captain Midnight radio program summaries for posterity.

3 See Appendix 4 for a list of these programs.

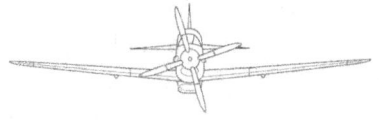

1

Ray of Revenge

(LATE 1945 TO EARLY 1946)

WORLD WAR II AFTERMATH

Upon defeat of the WWII Axis powers, Captain Stuart James Albright and his "Secret Squadron" paramilitary aviation group concluded their service as primarily an espionage and combat organization. But the Secret Squadron continued with its counterespionage and U.S. national security operations following the war.

In late 1945: Major Barry Steele retains his commission as a U.S. Army Air Corps officer, heading a military intelligence office that directs Captain Midnight's Secret Squadron. Captain Midnight reports to Major Steele, and commands all active and inactive Secret Squadron agents. Each active agent is a pilot who is assigned an "SS" number, which stands for "Secret Squadron" plus the numeric sequence. Inactive agents are in the Squadron's General Reserve and are not required to be pilots. They include the many listeners of the radio program, who joined the Secret Squadron by sending in Ovaltine labels in return for "Code-O-Graph" cipher badges[1] and associated Secret Squadron Manuals. The most prominent, *active* Secret Squadron agents are:

- SS-1 Captain Midnight (decorated WWI aviator and Secret Squadron leader).
- SS-2 Chuck Ramsay (an older teenager by the end of the WWII).
- SS-3 Joyce Ryan (an older teenager by the end of WWII).
- SS-4 Ichabod ("Ikky") Mudd (Chief Mechanic and a master technician).
- SS-11 Lyle William Kelly (a Secret Squadron Headquarters agent).

NAZI SECRET WEAPON

The end of World War II in August 1945 finds the Secret Squadron in action with scant respite. This is because British Intelligence informs Captain Midnight of the escape from Germany of a brilliant and infamous Nazi scientist. The fugitive is an applied physicist, Dr. Glaser, who has been developing a secret weapon far more destructive than the atomic bomb. Captain Midnight is also astounded when Colonel Fuchs of British Intelligence announces they believe Glaser has gone to the United States with Captain Midnight's greatest enemy over the years. That enemy is none other than the world's most dangerous master criminal, known only by his *nom de guerre* of "Ivan Shark."

As with "The Barracuda," gang-leader during WWII, neither Shark's true name nor background is known — only that Secret Squadron Manuals picture him as apparently of Eurasian descent, and that he seems either widowed or divorced. Most likely he is widowed — perhaps even at childbirth — because he and his daughter, "Fury," are never heard referring to her mother. Ivan Shark is an evil genius: enormously intelligent, highly educated, scientific, cosmopolitan, a master aviator, multilingual, energetic, charismatic, and a ruthless leader with designs for world dominion. Shark's three chief lieutenants are also expert aviators, and are identified by code names as well.

> FURY SHARK: Ivan's daughter (last seen at about age twenty, extremely bright and courageous — like Fu Manchu's daughter of the 1930s). Fury is believed deceased, having been missing in action since an American submarine's battle with Ivan Shark's U-boat in 1941.
>
> GARDO: A tough and devoted, but dimwitted agent, and consort of Fury's.
>
> FANG: A quiet, clever Chinese man who strangely vanished after WWII.

BLACK GULCH

Captain Midnight's Secret Squadron group soon learns that Colonel Fuchs's advisement is correct, and the Squadron agents succeed in tracing Ivan Shark and his band to Black Gulch, California. There, they learn the international criminal has a hideout carved in a mountainside near the Stanislaus River.

Captain Midnight and his companions (young Chuck Ramsay and Joyce Ryan, plus Chief Mechanic Ichabod "Ikky" Mudd) join forces with Sheriff Ballard and his deputies. Chuck Ramsay has uncovered evidence on where Shark's hideout might be concealed, and the pursuing parties drive two automobiles into the suspected mountainous area. They park their cars on the main road and warily make their way on foot. Suddenly, a camouflaged blind opens in a mountain slope ahead, and a hidden machinegun blasts at the Secret Squadron's and Sheriff's

Lockheed P-80 Shooting Star — First flown 8 January 1944, and introduced in 1945. PHOTOGRAPH: NACA, WITH SECRET SQUADRON INSIGNIA BY LEONARD ZANE

cars — cutting off retreat to the main road. Ivan Shark's men quickly surround the group of investigators. But Captain Midnight also acts swiftly. Via his "Pocket Locator" (a two-way, pocket-size dot-dash radio that uses flashing-light signals[2]), he orders Squadron Agent SS-11 (Lyle William Kelly) to lead a force of Secret Squadron jet fighters to Ivan Shark's hideout.

The pinned-down Squadron agents and Sheriff's officers manage to hold off Shark's men for only a short while. But it's long enough for three of Kelly's P-80 Squadron jets to arrive, diving from the skies to drive off the Shark group with strafing attacks. During the melee, a startling action surprises the investigators. Huge camouflaging drapes suddenly sweep apart in the mountainside, revealing a tunnel and aircraft catapult inside the cavernous base. Ivan Shark himself, plus his chief henchman Gardo and Dr. Glaser, burst out in a very fast "rocket plane."[3] Moments after

Shark's craft makes its swift escape, a mighty explosion devastates the cavern hideout, timed by Shark to obliterate his lair.

Upon investigating the rubble from Ivan Shark's destroyed base, the Secret Squadron does at least discover a small, battered steel case. At noon, in the workshop at the Black Gulch Airport, Ichabod Mudd cuts the case open. It holds a detailed map of the Patagonia region in South America, spreading from parts of Argentina to Chile along the South Pacific Coast.

While Ikky, Chuck, and Joyce study the map, Captain Midnight receives an enciphered message on his Pocket Locator. It's from Major Barry Steele at the Secret Squadron base in Grant City, Illinois (near Chicago). The message reports a high and mysterious vapor trail spotted by Navy aircraft carrier pilots in the South Pacific. The trail had appeared west of the Galapagos Islands, not far from Patagonia.

PATAGONIA

Ivan Shark's "rocket plane" reaches Patagonia, and Dr. Glaser resumes working on the secret weapon he began in Germany before WWII ended. His weapon is an extremely powerful disintegration-ray apparatus.

Captain Midnight receives permission from Major Steele to take his Secret Squadron agents to Patagonia, so as to track down the Shark organization and their collaborator, Dr. Glaser.

Midnight, Joyce Ryan, Chuck Ramsay, and Ikky fly to Patagonia in an amphibian. Just before they land, one of Ivan Shark's locally recruited spies (agent Y-64) sends a coded message to Shark, warning of Captain Midnight's arrival.

Secret Squadron Agent, Harry Sykes (SS-38), has been based in Argentina for some time. By a coded Pocket Locator message, he warns Midnight that information may have leaked about the Squadron's mission there. Captain Midnight and his group therefore take on assumed identities. Midnight pretends to be an American businessman, Andrew H. Preston, accompanied by his brother and his brother's son and daughter on a business and vacation trip. Ivan Shark is also masquerading as one Señor Bascombe, a local rancher; and he incites the airport manager's suspicions of the American businessman, Andrew Preston.

Midnight, Joyce, and Ikky go to a restaurant for lunch, and are tricked into entering a private dining room, where they are locked in behind heavy doors. Midnight immediately sends a Locator message to Harry Sykes for help. Just moments later, a trap door opens from under a throw-rug in the floor, and the smiling face of Harry Sykes appears. Sykes had suspected possible foul play at the restaurant, and had descended a stairway to the cellar below the dining room to reconnoiter.

Sykes quickly ushers his comrades into the cellar, and Ikky secures the trap door. The group heads for the stairway to exit the building, but then running footfalls sound along the passageway above. Concluding their disappearance from the dining room has been discovered, Midnight immediately leads his Squadron agents back up through the trap door into the dining room. Now finding the doors to the room open, they hastily escape from the restaurant.

Before long, Midnight determines Señor Bascombe is Ivan Shark, and Shark also discovers Andrew Preston is Captain Midnight. Midnight escapes Shark's men, and he and Ikky hurry to the airport to try to take off quickly. But Ivan Shark has managed to deceive the commissioner of police, Colonel Garcia, about the suspicious and potentially dangerous "Preston" party. So the Colonel meets Midnight and Mudd when they arrive at the airport. Upon inspecting Captain Midnight's amphibian, Colonel Garcia discovers machineguns and radar instruments, and so arrests "Andrew Preston" and his supposed brother (Ikky).

Shark is afraid that Colonel Garcia will release Midnight and Mudd from jail, so he hatches a plot against them. He, Gardo and Y-64 will enter the jail, feigning a visit. They will kill Captain Midnight and Mudd, in pretended self-defense against a claimed escape attempt. However, a coded Secret Squadron message is sent into the jail, promising that the agent who sent it will enter the jail sometime during the night.

In warder's uniforms, Chuck Ramsay and Harry Sykes help Captain Midnight and Ichabod Mudd battle Ivan Shark and his men. Joyce Ryan occupies the police during the struggle in the back jail recesses; and after a fierce fight, Shark and his two henchmen lie unconscious on the floor of the cell. The Squadron members bind and gag Shark, lock Gardo and Y-64 in the cell, and steal out of the jail carrying the unconscious Shark.

Commandeering Shark's car, Joyce and the Secret Squadron agents head for the airfield with their infamous prisoner. But Gardo and Y-64 soon gain release from the cell and organize pursuit. When the Secret Squadron group reaches the airfield, Captain Midnight directs Chuck and Mudd to carry the still bound, gagged, and helpless Ivan Shark into the shadows of some shrubbery near the hangar. Shark will thus be out of their way in a coming move to regain possession of their plane.

Captain Midnight sends SS-38 (Sykes) to inspect the hangar. Sykes runs back to announce that police officers guarding the hangar had apparently heard them drive up — and one of them is walking toward the hangar's rear door to investigate.

A struggle ensues between the Squadron members and the police — and then escalates when Gardo, Y-64 and the other Shark agents enter the fray. The Secret Squadron group barely manages to get into the amphibian — except for Harry Sykes, who rushes back to Ivan Shark's car. The Squadron amphibian hurriedly takes off and escapes — and so does Harry Sykes in Shark's car — leaving behind the international criminal and his band.

FLEEING PATAGONIA

Although his Patagonian operation has been discovered, mastermind Ivan Shark savors his next moves. While Secret Squadron reinforcements can soon be expected, he has secured an additional scientist to join in completing the powerful death ray mechanism, and he will relocate to a new base. The added scientist is another Nazi named Manfred Mueller. He knows that a second ray device is also needed to triangulate on a target in combination with Dr. Glaser's energy weapon, and he brings with him his own uncompleted device. Together, the twin ray weapons will form an immensely powerful disintegration ray apparatus that will span great distances.

TWIN RAY TRANSMITTERS

Dr. Glaser's and Manfred Mueller's twin disintegration ray transmitters are based on particle beam (directed energy) technology.[4]

SS-11 (Agent Kelly) flies a Secret Squadron P-80 fighter to rendezvous with Captain Midnight's amphibian at an airport in San Luis, Argentina. Kelly brings information about Manfred Mueller and his ray technology[5] that was obtained from European Squadron agents on Mueller's trail.

It is night, and while the two aircraft refuel, Captain Midnight gets a radio message from Harry Sykes, reporting that Ivan Shark and his gang are departing Patagonia in a big jet-transport plane. Sykes describes the large jet, which is headed east. Sykes is following at much slower speed in a small, sparsely equipped piston-engine plane, and he has lost sight of the big jet. Captain Midnight hurries to Kelly's P-80 and climbs aboard — directing Chuck, Joyce, and Ikky to track him by radar from the amphibian — while he will try to locate and intercept Shark's plane.

Precious time is lost as Captain Midnight scouts the night skies in vain for Ivan Shark's jet transport. During this frustrating search, the Squadron amphibian is at least able to rendezvous with Harry Sykes, and pick him up at a brief touchdown in central Argentina.

Continuing his search in the night gloom, Captain Midnight's radar finally detects a high-speed craft ahead and below. He descends and finally spots a large jet aircraft that fits Sykes's description. But Midnight's fuel is running low. He has no choice but to give up the chase and find the nearest airport. He reports the sighting to the Squadron amphibian behind him, and that the jet transport appears headed for the Argentine East Coast.

The jet transport is indeed Ivan Shark's plane, and its huge cargo bay carries Shark's "rocket plane" and the two uncompleted ray weapons. But the master criminal has noted that the chasing and then departing jet looked like a Secret Squadron craft. So he announces a cunning new plan to his agents aboard the transport.

Captain Midnight lands his fighter at an airport in eastern Argentina and refuels. The amphibian follows, and as soon as Midnight is able, he resumes flying toward Buenos Aires in the deepening night. But this time he does not detect the jet transport, and loses more time in the futile search.

As dawn breaks near the Buenos Aires Airport, the Secret Squadron commander spots an amphibian flying from the skies above the airport and out over the Atlantic. By its configuration of turret and tail guns, he recognizes the plane as one of Shark's fleet. Maybe Shark has switched planes!

Midnight chases the amphibian toward the rising sun, but he has no way of knowing that Shark and most of his gang are not aboard this craft. Instead, the amphibian is piloted by one of Dr. Glaser's German confederates, a mercenary who transports Dr. Glaser along with his partly built disintegrator weapon and one other crewman.

Captain Midnight's jet fighter — clearly marked with the Secret Squadron's winged-clock insignia — rapidly closes on the amphibian. The amphibian opens fire on Midnight's plane, with Dr. Glaser shooting from the multiple-gun turret and another agent shooting the tail gun. Midnight maneuvers, fires his machineguns, and knocks out one of the amphibian's engines. But not without cost. Glaser's turret guns score severe hits, striking Midnight's engine and tearing off part of the right wing. Now in mortal danger, Captain Midnight loops around in a last head-on pass. He fires heavily on the amphibian, crippling its remaining engine, and smashing the gun turret to bits. Dr. Glaser is killed instantly, and the damaged plane is forced down to the water.

Captain Midnight hastily radios the Secret Squadron amphibian, giving the location of Shark's craft and asking for its seizure by the

Gardo, Fury Shark, Fang, Ivan Shark. PHOTOGRAPH: STEPHEN A. KALLIS, JR.

Argentine Coast Guard. Then Midnight's engine fails, and the jet plummets toward the sea!

The disabled Shark amphibian lands on the ocean roughly, and its German pilot radios a message describing the battle and shooting down of the Secret Squadron jet.

The Secret Squadron amphibian flies beyond the Argentine coast — and soon spots an open parachute on the water. The craft lands and the Squadron agents rescue Captain Midnight. Then they power the amphibian on the water for about a mile to Shark's downed plane. The haggard German pilot and remaining crewman note the Squadron plane's armament. They see Joyce piloting — and Ikky, Chuck, and Harry wielding machineguns. Shark's two men raise their hands in surrender.

Chuck and Ikky board Shark's amphibian. They find Dr. Glaser's bullet-riddled body, and bear his uncompleted death ray weapon back to their own craft. Captain Midnight does not reveal his presence on board the Squadron amphibian, and the Argentine Coast Guard shortly arrives.

Once again, however, Ivan Shark's cleverness has served him well. After concluding he had been followed by a Secret Squadron jet, he had decided to divide his risk and maximize odds of escape. He had only touched down at an airport outside of Buenos Aires. This was simply to let off Dr. Glaser and his partially completed ray weapon, along with the German mercenary pilot and other gang member. He had ordered them to proceed quickly to the Buenos Aires Airport by truck, and then to take off in one of his amphibians from there. After the drop-off, he had continued with Manfred Mueller — taking the "rocket plane," the second ray weapon, and most of his crew to Montevideo, Uruguay. So while the Secret Squadron was busily tracking and battling his amphibian, Shark had landed at Montevideo, refueled and proceeded eastward across the Atlantic.

On his way beyond the South American continent, Shark picks up civilian radio news that Captain Midnight has crashed his jet plane into the ocean! Shark laughs maniacally that the plane was piloted by Captain Midnight himself! Oh, if only he could have been there to witness the end of Captain Midnight!

The Argentine Coast Guard arrests Shark's two agents and removes Dr. Glaser's body. The Coast Guard impounds the damaged amphibian, and extracts a confession from the German mercenary pilot about his destination. Ivan Shark had ordered the German to fly to Cape Town, South Africa for refueling; then to Somalia; and finally to a province in Northern India, not far from the Nepalese border, called Marchula. Shark's agents would then be in contact there.

The Argentine officials agree to keep Captain Midnight's survival a secret, and Midnight's amphibian refuels and heads for Africa.

MARCHULA

By the first of February, Ivan Shark and his organization are relocated in India's Marchula province, which extends below the Zanskar Mountain Range. The imposing peaks rise to an average altitude of nearly 20,000 feet. Shark and his gang establish themselves at a base in "The Valley of the Shadows," which nestles between mountains outside Marchula's sprawling capital city of Tanz. At this hidden base, situated at 34 degrees north latitude, Manfred Mueller continues working on the long-distance disintegration ray apparatus. It requires two separate devices, as well as atomic power to produce and transmit its enormous energy. And since Mueller does not know whether or not the Secret Squadron has captured the second device, he will have to construct another ray transmitter.

Captain Midnight and his companions pursue the arch-criminal Ivan Shark to the Orient, in an effort to capture him before he can use his deadly disintegration ray. The Secret Squadron picks up Shark's trail to the city of Tanz and its outskirts. It is dusk, near the great palace of the Shah Tanz, when Joyce suddenly spots Shark's chief henchman, Gardo, making his way not far from the palace.

Captain Midnight, Joyce, Chuck, Ikky, and Harry follow Gardo to a crude and vacant hut. Upon later entering, they discover the hut is merely a blind concealing a subterranean passageway. One of Ivan Shark's agents, "The Knife," notes Gardo's carelessness about staying unseen when entering the hut — because its passage leads directly to Shark's hideout. He informs his chief. In a rage, Shark orders The Knife to eliminate Gardo. The Knife pushes Gardo into a quicksand basin that borders the tunnel's exit, and leaves him there to die. Unaware of the quicksand, Captain Midnight and his Squadron agents make their way toward the place, but then see Gardo flailing and sinking into the death trap.

The Squadron members stay safely on solid ground and rescue Gardo. Capitalizing on the henchman's now grudging feelings against his boss, they get Gardo to reveal how to gain admittance into the arch-criminal's private office. Soon after and with guns drawn, they burst into the office and surprise Shark and the Nazi scientist Manfred Mueller. But Shark, although shocked at seeing the enemy he thought dead, refuses to admit defeat. He declares that he possesses a treacherous means to carry the Secret Squadron agents to death with him.

At this point, The Knife appears with more of Shark's men. In the fray that follows, Ivan Shark and his gang escape — together with Mueller and his ray weapon.

When the Secret Squadron agents pursue the Shark band, they soon find themselves in what is known as the "Pit of the Reptiles." It's a gaping rocky cavity, filled with thousands of deadly snakes, and Shark has activated a moving rock wall that will soon push them into the pit. Desperately searching for some way of crossing to the other side, the Squadron agents spot a rotten old rope hanging from a rusty metal rung above.

Shark tries to abandon his Tanz base, in favor of becoming master of the entire Marchula province. Midnight and his companions manage to use the perilous rope to traverse the pit, but Shark has set up an ambush on the other side. Shark has made good his own escape, and does not want to face Captain Midnight in a gunfight, so he has booby-trapped a cable-car railway trestle with explosives. The explosion blasts the trestle into the river below.

The river sweeps the fallen cable car into a subterranean channel and chasm, with the Squadron agents in the car. The Squadron members swim underwater, one by one, in the slim hope that when they are forced to come to the surface, the cavern's roof will rise again to provide some air-space.

NEW RULER

While the Secret Squadron struggles with its predicament, Ivan Shark assassinates the ruler of the Marchula province and establishes himself as the new ruler. The Nazi scientist Mueller resumes work on his deadly disintegrating ray.

The Secret Squadron agents swim in the subterranean channel, and into the huge hollow base of a massive stone idol within the great temple of Marchula. They decide to operate from within this sheltering idol, while Ikky searches for another escape route through the underground cavern and river channel. As Ikky leaves, Captain Midnight decides that Chuck and Harry must steal out of a concealed panel in the idol's base and venture into the city. Midnight and Joyce will also attempt to enlist the aid of Marchula authorities in trying to track down Shark's gang.

Unaware that Ivan Shark has become the masked ruler of Marchula, Captain Midnight seeks out the province leader for help in finding Shark. In doing so, Captain Midnight unwittingly becomes the master criminal's prisoner.

As the Squadron agents continually mistake Shark for the peaceful ruler of the Marchula province, Shark plays cat-and-mouse with them. Shark tends to overplay himself, though — because while pretending to be a friendly ruler, he orders Joyce arrested and imprisoned.

Chuck enters an area where Joyce had been, and hears Shark's sinister laugh, thereby discovering the masked ruler's true identity. But the discovery does Chuck no good, because he is promptly captured. Shark also apprehends the rest of them, except for Ikky, but at least they now know who the ruler is. That no longer matters to the evil mastermind, however, because he has secured the second disintegrator weapon back from the Secret Squadron's amphibian!

Chuck manages to hide his Pocket Locator and 1945 Code-O-Graph within the palace prison. The Squadron agents try to find a means to escape, and they soon succeed; but in doing so, Chuck is forced to leave his Pocket Locator and Code-O-Graph behind.

INTERCONTINENTAL WEAPON TOWERS

Meanwhile, Shark's disintegration weaponry nears completion. An absolute requirement is for Manfred Mueller to situate the disintegration ray apparatus at an altitude sufficiently unimpeded by earth's curvature to shoot the powerful beam directly at the targeted "great American city." The distance to the U.S. West Coast is over 8,000 miles.

Utilizing the Secret Squadron's amphibian, Manfred Mueller first flies to the city of Panka, in nearby Bhutan, taking the recovered disintegrator weapon and some of Shark's gang with him. The tiny country of Bhutan lies on the southern slopes of the eastern Himalayas, bordering Nepal and northeast India. Bhutan's latitudes extend between 26° and 29° north; some of its Himalayan mountain peaks exceed 23,000 feet. As with India's Zanskar Mountains, some 8,000 miles to the east of these Bhutanese mountains lie potential American West Coast targets:

> *San Diego, California at latitude 32° north.*
> *Los Angeles, California at 34° north.*
> *San Francisco, California at 37° north.*
> *Portland, Oregon at 45° north.*
> *Seattle, Washington at 47° north.*

Dr. Glaser's and Manfred Mueller's twin particle-beam weapons are atomic powered, rather than energized only by high-voltage electricity. As such, they extend greatly beyond the 250-mile range Nikola Tesla had described.[6]

Once in Bhutan, Mueller's group ascends to a high mountain plateau overlooking Panka and installs the weapon tower. Manfred Mueller aims the ray weapon at the targeted American West Coast city, and his accomplices build a temporary enclosure around the weapon's emitter near the top of the tower. Mueller leaves a contingency of men to guard the tower, and returns to Marchula to mount the second disintegrator apparatus on a high Zanskar mountain.

After Mueller's return, Ivan Shark leads a party to ascend the Zanskar mountain on horseback, abusing Marchulan bearers and the animals along the way. Shark's destination is a peak overlooking the city of Tanz, where Manfred Mueller and other Marchulans are working with the remaining disintegration ray weapon and tower.

[The enormous 8,000-mile target distance foreshadows technology beyond the disclosed range of even the U.S. Strategic Defense Initiative (SDI). The SDI program began, at least in earnest, in the 1980s. SDI devices consist of satellite-based, nuclear-powered laser and particle (commonly neutron) beam weaponry.[7]]

Manfred Mueller's and the late Dr. Glaser's apparatus consists of atomic-powered disintegrator beam weapons in coordination. San Diego is the most directly aligned target city, at 32° north — and bracketed by the Panka tower at 29° north and the Marchula device at 34° north.

While Shark's party ascends the Zanskar mountain, Captain Midnight and his Secret Squadron agents have escaped from Shark's palace prison in the Valley of the Shadows. Midnight then leads Chuck, Joyce, and Harry to pursue Shark's gang up the mountain.

As the Squadron agents ride ponies halfway up the mountain, Joyce is thrown from her mount and sprains her ankle. They pause and find their way to a cave where they tend to her. Meanwhile, Shark has also sent men to trail Midnight's party from below; and the Nazi scientist above learns the Secret Squadron is coming, too.

Shark's men find the cave where the Squadron agents hide, and with the Squadron members trapped, Shark soon arrives and gases them. But before blacking out, Captain Midnight is able to drop their three Code-O-Graphs and Pocket Locators into a crevice in the cave's floor so Shark cannot find them.

Upon recovering consciousness, Captain Midnight soon retrieves the Pocket Locators and Code-O-Graphs, and secrets them on his person. A Marchula native pleads with Midnight for deliverance of his people from their terrible new ruler, and gives his life so that Captain Midnight can get away and someday try to defeat Shark.

Enraged at Captain Midnight's escape, and distrusting his own men, the master criminal leads some of his band back down the mountain to return Chuck, Joyce, and Harry to the palace prison. Why does Shark bother to do this, rather than simply kill the Squadron agents on the spot? First of all, to lure his most prized prey — Captain Midnight — to try to rescue his comrades. Secondly, he wants the Secret Squadron agents to live long enough to agonize over their crushing defeat, upon his destroying the "great American city." However, the descending trek does delay Shark's disintegration progress, which rather annoys him.

Once again imprisoned in the palace jail, Chuck manages to retrieve his Pocket Locator and Code-O-Graph, and then tries to signal Captain Midnight via his Locator. But The Knife discovers what Chuck is doing and seizes the devices. Shark then lures Captain Midnight by sending a message in Chuck's name, telling Midnight that Chuck, Joyce, and Sykes will be executed in the Marchula Temple courtyard the next day.

On the Zanskar mountain peak above Tanz, Manfred Mueller works on the final stage of the disintegrator weapon. Upon the Zanskar completion, Mueller will coordinate the twin-tower/twin-country weapons, and Ivan Shark will throw the switch to transmit their horrible energies. The deadly rays will streak over the Tibetan Plateau, above China, and across the vast Pacific to destroy the "great American city."

The targeted city will neither know what hit it, nor from where the destruction came. And Ivan Shark gloats in Marchula, India, for he knows that he will continue wreaking immense global devastation. Shark's disintegration ray towers are brilliantly situated for both eastward and westward target obliterations, with no interfering mountains tall enough to block the rays for thousands of miles; and he also plans to install additional ray towers in other key locations. He will pulverize great cities, and go on to pound the *entire world* into submission! There will be no way to stop him in these remote Asian mountains, where he will aim his tower-mounted ray weapons by radio control — and also disintegrate any attackers into oblivion — be they land-based, or aircraft or missiles that he will blast out of the skies! For soon the whole world shall cower and tremble and bend and surrender to the absolute domination of Emperor Ivan Shark! Ivan Shark shall thus rule the globe, and he and his Axis Power servants shall exact their terrible revenge!

1946 CODE-O-GRAPH

Ichabod Mudd has also been busy. Ever since early 1942, Captain Midnight had charged him with designing each new Secret Squadron Code-O-Graph model.[8] Secret Squadron Headquarters has now carried out his engineering of the 1946 model, has built prototypes according to his exact specifications, and has rushed him a parcel by a special courier.

Ikky carries the new 1946 Code-O-Graphs with him, as he struggles to return to the Marchula Temple's hidden chamber by way of the underground river. Captain Midnight's 1946 coding device is the "Mirro-Flash" Code-O-Graph, and the first postwar one. It incorporates a plastic rotor assembly, as did its 1945 predecessor;[9] however, it has a brass (rather than steel) body, as did the early 1940s models.

The 1946 rotor assembly has a red plastic annular scale and a clear plastic knob. But instead of a magnifier, a polished metal mirror is inserted into the knob from behind.

1946 Code-O-Graph and Manual. PHOTOS: LEONARD ZANE, STEPHEN A. KALLIS, JR.

IMMINENT DISASTER

Ikky meets Captain Midnight in the hollow base of the Marchula Temple statue. While he and Midnight are free, what can they do to rescue their comrades? And they'd better do it quickly because Chuck, Joyce, and Harry Sykes are now led out to the Marchula Temple courtyard for execution.

Just as Ivan Shark watches the headsman's ax about to fall, one of the guards (a masquerading Ikky) foments a disturbance that interrupts the proceeding. Captain Midnight emerges unseen from the secret panel at the rear of the statue's base. He stealthily seals the panel, and he and Ikky then disrupt the deadly ritual into chaos. This farce postpones the execution, and Midnight and Ikky escape.

In hopes of locating their condemned comrades, Captain Midnight and Ichabod Mudd steal from the temple area to the nearby Marchula palace. But as they approach the palace, they are stopped by sudden flashes of sunlight in their eyes. They see Chuck, Joyce, and Harry at the window of the topmost floor — and Joyce signaling them with a small locket mirror. Captain Midnight returns the signal with the reducing mirror on his new 1946 Code-O-Graph. But he realizes that if he is to get a coded message to them that could save their lives, he must see to it that they somehow gain possession of a 1946 Code-O-Graph. He abruptly orders Ikky to accompany him back to the Temple idol.

BOKA-YIN'S DECREE

The three captive Secret Squadron agents are to be led to the public square, where this time they will be tied to ponies and dragged through the streets. In a desperate effort to communicate with his imprisoned agents, Captain Midnight attaches a 1946 Code-O-Graph near the tip of an arrow, and shoots the arrow to their cell's window-frame on the top floor. With the new Code-O-Graph now in their hands, Chuck, Joyce, and Harry are able to decode the message Captain Midnight flashes with the 1946 reducing mirror.

Captain Midnight's message says that all sentenced to death have the right to submit their case to the stone idol, Boka-Yin. The condemned Squadron agents soon demand this right, and are led to the Temple. There, to everyone's amazement, the idol speaks up. It pronounces the accused persons innocent, and informs the people their ruler is an impersonator who has killed the real Shah Tanz. The voice, of course, is that of Captain Midnight.

DISINTEGRATION RAY OBLIVION

Ivan Shark manages to escape from the enraged people, and tries to fire the disintegration rays. To stop the rays from going off, Captain Midnight gets into the Secret Squadron's amphibian and flies straight for the Zanskar ray tower! He bails out before the collision — as his plane smashes into the tower and topples it off the mountainside.

Shark and his gang hurriedly get away in their "rocket plane," and try to retrieve the remaining disintegrator weapon by flying to the high Panka plateau. But a snow storm overwhelms the craft's descent to the plateau, and the gang must bail out, as the "rocket plane" soon plows into the plateau and destroys the disintegrating-ray tower in a huge explosion!

With their mission completed, the Secret Squadron members head back to the United States in Shark's big transport plane. Time is short because a new international threat is developing and Major Steele awaits them.

> Captain Midnight's boss…was named Major Steel *[sic]*. He was played by an older actor — a fellow by the name of Jess Pew *[sic; actually Pugh]*, a real old nice guy and good actor.[10]

Left: Artist Erwin L. Hess drew the illustration of Major Steele facing Captain Midnight on Page 19 in the 1941 Better Little Book edition of *Captain Midnight and the Secret Squadron*. Right: Film actor Paul Birch was an excellent Major Barry Steele-type, including his slight Southern drawl, but he never played him. PHOTOGRAPHS: THE WANDER COMPANY; *THE 27TH DAY*. BOTH PHOTOS MODIFIED BY LEONARD ZANE

ENDNOTES

1 See Appendix 2.

2 See Appendix 3.

3 See *Radio's Captain Midnight — the Wartime Biography* ("*RCMWB*") Appendix 5 for what many such 1940s "rocket planes" actually were; namely, combination jet and rocket-engine aircraft, and sometimes employing only Rocket-Assisted Take Off (RATO) boosters as the "rocket" propulsion component.

4 A Wikipedia entry described directed-energy technology this way: "A particle beam weapon uses an ultra-high-energy beam of atoms or electrons (i.e. a particle beam) to damage a material target by hitting it, and thus disrupting its atomic and molecular structure. A particle beam weapon is a type of directed-energy weapon, which directs energy in a particular direction by a means of particle projectiles with mass. Some of these weapons are real or practicable; some are science fiction…

"In 1937, [Nikola] Tesla composed a treatise entitled *The Art of Projecting Concentrated Nondispersive Energy through the Natural Media*. This treatise is currently in the Nikola Tesla Museum archive in Belgrade. It described an open ended vacuum tube with a gas jet seal that allowed particles to exit, a method of charging particles to millions of volts, and a method of creating and directing non-dispersive particle streams (through electrostatic repulsion)."

5 A man named Thomas E. Bearden (whom Wikipedia has described as an inventor with little formal physics training) alleged in 2002 that a CIA report was obtained by a Freedom of Information Act request that described sighting a so-called "Tesla Globe." The purported sighting described a spherical "Tesla Globe" of electromagnetic energy that was used, not to protect an area, but to destroy a missile or other object in mid-flight. A questionable Internet site called rumormillnews.com added that a "Tesla Globe" is formed when two longitudinal wave beams are aimed, using an electromagnetic waveguide, for precise aiming of the so-called "Tesla howitzers" (i.e., "longitudinal wave interferometers").

An Internet site named angelfire.com reported claims made by a UFO enthusiast, named Christi Verismo, who described how a so-called "scalar energy weapon" might work. Verismo claimed two transmitters could send timed electromagnetic energy pulses, which meet, and either explode or extract energy. If two crossed beams are in so-called "continuous" mode, the created "Tesla Globe" or hemisphere can act as a continuous electromagnetic shield. The shield would destroy incoming weapons and aircraft entering it. If multiple beam frequencies are transmitted, then the "bottle" of energy is alleged: (1) to be able to be made any size, depending on the firing energy, (2) to be able to soften or melt metal, (3) to be able to create a so-called "nuclear-like" explosion, and (4) to be movable anywhere, either on the planet or through it. While these claims are extremely dubious, speculative and unsupported by evidence, they suggest similar 1940s speculations based on Nikola Tesla's pronouncements published in 1937, and also in the *New York Times* on 22 September 1940 (see Endnote 6 immediately below).

6 "Nikola Tesla, one of the truly great inventors who celebrated his eighty-fourth birthday on July 10, tells the writer that he stands ready to divulge to the United States government the secret of his 'teleforce,' of which he said, 'airplane motors would be melted at a distance of 250 miles, so that an invisible 'Chinese Wall of Defense' would be built around the country against any enemy attack by an enemy air force, no matter how large.'

"This 'teleforce' is based on an entirely new principle of physics, that 'no one has ever dreamed about,' different from the principles embodied in his inventions relating to the transmission of electrical power from a distance, for which he has received a number of basic patents. This new type of force Mr. Tesla said, would operate through a beam one hundred-millionth of a square centimeter in diameter, and could be generated from special plant that would cost no more than $2,000,000 and would take only about three months to construct." Quoted from "'Death Ray' for Planes," *New York Times*, 22 September 1940.

7   Refer to Wikipedia on the Strategic Defense Initiative.

8   See Kallis' *RCMWB*, *op. cit.*, p. 93.

9   See Appendix 2.

10   Quoted from an interview of actor, Jack Bivans, reported on homestead.com. He played Chuck Ramsay in the 1940s Captain Midnight radio program. Another Website, otrrpedia.net, reported that Jess Pugh was born in 1879, in Andersonville, Indiana. He had a slight drawl when speaking as Major Barry Steele on the Captain Midnight program.

2

Disappearing Ships

(1946)

WEST AFRICAN MENACE

The Secret Squadron agents return to Headquarters. There, Major Steele informs Captain Midnight that three American merchant ships have mysteriously disappeared. The ships were carrying food from New York to Marseilles. Steele suspects it is the work of private individuals, and that their purpose is to steal and sell the cargoes on the black market. Captain Midnight is assigned to investigate, without yet learning the perpetrators are a gang of ruthless outcasts based somewhere along the African West Coast. They are led by a powerful outlaw known only as "Congo."

Congo is already planning his fourth attack, and in New York two of his American agents — a man named Mr. Fabian and a sailor called "Monko" — await his orders. Meanwhile, Captain Midnight conceives a risky scheme by which he hopes to identify the pirates. He and Joyce Ryan board a cargo ship, the *Gray Eagle*, and wait to see if it will be threatened and captured by Congo. Fabian is also aboard the *Gray Eagle*, and although he serves Congo, he and his leader have never met.

When the *Gray Eagle* steams within a few hundred miles of the West African Coast, Congo's forces attack the ship. Fabian is killed, along with about thirty others. Captain Midnight removes the credentials from Fabian's body and masquerades as Fabian. While suspicious, Congo is for a time deceived that this is his agent.

Congo orders the bogus "Fabian" to kill Joyce, together with some other directives that expose Captain Midnight. The Squadron leader, Joyce, and several other people are made to walk the plank; but Captain Midnight manages to get his bonds cut first and frees the others after they plunge into the water. Although Midnight had arranged for a raft, Congo has his men throw oil on the water and set fire to it. Tongues of flame reach the raft, but Secret Squadron amphibian planes arrive, streaking down to rescue Captain Midnight and his companions. Congo, however, escapes to his base somewhere in West Africa.

Captain Midnight, Joyce, Ikky, and Chuck soon reunite and fly together in one of the amphibians. They get some leads on Congo and his marauders, and eventually pursue them by air. But close to the African mainland, Congo's fighter aircraft attack and shoot down the amphibian over a large island. Amid a wide river flowing in the island, Captain Midnight's crippled plane crash-lands on the central of three long islets.

Congo sends cannibal headhunters from the mainland to find and kill any Squadron survivors. A Chief named Zawata leads his savages across the ocean channel to the island, and they beach their canoes on the central river islet. Soon they discover the wrecked amphibian. But the Squadron members use hollow reeds to breathe through, while hiding below the surface of the river. Eventually the agents emerge undiscovered and make their way along the river bank. Joyce spies Zawata and his party moving on a path through clusters of mangrove trees and into dense undergrowth.

MYSTERIOUS ISLET

Captain Midnight suspects Congo's base may be nearby. So he and his companions wait until the tribal chieftain is well out of earshot, and then they trail him into the dense foliage. Upon following the savages nearly to the islet's upper tip, they see Zawata wave a torch toward the third islet upriver. But that islet is an illusion.

It turns out that Congo's base is not a tropical river islet, at all — but a cleverly camouflaged "baby flattop" aircraft carrier! It appears that a carrier-shaped islet in Palau — and the 6 August 1945 launch date of the "baby flattop" aircraft carrier *USS Palau* — were not simply coincidental with the tale of Congo's raiding ship. And the island where Captain Midnight's amphibian crash-landed? It was most likely Bolama, which contains a wide river and is located a few miles off the coast of Portuguese Guinea. Moreover, the nearby Bissau peninsula had also been inhabited by cannibals. *[Once again, author Robert M. Burtt had done his homework and applied his splendid imagination.]*

Just before nightfall, Zawata and his band paddle their canoes across the river to the island bank and head inland. Captain Midnight takes advantage of this opportunity to lead his comrades back to their cracked-up amphibian. From there, he is able to send a gradually failing radio message that identifies the disguised aircraft carrier. He requests bombing the most upriver islet. But Congo finds out about this and casts his

Above: Islet in the shape of an aircraft carrier in *Palau*. *Below: USS Palau*, launched on 6 August 1945 — an Escort-type, or "baby flattop," or "jeep" aircraft carrier. PHOTOGRAPHS: PALAU VISITORS AUTHORITY, NAVSOURCE PHOTO ARCHIVES

carrier adrift to float downriver. So the formerly central islet — with the marooned Squadron agents — is now the uppermost one, and Secret Squadron planes will bomb it heavily at daybreak.

When the attacking Squadron bombers approach within a few miles, the stranded Squadron members are able to use Ikky's Pocket Locator (unassisted by radio-repeater relaying) to communicate with the bombers and call off the assault. In the meantime, however, the disguised aircraft carrier has floated around several bends toward the sea and out of sight.

The Secret Squadron agents build a raft and cross the river to the main island. From there, they work their way downriver to search for the camouflaged carrier ship.

TRAPS AND COUNTER-PLAY

A criminal named "Mr. Smith" sends word to Congo that he will search the entire island and find and kill the Secret Squadron agents for a fee of $5,000. But Congo has another idea. He leads one of his slaves some distance from his Bolama island encampment, then shoots to wound the man as bait to lead Captain Midnight into a trap. As Congo has anticipated, after hearing the shot, the Secret Squadron members locate and tend to the wounded slave. They then follow his directions toward Congo's camp, when Joyce falls prey to another kind of peril. She falls into an elephant trap along the way. As her comrades try to extricate her, they are all captured by Zawata's cannibals. The next day, the Squadron members are to be sacrificed and cooked.

During a grotesque pre-feasting ceremony, Ichabod Mudd notices that Chief Zawata suffers the lower back pain of lumbago, which gives Mudd an idea. Learning via his Pocket Locator of a forecast heavy storm, Ikky declares to the savages that he is a great witch doctor. He balefully proclaims that Chief Zawata's aching back is the gods' punishment for Zawata's following the evil Congo; and that he, the great witch doctor, will punish the tribe even more by bringing furious rains and flooding! Ikky then bellows several incantations in jumbled Pig Latin. A fierce thunderstorm soon follows, and the greatly alarmed and repentant Zawata orders his natives to turn on Congo — which they do with zeal.

1946 Pocket Locator. Captain Midnight's two-way, flashing-light radio was believed by many in the 1940s to be only a daydream. But in fact, retro-engineering some working Pocket Locators of the era has proven feasible and successful.[1]

The 1946 model Pocket Locator features the following:

*1940s-vintage subminiature tubes, including indicating-light tube.
Ferrite-core and hand-wound coils.
90V tube-plate voltage and 1.5V tube-filament voltage.
4.4-mile minimum range over land.
A watertight, clear plastic case that withstands water depths.
Measures 6.5" x 3.875" x 1.625".*

1946-model Captain Midnight Pocket Locator: A green indicating light flashes in the center of the star. A watertight transmitting button protrudes from the emblem's center.
PHOTOGRAPH: TOORU KAWABATA

PLANS AND THREATS

Congo's camouflaged ship has floated across the ocean channel to the mainland, so the carrier looks practically like an extended part of the African Coastline. Meanwhile on Bolama Island, Congo flees from Zawata's tribe to a waiting plane that flies him to the mainland.

Captain Midnight had originally planned to be transported onto the

Olan Soulé played the part of Agent Kelly, SS-11, on radio and Aristotle "Tut" Jones in the *Captain Midnight* television program of the 1950s. He was the longest-playing Secret Squadron actor of the entire *Captain Midnight* broadcast era. PHOTOGRAPH: LEONARD ZANE

aircraft carrier, via a packing crate in another of Congo's island planes. But circumstances cause Joyce and Chuck to end up hiding in the transported crate instead, so Midnight must find some other means to reach the carrier. Midnight and Ikky split up to see if either of them can find a plane or power boat.

Congo's plane that carries the crate with Chuck and Joyce lands on the carrier, unloads the crate, and then takes off. The carrier floats from near the mainland out into the open sea.

When Chuck and Joyce emerge from the crate, they find the vessel deserted, and so attempt to pilot the ship. But Congo and his crew soon arrive and capture them.

Captain Midnight tries to keep Secret Squadron planes from bombing the renegade aircraft carrier, but he is without a radio, so he uses a native drum on the island to beat out a Morse code message that he hopes will be relayed to the aircraft. Ikky hears the drum message and uses his Pocket Locator to contact a nearing Secret Squadron amphibian.

Agent Kelly arrives with the amphibian, rendezvousing first with Ikky and then with Captain Midnight. After taking off, Midnight mans the controls and soon engages in an air battle with one of Congo's carrier fighters.

CARRIER CONFRONTATION

Sensing he is in grave danger, Congo decides to keep Chuck and Joyce as hostages. He orders one of his assistants, named "Hyena," to take them below. Chuck uses ju-jitsu to knock Hyena down several steps and into unconsciousness. He picks up Hyena's Tommy gun, and then he and Joyce ascend to the landing deck. Chuck and Joyce sneak to a radio room, but are trapped there. They are forced to surrender, and will be shot after the carrier's planes return.

In an incredible feat of flying skill with the amphibian, Midnight wins the air battle with the Congo fighter plane, forcing the fighter down on the African mainland. Midnight lands, and Ikky and Kelly capture the fighter pilot. Ikky and Midnight quickly fix the carrier plane well enough to fly, and Captain Midnight climbs aboard and heads back to the carrier with it.

Midnight roars the last and belated fighter plane onto the aircraft carrier and disrupts the execution. With the plane's machineguns and his pistol, he holds everybody at bay long enough for the Secret Squadron bombers to arrive and force Congo's surrender. Washington dispatches two destroyers to bring in the pirate carrier, and Captain Midnight and his Squadron comrades finally look forward to a relaxing vacation.

ENDNOTES

1 See Appendix 3 for detailed specifications and photographs of reconstructed, working 1942 and 1946 Pocket Locator models.

3

Deadly Biological Weapon

(1946)

NORTHERN MEXICO

The Secret Squadron group arrives to vacation at a ranch in Northern Mexico. However, a vacation is not what they get. While Captain Midnight sits talking with his host, the hacienda owner Señor Gonzales, an old scientist named Professor Matthews rushes into the hacienda from his nearby desert camp. Matthews has been conducting an experiment at the camp and announces that a highly valuable test tube has been stolen from his laboratory. Matthews is joined by his laboratory and personal assistant, Juan Madero. Unknown to Matthews, Madero has perpetrated the theft, but has been unable to make a getaway.

Madero is in the employ of a gang of criminals led by an unidentified figure whose description tallies with that of Señor Gonzales himself. Now in the living room of the hacienda, the professor makes a stabbing statement. The test tube contains a germ culture that can be turned into a deadly bacterial weapon. Captain Midnight asks a number of penetrating questions that eventually lead to Juan Madero's being exposed as the thief. Madero is taken into custody, but only after he has disposed of the test tube.

A wealthy and respectable Mexican ranch owner named Ernesto Mendoza turns out to be Ivan Shark. He insists that critical injuries he suffered when tumbling down the mountain in Panka have restored his sanity, and that he is profoundly regretful and ashamed of his past misdeeds. Captain Midnight, however, is certain that Shark is responsible for the theft of the test tube.

Joyce and Chuck sneak into Shark's area. But they are rendered unconscious by odorless, colorless gas, and are then injected with some of Professor Matthews's menacing serum. However, due to an incomplete formula, the experiment proves unsuccessful, with no adverse effects on Chuck or Joyce. Unaware they had been injected, they are returned to Captain Midnight — along with excuses that the reformed "Señor Mendoza" had been concerned for their health after they "fell unconscious" from possible allergies to nearby toxic plants. He therefore "kept them under observation until their health proved sound, so nothing would cast aspersions on the quality of care they received." Ivan Shark profusely apologizes for the unfortunate incident. But despite this conduct, Shark soon captures the old professor and tortures him in an attempt to gain the biotoxic formula.

Professor Matthews manages to hold out and get away from Shark. He then writes out the unperfected formula and gives it to Captain Midnight. The Secret Squadron commander has Señor Gonzales lock the formula in his safe at the hacienda.

Barry Steele sends his secretary to Mexico to assist Captain Midnight. Ivan Shark decides to intercept the secretary and replace her with — of all people — Fury Shark! It turns out the international criminal's daughter did not die in the 1941 battle between the Shark and U.S. submarines. Moreover, Fury will not be recognized by the Secret Squadron, because through plastic surgery and her own clever powers of mimicry, she has adopted a new appearance and personality.

DAUGHTER'S DECEPTION

Fury Shark, changed beyond recognition, presents herself to Captain Midnight as secretary Ann Reynolds. While the Secret Squadron agents have no way of knowing she is Ivan Shark's daughter, her rather prying manner arouses some suspicions, and they do not turn the biological formula over to her. Instead, Midnight asks her to assist in capturing Ivan Shark! This would be done by trying to locate the stolen test tube that Midnight suspects Shark has. If Shark does have it, he can be arrested with the condemning evidence.

Captain Midnight remains under the misimpression that Fury Shark has died, and so the disingenuous Ann Reynolds — whom he tells is "both attractive and intelligent" — could apply for a position to assist Shark. Fury can't help cooing, deep-voiced and seductively, "Thank you, Captain," at the compliment.

Midnight believes Shark must greatly miss his daughter and would be receptive to someone like Miss Reynolds, who has "admired and envied Fury and her exciting and adventurous life." So Captain Midnight sends "Miss Reynolds" to approach Shark.

Fury and her father cannot contain their delicious mirth when they meet. Shark gleefully advises his masquerading daughter to inform Captain

Left: Sharon Grainger played Fury Shark from 1940-1949 — the impersonated Ann Reynolds after plastic surgery? *Right:* Erwin L. Hess illustration in *Captain Midnight and the Secret Squadron*. PHOTOS: PHOTOFEST, THE WANDER COMPANY

Midnight that he has accepted her as an assistant — while he launches a counter-trap to undo Captain Midnight. Ivan and Fury Shark are such delectable master villains!

Ikky soon delivers a coded message to Captain Midnight. It's in reply to a radio inquiry Midnight had sent to Major Steele for a description of Ann Reynolds. The message says Ann Reynolds is 5'-3," with brown eyes and dark brown hair. But the woman representing herself to Captain Midnight is at least 5'-7" tall, has blue eyes and light brown hair. This confirms Midnight's suspicions that the bogus Ann Reynolds must be one of Ivan Shark's agents, so Midnight conceives a counter-counter-trap to outwit Ivan Shark.

Later, the Secret Squadron manages to foil Shark and also to discover and free the real Ann Reynolds, whom Shark has secretly held prisoner and kept semi-starved. Upon her rescue, Ann Reynolds tells Captain Midnight something startling: Fury Shark is alive. Fury has had plastic surgery to change her appearance, and she is the one who has impersonated her. Captain Midnight is amazed that the Shark organization has been able to keep Fury's secret for so long — and also that Fury was so effective in masking her identity. Midnight should have recognized those glinting blue eyes.

It finally seems that Ivan Shark and his lieutenants are to be delivered into the hands of justice. But then a man called "Fingers," who is Shark's henchman, unexpectedly appears and slips up behind the Secret Squadron agents with a submachine gun. A counter-counter-counter trap! Ikky, however, manages to get away and take Ann Reynolds with him.

Because Ann Reynolds is weak, Ikky decides to fly her back to Secret Squadron Headquarters in the United States for care and recuperation. He also radios the Mexican authorities to pursue and arrest Ivan Shark.

Meanwhile, the dastardly Ivan Shark forces Señor Gonzales to open his safe, and Shark seizes the uncompleted bacterial formula. He then orders Captain Midnight and his two companions into a plane, planning to fly them out over the Mexican desert and send them plunging to their deaths. Simply shooting his enemies is again not elegant enough for Shark. He is an artist and must also inflict suspenseful mental torment. But when the international gangster learns that the Mexican authorities are pursuing him, he decides to abandon the plane himself. Leaving the Secret Squadron agents securely bound on the cabin deck, Shark sets the controls downward, and with Fury and Fingers parachutes to the sands below.

Midnight manages to get free, and save himself and his two agents from death by crash-landing the plummeting plane. But the written, though still incomplete, bacterial formula is now in Shark's hands. The three Secret Squadron agents are stranded in the desert, with the crashed-landed plane now a useless wreck.

SHARK'S NEW ACTIONS

Ivan Shark hastens back to his hacienda and turns over the unperfected bacterial formula to a sinister scientist in his employ. The scientist is named Dr. Habib, and his job is to complete Professor Matthews's germ discovery, which includes developing this biological menace into an aerosol disease bomb! With this kind of powerful weapon, the international criminal will be able to terrorize and extort whole nations.

While Shark has Dr. Habib work on disease bomb synthesis, the three Squadron agents manage two things: first to reunite with Professor Matthews and second to return to Shark's hacienda area. By Pocket Locator, the three agents confer with Ikky and Ann Reynolds — the two of whom now fly in a Secret Squadron plane on their way to U.S. Squadron Headquarters. Miss Reynolds informs Captain Midnight of something else she overheard from her Shark captors: the secret signal the gang members use to gain admittance into Ivan Shark's laboratory. Captain Midnight decides to enter the laboratory and carry out Professor Matthews's directions for destroying the formula's ingredients and synthesizing equipment.

Captain Midnight, Chuck, Joyce, and Matthews gain access to Ivan Shark's laboratory. But a fierce struggle soon follows, and the laboratory catches fire. Dr. Habib is lost in the terrible blaze. But Ivan and Fury Shark escape — capturing and spiriting Professor Matthews away with them.

At a remote cottage, Shark tortures the professor in a renewed attempt to force him to reveal the full secret of the disease bomb — which Matthews apparently does know. But when the master criminal fails to break the professor, Shark decides to take him to another place where something else might be utilized to gain the desired results.

Captain Midnight follows Shark's trail to the now abandoned cottage. Even though deserted, Midnight discovers the professor has managed to leave a clue that indicates where to search for him. As night approaches, Captain Midnight flies with Chuck and Joyce to the city where they think Shark's group may have relocated. During the flight, however, their plane is suddenly struck by heavy machinegun fire. Captain Midnight, Chuck, and Joyce are forced to parachute to the desert below.

WHISPER

Knowing Ivan Shark will quickly send a search party out to destroy them, the three Squadron agents decide to hide behind some boulders in the vicinity of a great stone column not far from their crashed airplane. The darkness deepens, moonless and black, and then a secret passageway suddenly opens at the base of the column! A man called "Whisper" leads twenty-two men out of the passageway and toward the wrecked plane. All the men carry rifles.

As Whisper and his band slowly surround the crashed plane, Midnight leads Chuck and Joyce silently and swiftly through the darkness to the stone column. On reaching the pillar, the three crouch inside a deep niche near the underground entrance — when two more of Whisper's guards emerge from the secret portal. The three Squadron agents immediately overpower the guards and drag them into their recess. But on hearing more sounds of footsteps in the passageway, below, they realize Shark has sent another search party. Captain Midnight pulls a long Mexican serape off a guard they overcame and wraps himself in it. He has Chuck do the same, then plops a big sombrero on Joyce's head and announces they will slip out and join the search party.

VIZCAY

Midnight, Chuck, and Joyce persuade the searchers that they are agents of Ivan Shark from the city of Vizcay where Shark is located. But they are simply led right to Ivan Shark. By bold action and deception, however, the three Squadron agents soon manage to free Professor Matthews and get away from Shark with the professor. But small groups of armed men shortly search every corner of the city to find them.

The three Squadron members and Matthews seek refuge in an old abandoned well. As their presence is about to be discovered, their flashlights reveal a stone panel in the well's shaft that opens to a subterranean passage. The passage angles and descends sharply and deeply, then levels and re-ascends for a steep, short distance to level off again and continue. The dip had evidently been a water trap, but is now as dry as the well. The tunnel winds, leading them to a maze of tall corridors with ceilings supported by ornately carved stone columns. The column shapes and designs appear to be Aztec.

AZTEC TREASURE

Continuing through one of the subterranean corridors, the Squadron agents and Matthews enter an ancient chamber. Inside the big stone room, they discover vessels containing a breathtaking fortune in Aztec gold and jewels! They then hurry back to the main passageway. They don't suspect, though, that Ivan Shark has learned of their retreat into the well — and is now also on the way to discovering its secret.

Shark soon traps the Squadron agents and Matthews in the underground Aztec complex. Because Matthews is the only one who knows the full secret of the germ bomb, Shark cannot simply start shooting and risk killing or incapacitating the professor. Shark therefore proposes a bargain to Captain Midnight, in return for Professor Matthews, and Midnight asks for an hour to consider it. The Secret Squadron agents retreat into the Aztec treasure chamber — with Shark noting its entry — and equip themselves with gold coins, diamonds, and a small dagger. While they do this, Shark ascends back through the well and sends Fury in a helicopter to his hacienda to get some truth serum for using on Professor Matthews. Meanwhile Captain Midnight and his group emerge from the treasure chamber, and by probing some fine fissures with the dagger, they soon discover another hidden stone panel in the subterranean passageway.

Within the hour, Fury returns in the helicopter and lands in Vizcay's public square. Just as she disembarks, the three Secret Squadron agents and Matthews escape through a secret exit from the underground passageway. They try to reach the helicopter to get away, but Shark, Whisper, and his men capture all of them.

Returning to the newly discovered Aztec exit portal, Shark leads Whisper, his gang and their captives back down into the maze of underground corridors. With the help of Whisper and his men, Shark confiscates Midnight's Aztec antiquities. He then has Whisper's men bind Captain Midnight, Chuck, and Joyce to the stone pillars. As the Secret Squadron agents helplessly watch, he injects sodium pentothal truth serum into the veins of Professor Matthews.

While the truth serum begins to take effect, Captain Midnight tells Whisper that Shark knows where the whole Aztec treasure is, and Shark has not told Whisper because he intends to steal it all for himself. The criminals turn on Shark and Fury, and the two flee with Professor Matthews as their prisoner. Captain Midnight, however, manages to persuade Whisper's men to untie him and his two colleagues.

SHARK'S GETAWAY

Shark and Fury try to get away in the helicopter with the professor, but Whisper and his gang force the craft down with machinegun fire. Ivan Shark and his party abandon the crippled helicopter, but Shark immediately hijacks a car. He races in the vehicle with Fury and Matthews across the sand toward a neighboring town. By this time, though, the truth serum has worn off.

Captain Midnight, Chuck, and Joyce abandon the Aztec treasure and slip through the underground passage to freedom. They search Shark's disabled helicopter and find a map. The map shows penciled markings toward a place to the south that is labeled, "Castellani." At this point, Captain Midnight also receives a Pocket Locator message from Ichabod Mudd. The message says Ikky is now flying back into Mexico in a Secret Squadron plane.

CASTELLANI

With Professor Matthews as their captive, Shark and Fury head for the Mexican colony of a man named Castellani. He is an ominous master of the hypnotic arts, and Shark plans to place Matthews under hypnosis and compel him to reveal the secret.

Meanwhile, Ikky flies his plane to rendezvous with his Secret Squadron comrades outside the city of Vizcay. Captain Midnight, Chuck, and Joyce board Ikky's plane, and they all head for Castellani's colony.

Upon arriving at the colony, the Secret Squadron party encounters a shock. They are accosted by hundreds of robot-like men, who are slaves of the master hypnotist! The four Squadron agents are led into the presence of Castellani, but the Secret Squadron leader outwits the hypnotist, who is forced to flee through a panel.

From another part of his mansion, Castellani uses a public address system to command ten of his men to put an end to the Secret Squadron agents. But the mentally enslaved men are so robotic in their awareness and actions that Captain Midnight's group is able to circumvent them and get away.

The arch-criminal Shark now arrives unheralded with his prisoner, Matthews, and Captain Midnight is unable to prevent them from entering the mansion. Castellani captures Ikky and decides to toy with him rather than simply kill him off. So he reduces Ikky to a state of deep hypnosis, and then by suggestion, persuades the Secret Squadron agent to bow humbly before the international gangster, Ivan Shark. The master criminal is delighted at this parlor amusement and laughs with gusto.

But Captain Midnight, Chuck, and Joyce soon manage to trap Shark and the hypnotist Castellani — until Fury Shark appears in the doorway, armed with a submachine gun. Fury wants to kill her enemies on the spot, but Captain Midnight shrewdly suggests to Castellani that he and his companions can be transformed into the hypnotist's personal slaves — just as Ikky has. Ivan and Fury Shark snicker with pleasure at that idea, too — for the time being — and Shark also wants Captain Midnight to bow to him in humble submission. So the Squadron leader and his three agents are led into the carriage house, while the master hypnotist proceeds to extract the secret of the disease bomb from Professor Matthews. But Castellani soon changes his plans. Instead of being paid a fee, he decides he will keep the professor's secret for himself, and then kill both the Sharks and the Secret Squadron agents.

That night in the carriage house, Captain Midnight inflicts painful, but harmless pressure against Ikky's arm with his finger joints. This succeeds in breaking Ikky's hypnotic spell. Midnight then conceives a daring plan of escape. While Ikky distracts their guard's attention, Midnight seizes a pole and strikes the light bulb directly overhead. The Squadron agents rush up to a hayloft, and then plunge back down. The shock of bodily impact on the guard suddenly releases him from Castellani's power. He vows vengeance on the awful man who had enslaved him.

Meanwhile, the master hypnotist has succeeded in extracting the full secret of the immensely destructive disease bomb from Professor Matthews. Castellani intends to use this knowledge for his own purposes, and he orders a slave to round up more men to kill Captain Midnight and his companions. The slave exits the office to carry out this command. Soon after, Castellani rises from his desk to leave the office. But then Fury Shark suddenly bursts in with a drawn gun and orders him on pain of death to surrender the germ bomb secret. The master hypnotist bows in submission — but with one hand behind his back, secretly activates the P.A. microphone on his desk.

Captain Midnight sends his former slave guard to lure Castellani into a trap. And just as the master hypnotist is about to write Matthews's disease secret for Fury, the freed guard arrives. At the same moment, the Secret Squadron agents find themselves surrounded by a gang of slaves that has been ordered to wipe them out. But then without warning, the guard sent to lure Castellani suddenly whips out a gun and fires three shots into the hypnotist's body!

As he slumps down, Castellani clutches his P.A. microphone and issues a post-hypnotic command that releases his men from their enslaving trances. But before Castellani can utter another word, he collapses in death — while a great change comes over the crowd of robot-like men.

Captain Midnight is quick to take advantage of the former slaves' desire for revenge, and he urges them to help capture the arch-criminal Ivan Shark and his daughter Fury.

THIEVING FINGERS

Deprived of the deadly disease bomb's secret, Shark and Fury are forced to flee from the colony and leave Professor Matthews behind. Without skipping a beat, though, Shark revises his plan. He will gain a fortune by stealing the priceless Aztec treasure that is hidden in the city of Vizcay. However, he does not know that his treacherous agent Fingers — together with a gangster named General John Hubbard — are at this moment engaged in a fierce gun battle with Whisper's gang for possession of the Aztec treasure!

Ivan Shark returns to the great rock pillar in the desert to rejoin Fingers. But he learns the treasure has already been stolen, and he correctly surmises that his former henchman Fingers is the thief. Shark immediately decides to head to Mexico City in hopes of picking up Fingers' trail. Mexico City is the destination of the Secret Squadron agents, too. As yet unaware of the Aztec treasure's fate, they plan to inform the Mexican Government of its location in the city of Vizcay.

AZTEC SUN-GOD RING

Meanwhile, two planes bearing the valuable collection of Aztec gold and jewels have landed in a Mexican town just south of the U.S. border. And now, in a private room at the rear of a small restaurant, Fingers speaks with the clever American gangster, General John Hubbard. Fingers and Hubbard soon send a letter to the Mexican government, demanding ten million dollars for return of the ancient Aztec treasure, and they send a ring as a mark of identification. This ring is engraved with central elements of the ornate Aztec calendar, and is topped with a blood-red ruby.

Mexican government officials welcome Captain Midnight and request the Secret Squadron's assistance in finding the Americans who have stolen the priceless Aztec treasure. Authorizing Captain Midnight to act as Mexico's special representative in this matter, the authorities hand over the Aztec Sun-God ring sent by the criminals for Midnight to wear on his own finger. They also provide several copies of the ring, especially fashioned for Secret Squadron agents, in order to confuse the thieves. This is part of a plan whereby Captain Midnight promises to track down and retrieve the treasure for the Mexican government without paying the ransom.

At the Mexican-U.S. border, a paid agent of Ivan Shark waylays Captain Midnight, seizes the original ring and flees with it. While the Secret Squadron agents carry on a futile search for the man, Shark and his daughter, Fury, fly straight to a tourist camp with the ring, where a meeting with the gangsters' representative named Malone has been arranged.

Ivan Shark wears the Aztec ruby ring, claiming to be the Mexican government's representative to negotiate for the treasure. Handing the ring to Malone for inspection, he tries to ply from him where the Aztec riches are concealed. Shark learns only that the treasure is hidden somewhere in

Pacific City (across the border in the USA). But Malone is also shrewd and clever, and he soon discovers Shark's identity. At this moment, the Secret Squadron agents also reach the camp, and Shark fires his automatic point blank into Malone's body! Then he flees toward his waiting plane.

Chuck and Ikky pursue Shark, as Joyce and Captain Midnight stay behind and tend to the dying gangster Malone. Upon asking him where

Aztec Sun-God Ring, patterned after the Calendar Stone of the God *Tonatiuh*. RECONSTRUCTION OF THE CLAIMED "ORIGINAL" RING AND PHOTOGRAPHS: LEONARD ZANE

the treasure has been concealed, Malone's only answer is to give Captain Midnight the original Aztec ring that he has gotten from Shark. At this moment, Fingers steps out from the shadows. He has observed the goings-on, and reveals to Captain Midnight that he is General John Hubbard's chief partner.

Midnight explains he is authorized by the government of Mexico to pay the ransom in return for the Aztec treasure, upon learning its location and obtaining it. Fingers demands the ring to take to the general, and promises to return with the location information if Midnight brings the ten million dollars. Captain Midnight performs a surreptitious switch, giving Fingers an Aztec Sun-God Ring copy, and Fingers swiftly departs.

GENERAL JOHN HUBBARD

The gangster, General John Hubbard, inserts a small piece of paper in an astonishing secret compartment of the duplicated Aztec ring. The paper bears the address of his waterfront warehouse and says to come at seven p.m. He orders Fingers to deliver the ring to Captain Midnight late that afternoon. But Captain Midnight has not been idle. Eager to track down the treasure before meeting with General John, he finds a clue to the location of Hubbard's warehouse in the files of the Pacific City newspaper. He then heads for the warehouse with Chuck, Joyce, and Ikky.

Capt. Midnight's AZTEC SUN-GOD RING Secret Compartment

HINGED SECRET COMPARTMENT DOOR, REFLECTING RUBY CAPSTONE BOTTOM

OPEN SECRET COMPARTMENT

SEALED SECRET COMPARTMENT DOOR, WITH CENTER LATCH NUB AND LOWER CORNER PULL KNOB

"ORIGINAL" OR "AUTHENTIC" RECONSTRUCTION AND PHOTOGRAPH: LEONARD ZANE

Ivan Shark and his daughter, Fury, are also hot on the trail of the treasure, and they spot Fingers on the street. They accost him at gunpoint, forcing him to accompany them to their hotel. There, Shark seizes the (believed original) Aztec ring from his former henchman, opens it, and reads the address within. Triumphantly, he and Fury hurry for the warehouse with Fingers as their prisoner.

Fog hangs heavy and almost impenetrable around a wood-framed waterfront warehouse. After groping and making their way inside, Ivan Shark, Fury, and Fingers meet General John Hubbard. Inside a recess in the nearly dark building, they offer to pay Hubbard a million dollars for the treasure. Being only a fraction of what the treasure is worth, Hubbard indignantly refuses. Shark draws his automatic and threatens Hubbard.

The General nods at the shelves of only textiles and laughs. Did anyone think he was foolish enough to expose himself at the same place where the treasure is hidden?

Shark says he will shoot Hubbard immediately if he doesn't reveal the secret. While Hubbard knows he's very valuable to Shark, he's not particularly inclined to call his bluff — especially when he also catches a glimpse through the windows of Secret Squadron agents emerging from the mists outside. He haltingly complies with Shark's demand, whispering very slowly to the international criminal. But then Shark spots the approaching Squadron agents, and he orders the general and Fingers to move quickly and quietly between rows of shelving where none of them can be seen.

Captain Midnight, Ikky and Joyce enter the building as Chuck remains on guard in front. Finding the place seemingly deserted, the three Squadron members begin to search. With the Squadron agents closing in, Hubbard suddenly thrusts Fingers as a shield, shoving him into Shark and racing for the door. Shark's automatic goes off, knocking Fingers to the floor. Exiting the building, the general rushes past Chuck, who turns to follow — but Hubbard disappears into the thick fog blanket. Back inside, Ivan Shark pulls an incendiary grenade from a pocket. As he and Fury bolt out of the building, he hurls the grenade behind them. It explodes inside the warehouse in a blazing blast. Chuck fires his pistol at the fleeing Shark and Fury, forcing the pair to run for cover. Inside the building, Midnight and Ikky lift Fingers and carry him as Joyce leads the way around flaming debris to the outside.

Escaping the burning warehouse, while carrying the wounded Fingers, Captain Midnight and Ikky follow Joyce to join Chuck in the thick fog outside. Chuck waves them all down, as he points toward some parked vehicles that squat like phantoms in the mists. Chuck then steals closer to the metal hulks, crouching and hiding below a loading dock. Suddenly, Shark and Fury rush from behind the vehicles — and the unseen Chuck manages to overhear Shark tell Fury the treasure is aboard Hubbard's fast launch that will soon leave the bay. The arch criminal and his daughter race into the mists toward some commercial boats moored along the waterfront.

Chuck returns to his comrades who kneel beside Fingers. The failing henchman begs them to make General Hubbard pay for what he has done to him, draws a last breath, and dies. Staying with the body, Ikky will contact the police. Captain Midnight leads Chuck and Joyce to pursue Shark and Fury.

LIGHTHOUSE

Shark decides to seize a sightseeing boat and go after General John Hubbard, but the very poor visibility holds him back. Close behind, but undetected in the dense fog, Captain Midnight whispers to Chuck and Joyce to get ready to stow away in the same boat and let Shark steal the treasure for them! While Shark searches for an easily captured vessel, Chuck and Joyce wait in hiding at the waterfront, but Captain Midnight does not. He soon secures a small, fast cabin boat to pursue the general on his own.

Meanwhile, General John has reached the lighthouse at the mouth of the bay. He arranges for the lighthouse keeper, a man named Gibbs, to hide the precious treasure in an almost inaccessible spot. Hubbard then conceals his launch in an enclosed slip near the lighthouse.

A short time later, Captain Midnight reaches the lighthouse. He asks the keeper if he knows General John Hubbard or if he has seen anyone answering his description. Gibbs coyly says only that he knows the general, but offers nothing more. Gibbs's manner incites Midnight's suspicions. He tells Gibbs he has something the general is interested in, and stepping out of Gibbs's view, writes out a small message and slips it into the secret compartment of a copied Aztec ring. Hoping to draw Hubbard out of hiding, Midnight turns back to Gibbs and hands him the ring to give to Hubbard. He tells Gibbs he'll stay moored outside in the boat to wait out the fog.

Very soon afterward, General John — hiding in an upper lighthouse room — gets the ring from Gibbs. He opens the secret compartment and reads the small note. The note says, "FULL REWARD IS YOURS NOW." Because of the ring, Hubbard figures the message is from Ivan Shark, and that Shark would finally rather pay well than risk losing the treasure. So General John walks blindly into the trap on Midnight's cabin boat, and Midnight apprehends and binds him for doing away with Fingers. Captain Midnight sends a Pocket Locator message to Chuck and Joyce, telling them to get the police and Ikky because he has captured Hubbard and is bringing him.

Captain Midnight returns with his prisoner to meet Chuck, Joyce, Ikky, and the police officers. But Shark had left earlier in a large boat, doubtless even passing Captain Midnight in the mist!

Ivan Shark arrives at the lighthouse. He intimidates Gibbs at gunpoint, and Gibbs informs him that the treasure is hidden in an underwater chamber, accessible only at low tide. The arch criminal enters the lighthouse and waits for the opportunity to remove the loot. But Gibbs — worried at having double-crossed General John — cleverly uses the lighthouse beacon to send out a signal asking the gangster to come at once. Midnight sees the signal and understands it. He orders Chuck and Joyce to sail out to the lighthouse to investigate.

Because of murder charges Captain Midnight and Ikky make to the police about the slain Fingers, the officers arrest General John Hubbard and haul him off to jail. Midnight and Ikky then head out to the lighthouse, where Chuck and Joyce had arrived a half-hour before. But Captain Midnight does not suspect what serious trouble his young agents are in.

Chuck and Joyce had met the lighthouse keeper, and upon their asking him questions, he attacked them. They overpowered him and used his keys to gain access into a small airtight room. To their amazement, they found a chest containing the Aztec treasure. But even as they stared at the discovery, the arch-criminal Ivan Shark appeared just outside the chamber. Kicking the door shut and locking it, Shark imprisoned both Chuck and Joyce within.

Now — as Chuck and Joyce frantically twist the doorknob of the low chamber — they hear Shark's strident laughter. Joyce hurriedly sends a Pocket Locator message to Captain Midnight, and Shark's glee soon turns to alarm when he spots a small cabin boat moving swiftly toward the lighthouse. It carries Captain Midnight and Ichabod Mudd — and about a mile behind the boat, a Coast Guard cutter speeds on the way, too! Without a moment to spare, Shark is forced to abandon the Aztec treasure and rush to the enclosed boat slip. Breaking the slip open and piloting General Hubbard's fast launch, he hurriedly flees toward a tiny and obscure mainland cove.

Captain Midnight and Ikky leap from their boat onto the lighthouse shore, and sprint to the tower. Racing to the deck above the underwater room, they desperately break and pry through its ceiling, finding Chuck and Joyce unconscious inside. They lift and carry them to ground level, where they meet the lifesaving squad from the Coast Guard cutter. The squad immediately administers oxygen to resuscitate and save the young agents.

The Coast Guard assists the Secret Squadron in retrieving the Aztec treasure, and placing it in safekeeping for turning over to the Mexican government. All Aztec artifacts will be returned, including the original Sun-God ring.

Ironically, Ivan Shark has gotten away with at least one of the accurate gold copies of the Aztec ring, in addition to the other ones retained by Captain Midnight and his immediate group of active Squadron agents.

While the ring is a bitter reminder for the covetous Ivan Shark, Captain Midnight creates much happier memories for his own followers. The Secret Squadron leader arranges for souvenir facsimiles of the original ruby ring to be made available to all Secret Squadron members.

But all is not settled. Before long — and with the aid of legal counsel that argues insufficient evidence, together with pulling some political wires — General John Hubbard secures his release from prison. Upon his release, he is shocked to learn something: only one of his candidates for city office has recently been elected in Pacific City, and the new administration in power is determined to run the general out of town. But Hubbard is not one to retreat into obscurity. He wastes no time laying plans for regaining control of Pacific City.

Top: "Original" Aztec Sun-God ring with "secret compartment." 14k gold, cultured ruby capstone, plus five small "Holy Day" rubies inset on each side. Created by Leonard Zane as an "authentic" reconstruction. *Bottom:* Brass, 1946 Aztec Sun-God radio premium ring. Its "secret compartment" is in the hollow plastic capstone that slides away from two, gripping metal collars.
PHOTOGRAPHS: LEONARD ZANE

HOW TO USE THE SECRET COMPARTMENT

Place your thumb against the side of the stone directly above the shaft of your ring. Press gently—and watch the stone slide out, revealing the hidden compartment underneath. Note how you can hide a short note written on thin paper —to pass along to a friend who knows the secret of the hidden compartment and how to open it.

To close your ring, simply press the stone back in place. Be sure the edges of the stone are in the metal grooves at the sides.

Published by
SECRET SQUADRON HEADQUARTERS
360 N. MICHIGAN AVENUE
CHICAGO, ILLINOIS

The Story of Your SECRET SQUADRON MYSTIC SUN-GOD RING

by
CAPTAIN MIDNIGHT

YOUR NEW OFFICIAL S.S. RING—
Celebrating our Secret Squadron Adventures in Mexico, Ancient Home of the Aztecs

Every organization has an official ring for its members, bearing insignia derived from campaigns or exploits in which the organization has performed outstanding service. Here is your very own official Secret Squadron ring. I hope you will wear it always as a mark of your membership in the Secret Squadron, and as a reminder of our Secret Squadron adventures in the land of the Aztecs, of which this ring is a symbol.

The Aztecs, as you may know, lived and reigned long ago in the country we now know as Mexico. Like most ancient people they worshipped many gods. Their best-known god —called TONATIUH, the Sun God—is shown as the Aztecs pictured him on the side of your ring. Montezuma and other famous kings of the Aztecs worshipped this Sun God as the giver of all power and made human sacrifices to him on the high altar of the Sun God's temple.

The red plastic stone in your ring symbolizes the altar of the Sun God's temple. Its rich, brilliant color simulates the deep red glow of a genuine ruby.

Although the Aztecs were masters of such sciences as astronomy and mathematics they believed in many superstitions which we call savage or childish today. One of their superstitious signs, the sign for "good luck" which was believed to safeguard the wearer, is shown below the picture of the Sun God on the shaft of your ring.

But your new official Secret Squadron ring is far more than simply a handsome ring with interesting Aztec designs. It contains an amazing special feature you will find of great importance in Secret Squadron activities—an ingenious secret compartment carefully concealed so that "outsiders" cannot possibly discover it.

This secret compartment, cleverly hidden beneath the stone in your ring, can be very useful to you in carrying secret information and passing it along to friends who will seem to others to be merely examining your ring. Directions for opening this secret compartment are given on the next page. I know you will guard this secret by showing the hidden compartment only to loyal friends of the Secret Squadron.

Capt. Midnight
"SS-1"

Aztec Mystic Sun-God Ring instruction leaflet. PHOTOGRAPH: LEONARD ZANE

4

Pacific City Peril

(1946)

GENERAL JOHN HUBBARD'S PLOT

General John Hubbard's scheme is underway. Pacific City's newly elected mayor is run down by an auto and mortally injured. The car that struck him belonged to young Jim Malloy. The man at the wheel was a gangster nicknamed "Torpedo," who forced Jim to lend the car and take the blame for what happened. The completely innocent Jimmy Malloy gives himself up; and Mr. Arnold, who is the successor to the dead mayor, accepts his confession. But Joyce Ryan had caught a fleeting glimpse of the death car's driver. She refuses to believe Jimmy Malloy is guilty and expresses her doubts to Captain Midnight. The captain shares her skepticism.

While Malloy confesses it was he who had run down and killed the new mayor of Pacific City, Captain Midnight suspects it is a false confession, and that Jimmy is shielding someone from the gangster General John Hubbard. Captain Midnight soon learns that Jimmy's future father-in-law had once been an unwilling associate of Hubbard's. So Midnight concludes it was General John who had the mayor killed and who forced Jimmy to take the blame by threatening to expose the girl's father. Captain Midnight is determined to find records to support the idea. So under cover of darkness, he and his Secret Squadron agents creep up on Hubbard's large manor, and climb in the window of the study. But the gangster has already been informed of their plan.

As the Squadron agents climb through the window, they find themselves surrounded by machineguns. General John forces them into a small, soundproof steam room and locks the door, intending to scald them to death. But thanks to Captain Midnight's resourcefulness, they escape through an aperture in the wall that houses the ventilator fan. The Squadron members make their way up a stairway, still determined to find the papers they seek.

Meanwhile, the new Mayor Arnold is so severely beaten that he is forced to resign. Only one man now stands between General John and control of the town, and that is Commissioner Fordham. The commissioner is a licensed pilot, and Hubbard plans to dispose of him in what will appear to be an accidental plane crash. The General sends Fordham a telegram from New Orleans (the state capital at this time), which ostensibly comes from the governor. The telegram arrives while the commissioner is conferring with Captain Midnight. The message directs Commissioner Fordham to fly to the governor's headquarters for an emergency meeting. Fordham shares the message with Captain Midnight, saying he will have to finish their business later. Somewhat suspicious, Captain Midnight persuades the commissioner to delay his departure for a couple hours, so that Chuck Ramsay and Joyce Ryan can bring some information on General John Hubbard to show the governor. The commissioner consents, and before long, Chuck and Joyce arrive and hand Fordham a written summary of General John Hubbard's alleged crimes.

IMPERILED COMMISSIONER

Unknown to the Secret Squadron and the commissioner is that General John has earlier placed an altitude-sensitive bomb in the cockpit of Fordham's plane. The bomb contains anesthetic gas and will explode when the plane is over the mountains that rise up to 8,000 feet. Also unknown to Commissioner Fordham is that Captain Midnight and Ikky have decided to protect him from dangers, by secretly concealing themselves in the cabin of his plane. None of them, however, discovers the gas bomb.

The gas bomb explodes at the preset altitude, the commissioner quickly loses consciousness, and the plane falls into a dive. As the aircraft plummets toward a mountain, Captain Midnight and Ikky scramble from the cabin into the cockpit. Ikky drags Fordham away from the fumes, and begins strapping a parachute on him, as Midnight takes control of the craft and levels it out. Captain Midnight is almost overcome by the gas and has to duck back into the cabin. He and Ikky then hurriedly don parachutes, and Midnight orders Ikky to tie a length of rope to the ripcord handle of Fordham's chute. Holding onto the rope, they throw the commissioner's unconscious body out the cabin door and pull on the rope to open the parachute. Captain Midnight and Ikky then bail out of the doomed plane, and the three float down to the mountainside.

General Hubbard had stationed Torpedo in the mountainous region where Fordham's plane was to have gone down, and Torpedo witnesses an exploding crash in the far distance near a mountain peak. He radios Hubbard the news of Fordham's death — but then shortly spots parachutes opening, and grimly tells his employer of the escape. Hubbard angrily orders Torpedo to determine the parachutes' exact location.

The Secret Squadron agents and Commissioner Fordham land near a logging camp, which Torpedo soon discovers and communicates to General John. The general sends goons up to kill the Secret Squadron agents and Fordham who is now revived. The thugs spot their intended victims, chasing and trapping them at the bank of some raging rapids.

The apparently cornered Captain Midnight, Ikky, and Fordham find a flume in the water's rocky bed and throw several loggers' planks in the rushing water. Stretching themselves out on the boards, they plunge down and ride the torrent through the trough for some distance. Presently, the flume's end suddenly appears ahead of them, but they manage to hurtle towards a jumping off place and extricate themselves. Thus eluding their pursuers, they continue their mountainous descent and eventually make their way back to Pacific City.

Learning that Captain Midnight, Ikky and Commissioner Fordham have reached Pacific City, General John Hubbard is determined to get rid of them in short order.

It is night, and soon after escorting the commissioner to his home and walking into the street, the Secret Squadron leader and Ikky encounter a police squad car that roars up and screeches to a halt in front of them. Two policemen, corrupted by the general's payoffs, swiftly get out of the squad car to arrest them. But Midnight and Mudd overpower the officers. Alarmed at the mounting danger, the Squadron agents haul the crooked policemen into Fordham's home and strip off their uniforms. After binding and gagging their captives, Midnight and Ikky don the police uniforms and then drive the commissioner off in the squad car. They head for the home of Dick Daniels, who is editor of the *Pacific City Herald* newspaper. On the way, Ikky contacts Chuck and Joyce by Pocket Locator, telling them to drive to meet them at the Daniels residence.

Upon learning the menacing events, Dick Daniels suggests disguising the commissioner and protecting his life by taking him out to the

"Floating Pleasure Palace." It's an abandoned gambling ship anchored in the Gulf outside the three-mile limit. Captain Midnight directs Chuck and Joyce to drive the now-disguised commissioner to the waterfront and to take him out to the Pleasure Palace. Midnight and Ikky will provide further protection by following in the police car.

Hubbard's chief aide, Torpedo, is on Chuck and Joyce's trail. He secretly follows them and their unidentified passenger from the Daniels home to the wharf. But because of the nearby police car, Torpedo makes no move against his quarry. Upon watching the three board a launch and leave the dock, Torpedo radios General John.

From his suburban manor, the general orders Torpedo to wipe out the occupants of the ship. He then calls police headquarters to send a squad car to pick him up and drive him into town.

Guess which squad car, fresh from the wharf, goes to collect the general? In a short while, Captain Midnight and Ichabod Mudd — still in their appropriated police uniforms and now facially disguised, too — drive General John down the winding drive of his manor to the street. Suddenly, they hear a violent explosion out in the bay. From the gangster's own lips, they hear that Torpedo has blown up the abandoned gambling boat where Commissioner Fordham, Chuck, and Joyce had been hiding!

Thanks to Joyce's keen eyes, however, she had earlier exclaimed to Chuck that the pilot of the approaching motorboat was the same man who had run down the Pacific City mayor. Chuck drew his gun, and seeing this, Torpedo leapt from the boat into the water.

As the pilot-less motorboat draws closer, Chuck takes careful aim at some dense bundles in it. With expert marksmanship, Chuck shoots at the bundles, which turn out to be TNT, and a huge explosion erupts while the motorboat is still many yards away.

The big blast also wrecks the launch on which the three survivors had hoped to escape, though. Joyce sends Ikky a Pocket Locator message that two speedboats are closing fast on the ship! With the speedboats now approaching, all three ship's survivors have no choice but to jump overboard and try to swim unseen to shore.

General John Hubbard's henchmen close in with their speedboats. The gang retrieves Torpedo and also captures Fordham, Chuck, and Joyce. Torpedo then leads the gangsters and their captives to a remote inland area where an old coal mine lies abandoned. They force their victims far into the bowels of the mine, and then down a deep and sheer vertical shaft, with a promise that they will never again see the light of day.

GROWING TREACHERY

Meanwhile, Captain Midnight worries that their commandeered squad car will soon be pursued by the Pacific City Police. So he heads back for the wharf to switch to Chuck and Joyce's car. Their backseat passenger, General Hubbard, now knows his companions are his Secret Squadron enemies. Furtively reaching forward and low, the general retrieves a pouch from under the front seat and tucks it inside his jacket.

Arriving at the wharf, Midnight and Ikky force Hubbard into Chuck and Joyce's car. They drive along coastal hills, nearing the area where they had seen the two speedboats disappear, and General John seizes his chance. He draws a pistol out of the pouch, but Midnight spots the general's quick move, and from the driver's seat wrenches Hubbard's hand. Amid the sudden struggle, Midnight loses control of the car. The wayward vehicle careens off the road and crashes into a tree at the foot of an embankment — knocking Midnight and Ikky unconscious.

The stunned gangster soon recovers from the crash, and raises his pistol at the two limp forms in the front seat. But just then, a motorist who had witnessed the accident stops to offer aid, and General John is forced to accept a ride to town, leaving Captain Midnight and Ikky in the wrecked car. When Hubbard reaches his home, his mood is greatly buoyed when he learns of the captives in the coal mine, and he roars with laughter.

Captain Midnight and Mudd recover, and by morning reach a telephone to call Dick Daniels at the *Pacific City Herald*. Daniels sends a car to get them, but when they arrive at the newspaper office, a stooge of General John's telephones Hubbard to inform him. After ringing off, Hubbard immediately telephones the paper. In a disguised voice, he leaves an anonymous tip that the commissioner and a couple others are trapped inside the remote and abandoned coal mine.

The Secret Squadron commander and Ichabod Mudd warily descend into the mine. With all the Squadron agents and Commissioner Fordham now in the coal mine, General Hubbard springs his trap. He sets off an explosion that seals the entrance under hundreds of tons of impenetrable rubble.

Deep below, the tunnel captives desperately dig into a fissure in the wall behind them. After a great deal of effort, they break through to find a winding passageway. Several hours later, they emerge under the starlit sky.

FRUITS OF SCHEMES

The following day passes into early evening, with General John Hubbard convinced that the blast has spelled the end of his enemies.

He pays a visit to Dick Daniels at the *Herald*, who is still at work in his glass-walled editor's office. Bringing a well-known citizen with him, who is also one of his long-time agents, Hubbard informs Daniels that in the commissioner's absence his agent is to be declared mayor of the city. And this will be only a first step. After that, the general will expand his influence to statewide and eventually even nationwide proportions. The general's megalomania is now fully revealed. Hubbard also says that since the editor knows too much, he will of course have to pay with his life.

The Secret Squadron agents drive Commissioner Fordham to the front of the *Herald* building. Wanting to catch Dick Daniels before he leaves, Captain Midnight asks Joyce to go up quickly and inform Mr. Daniels they have arrived. As Joyce enters the building and ascends the stairs, she spots the back of General Hubbard's menacing figure looming through the glass partitions of the editor's office. She rushes back and tells her colleagues.

With drawn pistols, Captain Midnight, Chuck and Ikky climb the stairs in the *Herald* building, leaving Joyce behind to protect Commissioner Fordham. Upon spotting General Hubbard in the editor's office, Midnight yells to Hubbard that Commissioner Fordham and the Secret Squadron are all safe, and that the commissioner will take his rightful place as mayor of Pacific City. Midnight sternly declares that General Hubbard's scheme has failed. Cornered and shrinking back from a battle where he is outgunned, General John Hubbard is forced to surrender. That same night, Torpedo turns state's evidence, signing a confession that reveals Hubbard's long series of crimes.

5

The Holiday Beach Weapon

(1946-1947)

INTERNATIONAL SCIENCE CONFERENCE

The police commissioner of Holiday Beach, Florida meets with Major Barry Steele at Secret Squadron Headquarters in Washington. The commissioner appeals for help in rounding up a gang of thieves that has been terrorizing the town. An international science association will soon hold a conference at the resort, and so there's a danger that important scientific secrets might be stolen. This strongly interests Major Steele.

Captain Midnight and his Squadron team arrive at the resort and enjoy some recreation. Before long they get an exclusive chance to ride the Silver Streak — the new rollercoaster at the Holiday Beach Amusement Park. But at the rollercoaster's first drop, a front wheel comes loose and the cars jump the tracks and plunge down. The imperiled agents leap from the cars, grip rail ties, and then gradually work their way down the hazardous descent to safety.

Captain Midnight believes what happened was no mere accident. He leads his companions to the big top. As the show is about to begin, Midnight's attention is drawn to a female bareback rider. She is masked, and wears a jade pendant similar to one the Countess of Hertel had recently reported stolen. Captain Midnight does not know the masked equestrian rider and the countess are one and the same — and that she is also a member of a carnival gang of thieves. After she finishes her act, the Secret Squadron agents slip out of the tent and confront her. Upon questioning, the countess removes her mask to reveal her identity. She tells them she is wearing only costume jewelry, not the real pendant that is still missing. But the jade pendant looks so real that the Squadron leader is dubious.

Captain Midnight realizes that a carnival parade would form a perfect distraction for someone intending to pull another robbery. What he does not know is that the carnival master, "Uncle Ben," heads the carnival gang — and that Ben has ordered the lion tamer to release his most savage lion in the public square.

The Secret Squadron agents are quartered at the Tivoli Hotel that borders the public square — when suddenly, the ferocious lion appears in the square and terrorizes the vacationing people. Inside the hotel, Midnight and Joyce race up several flights of stairs, and he raps on the door of a room belonging to a man known to be a hunter. Getting no response, Midnight breaks through the door, seizes a rifle, and spots the lion from the window. With two shots he kills the beast. He then withdraws to rejoin Joyce in the hallway — when a sudden explosion rocks the hotel from the main floor! Suspecting a related crime, the Secret Squadron leader and Joyce hurry down to the lobby, and find the steel door to the hotel vault blown open and a large jewel stolen.

Thanks to a sharp observation by Ichabod Mudd, the Secret Squadron manages to retrieve the stolen jewel so quickly that news of the robbery does not reach the press. Despite the lion incident, the hotel blast, and foiled theft, the meeting of renowned scientists from various nations will proceed in Holiday Beach as scheduled. But Captain Midnight senses grave danger. Unless the gang of thieves operating in this fashionable winter retreat is captured, he warns that the criminals may turn from robbing precious stones to far more precious scientific secrets — discoveries that might be convertible to weaponry of major military importance.

THREATENING SCIENTIST

The danger Captain Midnight warned of is more imminent than even he suspects. An unscrupulous scientist named Dr. Salvin has hired Uncle Ben, the old carnival master, to steal certain important scientific papers from the conference and radio back coded messages to him. Uncle Ben soon learns the Secret Squadron agents have tracked the thefts, and are trying to locate the transmitter, so he moves the device to a mausoleum in an abandoned graveyard.

Joyce and Ikky follow Uncle Ben's trail to the graveyard, but when they arrive, they find themselves suddenly surrounded by a gang of men armed with submachine guns. The leader of the gang orders them into a stone crypt that stands in the middle of the cemetery. After they go inside, the gang-leader seals the door behind them, so their only hope is to contact Captain Midnight by Pocket Locator. Then carbon monoxide gas begins pouring into the tomb!

Back at the hotel, Captain Midnight has been trying to crack Dr. Salvin's code. Just as he finds the key to the cipher, his Pocket Locator signals a coded message that his Squadron comrades are in extreme danger. Midnight and Chuck rush to the cemetery, drive off the criminals, break into the crypt, and rescue Joyce and Ikky.

Dr. Salvin has heard about Code-O-Graphs and resolves to obtain one. He wants to disrupt the Secret Squadron's communications, and also to develop a mechanical device of his own to encipher messages that cannot be broken. Realizing Captain Midnight had cracked his own code, Salvin sends out a coded missive describing the whereabouts of his laboratory in a swamp; and just as he has anticipated, Midnight intercepts it.

Dr. Salvin's intercepted message is so detailed and obvious about his laboratory's location, that the Secret Squadron leader suspects the message is probably a plant. Nonetheless, he decides to act on it. This is because he wants to try to capture Salvin before the menacing scientist can gain possession of a valuable scientific secret. It's a mysterious and precious formula created by another member of the scientific conference named Professor Hodges.

Captain Midnight leaves Ikky behind to guard Professor Hodges. Then he, Chuck and Joyce plunge into the depths of the Everglades. They are unaware their approach is spotted from a high lookout platform on an islet amid the great surrounding swamp.

Dr. Salvin traps Captain Midnight and his two companions. The moment they fall into his hands, he subjects them to a hasty search, seizing their Pocket Locators and hoping most of all to get their Secret Squadron Code-O-Graphs. When Salvin is unable to find any Code-O-Graphs, he orders his men to take the prisoners to his hideout and lock them in a laboratory cell. What Salvin does not know is the Secret Squadron agents have their Code-O-Graphs concealed inside lining pouches of their clothing.

On the way to the hideout, Captain Midnight manages to escape by plunging into a dense thicket. And once inside the laboratory cell, Chuck and Joyce hide their Code-O-Graphs under a loose floorboard.

Captain Midnight makes his way to the hideout's radio room, pulls out his Code-O-Graph, and begins to tap a message to Ikky at Holiday Beach. But his presence at the transmitter is discovered, and the message is interrupted by the entrance of Dr. Salvin and several of his men with machineguns. Despite Captain Midnight's effort to save it, his Code-O-Graph comes into the scientist's possession. The Secret Squadron leader is then hauled back to the laboratory cell and imprisoned with his young comrades.

Ichabod Mudd has received enough of Captain Midnight's message to learn the general location of Dr. Salvin's hideaway in the great swamp, and that his Squadron colleagues are in dire trouble. So he decides on bold action. He secures a large flatboat and motors into the swamp. As his craft moves along, he notes oil seepage on the water's surface. In the hideout's area, Ikky sets the floating oil ablaze. Besides causing consternation among the fauna, including rushing alligators, the blaze greatly threatens Ikky himself.

During the fire and chaos Captain Midnight, Chuck, and Joyce manage to escape the prison — but Dr. Salvin and his group disappear down a tunnel in the hideout without a trace. Midnight, Chuck and Joyce work their way through the swamp, winding between the flames that repel the gators, while at the same time using huge leaves to brush away the flames. Finally, they spot Ikky and his flatboat.

After wading through the mud and grimy water to the safety of Ikky's boat, the Secret Squadron agents return to their quarters to clean up and change clothes. Later, Captain Midnight directs Ikky to send him a bogus message via Ikky's Pocket Locator, using the 1946 Code-O-Graph. Midnight knows Dr. Salvin can intercept the transmission with the stolen Pocket Locators, and can also decode it with the now compromised 1946 Code-O-Graph. The message says Professor Hodges will bring his papers and meet them at a certain roadside inn on Highway 70 at eleven p.m. In reality, Midnight ensures that Professor Hodges will remain at the Tivoli Hotel and Ikky will precede Captain Midnight, Chuck, and Joyce to the inn.

Lured by the coded message, the menacing Dr. Salvin arrives at the Highway 70 inn an hour early at ten p.m. — ready to lie in wait for Professor Hodges and seize his precious papers. Instead, Dr. Salvin finds Ikky waiting there with a drawn gun. Just when Ikky captures Salvin and retrieves the stolen Code-O-Graph, though, the tables are turned by the entrance of Uncle Ben and his criminal gang. With the 1946 Code-O-Graph once more in Salvin's possession, he orders Ikky to be removed to a more isolated spot and eliminated.

"WHISTLING" CODE-O-GRAPH

The criminals force Ikky into a truck and start down the remote highway to a secluded spot where they plan to kill him. But at that moment Captain Midnight, Chuck and Joyce appear on the road. Ikky spots them and swiftly draws his new 1947 Secret Squadron "Whistling" Code-O-Graph from his pocket. He blows loud, piercing blasts: three short, followed by three more short for Morse code "S-S."

Recognizing the Secret Squadron distress call, Captain Midnight leads Chuck and Joyce to Ikky's aid. A gun battle follows, in which Uncle Ben and his accomplices are killed, and Midnight, Chuck and Joyce rescue Ikky.

The 1947 "Whistling" Code-O-Graph is a cipher disk mounted on the side of a plastic whistle. The whistle's body is blue and the rotor is red. The 1947 is the first Code-O-Graph to show Captain Midnight's winged-clock insignia, which is also emblazoned on the 1948 and 1949 models.

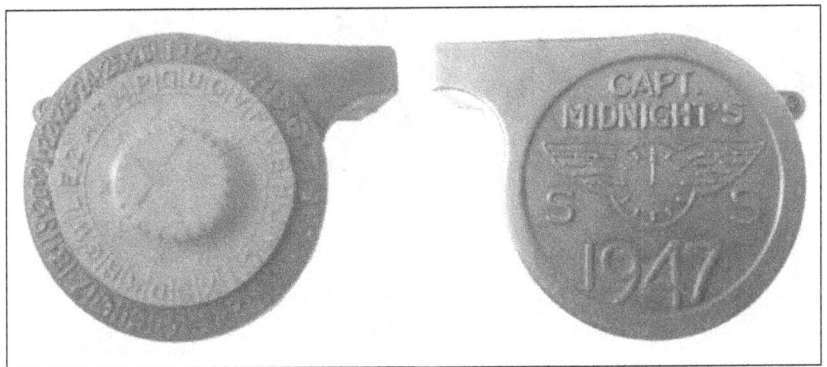

1947 "Whistling" Code-O-Graph. PHOTOGRAPH: LEONARD ZANE

PROFESSOR HODGES' SECRET

Through the late Uncle Ben, the Countess of Hertel has learned Professor Hodges' papers are extremely valuable, and while the Secret Squadron agents have been away, she has managed to trick Professor Hodges and steal his papers. The countess then sends a message to Dr. Salvin, to arrange a meeting at a Holiday Beach restaurant in order to sell him the scientific documents.

The Secret Squadron agents return to the hotel to join Professor Hodges — and discover his valuable papers are missing. Meanwhile at the restaurant, Dr. Salvin informs the countess that the papers she has stolen comprise a formula for a new and deadly radioactive substance known as Nosterium. The countess asks for a million dollars from Dr.

Salvin in exchange for disclosing the papers' whereabouts. On hearing this, he seizes her angrily and forces her under threat of death to blurt out the truth. He then hurries away with this knowledge.

A short time later, the countess seeks out Captain Midnight; and to avenge herself for Salvin's brutal treatment, she reveals to Captain Midnight that the papers are in her dressing room at the amusement park.

The 1947 Secret Squadron Manual, though only a pocketsize measuring 6" x 4-3/8", still has 16 pages like its predecessors. The 1947 Manual also displays some subtleties on the cover. The pilot boarding the P-40 seems to have rather Asian facial features, and a short-skirted female runs among male colleagues in the background. Captain Midnight is both technically and socially advanced for the 1940s era. PHOTOGRAPH: LEONARD ZANE

Reaching the amusement park in the dead of night, the Secret Squadron agents discover Dr. Salvin trying to escape with the precious formula. When they pursue him, he dashes into the building called, The House of Horrors. In a series of gruesome and macabre chambers, not only does the sinister Dr. Salvin elude capture, but he also manages to grab Joyce. Dragging her along, he hauls her through a maze of passages and over a bed of artificially lighted charcoal into a dark nook. There, while gagging her, he boasts that this House of Horrors is only child's play — while Satan's Cay will spawn real and great horrors! With drawn gun, Salvin then spirits Joyce away — but not before she has managed to scrawl something on the wall with a piece of charcoal.

A short time later Captain Midnight, Chuck and Ikky turn on all the lights in The House of Horrors, and they search everywhere for the lost Joyce. Finally, they reach the chamber where some black wall-scrawling reads: "Satan … …" Again, the two groups of three dots represent "Secret Squadron," and Captain Midnight concludes that "Satan" must indicate where Joyce will be taken.

Poseidon Undersea Resort, Fiji. PHOTOGRAPH: POSEIDON UNDERSEA RESORTS

SATAN'S CAY

In the morning, Captain Midnight checks maps of the area for the word, "Satan," and discovers a small island off the coast named "Satan's Cay." So he, Chuck, and Ikky fly their amphibian over Satan's Cay. It is an atoll in the Florida Straits that consists of a steep rock crater, which completely surrounds a lagoon. But seeing no signs of life or habitation in the barren place, the Squadron agents land the amphibian in a bay at a nearby island. Questioning the islanders, they learn that a boat sailed to Satan's Cay yesterday, and this was unusual because of its impassable rock walls.

Captain Midnight acts on the islanders' observation, motoring out in a launch with Chuck and Ikky to Satan's Cay. When they arrive, they circle the atoll and seek some passage through the rock barrier. Midnight suspects the mostly sunken crater would make a perfect enclosure for a hidden underwater base — and he is correct — for the encircling stone cliffs hide Dr. Salvin's mysterious underwater stronghold. Within his submerged fortress, he keeps Joyce prisoner.

Suddenly, Chuck points to a small submarine heading straight for the atoll. Chuck, Captain Midnight, and Ikky watch the craft dive only a hundred yards before reaching the cliffs. The Secret Squadron agents move their boat into a small craggy inlet, near where the submarine disappeared. Chuck swims in search of an entrance through the rock, but a barracuda attacks him and Captain Midnight is forced to fire a shot to kill the ferocious fish. After the shot, a few human faces peer over the rocky ridge above — Dr. Salvin's guards. So Midnight now knows this indeed must be a hidden base. He, Ikky, and Chuck quickly motor back to the nearby island.

EPSILON RAY

At his covert underwater bastion in Satan's Cay, Dr. Salvin intensely studies the properties of Nosterium. He will use Professor Hodges' secret to create his own deadly energy weapon that fires Epsilon rays.[1] In a burst of creative frenzy, Dr. Salvin writes out equations for generating Epsilon rays from Nosterium, keeping his papers together with the Nosterium formula.

Having returned to the island where their amphibian is moored, the Secret Squadron agents realize they cannot safely approach Satan's Cay again. But then Captain Midnight spots a U.S. Navy submarine in the distance, and announces a daring plan.

Captain Midnight and his two agents fly their amphibian low over the U.S. Navy submarine and signal the officers on the conning tower. After soon communicating by radio, and following an additional radio request to the sub by Major Steele from Washington, the navy commander agrees to allow Captain Midnight to come aboard for a brief conference. The amphibian lands near the submarine, and in the meeting that follows, the navy commander agrees to scout the waters beneath Satan's Cay for an underwater passage. While this action is underway, Chuck and Ikky will circle in the amphibian at about 500 feet above the lagoon and prepare to land there if necessary.

The navy U-boat submerges, with Captain Midnight aboard, and searches the area where Midnight and his agents saw the small submarine dive. There is indeed an underwater maw in the rock, and the navy sub proceeds through the passage into the cay's lagoon.

FORTRESS IN THE SEA

Dr. Salvin's mysterious base extends beneath the water, along part of the rock wall lining the lagoon. Through thick glass windows of his undersea fortress, Dr. Salvin watches the navy submarine enter the heart of Satan's Cay. The huge underwater vessel blocks escape by Dr. Salvin's own submarine that is housed in an enclosed underwater pen. His base discovered, Dr. Salvin now makes desperate moves.

The sinister Dr. Salvin collects the deadly Nosterium and Epsilon plans, grabs Joyce, and leads her and his men into his submarine inside the sealed pen. A sonar signal from Salvin's sub opens the pen's portals; and he hurriedly pilots the craft in shallow depth *above* the navy U-boat — so as to try to escape the lagoon. Flying overhead in the amphibian, Chuck and Ikky note the brazen maneuver; and while they must assume Joyce is most likely aboard the small sub, they take a great risk by firing machinegun bursts at Salvin's vessel. This causes some minor damage — and as Chuck and Ikky had hoped, Salvin's submarine surfaces in the lagoon!

Angeline Orr as Joyce Ryan.
PHOTOGRAPH: MAURICE SEYMOUR

Dr. Salvin soon ascends the conning tower of the narrow vessel, grasping Joyce as his hostage. Chuck lands the amphibian in the lagoon, and from the cockpit, he and Ikky clearly see Salvin holding a gun on Joyce.

Sensing a need to be above water to observe what is going on, Captain Midnight persuades the naval commander to surface the navy submarine. When the navy U-boat rises above water, the commander and Captain Midnight swiftly ascend the conning tower — to face Dr. Salvin and Joyce in the tower of the other sub.

Salvin threatens to kill Joyce if the navy submarine and the amphibian do not withdraw and let his vessel through the passage. Captain Midnight calls to Joyce that brighter times will come. Then Midnight momentarily blinds Dr. Salvin with a signal mirror — and Joyce seizes the opportunity to break free and leap into the lagoon!

Now knowing he has no alternative but to act immediately, Dr. Salvin disappears down the conning tower and his U-boat dives. As this happens, Chuck and Ikky power the amphibian on the surface to rescue Joyce, then come alongside the naval submarine to pick up Captain Midnight. Before leaving the navy sub to board the amphibian, Captain Midnight asks the commander to chase Dr. Salvin's submarine. There might yet be some chance of apprehending the scientist and recovering the extremely valuable plans that he has stolen. The navy commander agrees to pursue Salvin's submarine by sonar-tracking.

UNDERSEA BATTLE

Captain Midnight boards the amphibian, and the naval craft submerges. But the delay has been long enough for Dr. Salvin's submarine to escape the lagoon through the subterranean passage. When the amphibian takes to the air, the Secret Squadron is able to see Dr. Salvin's vessel and the pursuing navy sub in the clear waters at moderate depth. Then an underwater drama unfolds. From an aft tube, Dr. Salvin fires a torpedo at the chasing navy submarine, and then his sub speeds into the deep waters of the Florida Straits!

Salvin's torpedo narrowly misses the naval sub, and so the navy commander takes no further chances. He fires two bow torpedoes, and one of them strikes Dr. Salvin's submarine and blasts it apart!

Dr. Salvin's shattered U-boat sinks in clumps of mangled steel and disintegrating fragments. The navy submarine surfaces and confirms the kill by radio to the Secret Squadron's amphibian. The sinister Dr. Salvin and the formula for the Epsilon ray now lie deep at the bottom of the Florida Straits.

ENDNOTES

1 According to Wikipedia, the term "Epsilon ray" was coined by British Nobel Laureate Physicist, J.J. Thompson, the man also credited with discovering the electron. "Delta radiation" or "secondary rays" are high-energy electrons or alpha particles (helium nuclei) emitting from a source. If the particles are extremely high energy, and crash into one another, then other types of radiation decay can occur following the secondary decay. Such "tertiary radiation" is sometimes described as an Epsilon particle or "ray." Thompson's term "Epsilon ray," however, is obsolete and no longer used.

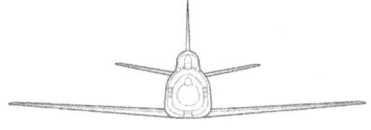

6

The Slave Smugglers

(1947)

BARE-HANDED BRUTALITY

An air of baffling mystery hangs over the whole week. With Dr. Salvin and the formula for the Epsilon ray at the bottom of the Florida Straits, Captain Midnight is flying back to Washington when he picks up an intriguing distress call. The call comes from a private yacht named *Angela*. The vessel is sailing near the Bay of Fundy (between New Brunswick and Nova Scotia, including a small portion along the Maine Coast). The message says the *Angela* is under attack.

Flying northward to investigate, the Secret Squadron agents find the craft stranded on the shoals of a small uninhabited island. They board only to discover that all three members of the crew are dead, murdered in a mysterious and incomprehensible way. For though they were armed, they've apparently been strangled by a single individual! The marks left on all three throats indicate a missing little finger on the right hand.

Midnight puzzles over how one person could have done the job. But there was actually more than one person. In fact, a great many of such persons are being smuggled into the United States from some distant, strange land. Their leader is simply known as "The Chief," and they are part of a great plot to attack America.

One of these brutal savages dresses and speaks like an ordinary American citizen, but with just a tinge of an exotic accent. He applies for a job at a naval ordnance plant. When he is turned down, he proceeds to strangle the employment supervisor. The Secret Squadron agents — now re-outfitted with 1947 Code-O-Graphs, Pocket Locators, and other equipment — speed to the scene. They find the circumstances of the death are the same as those surrounding the yacht's crew. This time, though, there is a clue: the killer has accidentally left his reference card behind. It leads the Squadron agents to a rooming house where he's been staying. The housekeeper there, Mrs. Vance, tries to keep them out. But they search his room and in a desk drawer find a tiny, white carven idol of a tribal god. Deciding the man may return for it, Captain Midnight leaves Chuck and Joyce behind to watch for him, while he and Ichabod Mudd track down other clues. Midnight orders them to keep in touch with him through Pocket Locators and the 1947 Code-O-Graph codes.

Meanwhile, the killer — called Jorgensen — has gone to New York City to report to his immediate superior, a man named Mr. Talon. The superior reprimands Jorgensen for jeopardizing what he cryptically calls the "Chief's Master Plan." There must be no more killings by Jorgensen and his compatriots, he says, until the day of the "great attack." Jorgensen consents and returns to his rooming house to get his idol. As the week ends, the confrontation between the killer and Chuck and Joyce is imminent.

The housekeeper, Mrs. Vance, is also a member of the subversive organization. On Jorgensen's return, she informs him that federal agents have searched his room. When he finds his idol stolen, he goes berserk and vows to kill the agents. Throughout the scene, Chuck and Joyce cling to a trellis just outside the window. Upon hearing that Jorgensen and Mrs. Vance are going to New York, they decide to sneak along with them in hopes of discovering what's afoot.

Chuck and Joyce send a coded message to Midnight, who accepts their plan and also says an anthropologist reports that the idol is utterly unlike the work of any known primitive tribe. The youths then climb into the trunk of Jorgensen's car. Midnight and Ikky follow in their own car from an appreciable distance behind.

Out on the highway, Jorgensen's rear tire blows out, and Mrs. Vance opens the trunk to get the jack. Seeing Chuck and Joyce, she slams the lid on the two before they can act, locking them in the trunk. They feverishly send a distress signal to Captain Midnight, as Jorgensen drives on the flat tire up a hill overlooking a riverbank. Then he releases the brake and hops out with his accomplice. It looks as though Chuck and Joyce are rolling down into a watery grave. But Midnight's auto quickly appears — racing across an open field and crashing into the death car just before it reaches the bank. The car rolls over and bursts into flames, but Chuck and Joyce are extricated before being roasted alive.

TALON'S EMPLOYMENT AGENCY

Jorgensen and Mrs. Vance force a passerby to give them a lift to New York. They plan to return to Mr. Talon at his business — which is an employment agency front that places Jorgensen's fellow nationals in strategic spots throughout the country. The plot is to prepare for the day of the great attack. The Secret Squadron agents again manage to pick up the trail.

Jorgensen and Mrs. Vance reach Talon's employment agency and confer with him in his private office. The door between his office and the outer one is topped by a transom that is slightly open. Captain Midnight, Chuck, Joyce, and Ikky arrive at the agency a short time later, and ask the secretary in the front office to see Mr. Talon. The secretary calls Talon on the inter-office line, relaying the request by "Captain Midnight and his associates." In the private office, Jorgensen pulls out his revolver and stands on a chair so he can aim at the visitors in the next room. He murmurs that he will make his first shot at Captain Midnight count.

Mrs. Vance fears that a quadruple murder in Talon's office would lead to an investigation that could expose the whole master plan. She tips the chair on which Jorgensen is standing and so prevents his firing the gun.

When Talon meets the Secret Squadron agents in the outer office, he feigns complete ignorance of Jorgensen. But while talking with Midnight, he receives a telephone call. He awkwardly assures the caller that he will call back, at the same time scribbling down a phone number. Seeing the number, and shrewdly guessing from Talon's behavior that the call may have something to do with Jorgensen, Midnight bids goodbye and leads his agents out of the office.

MANHATTAN MANSION

At the police station, Midnight learns the place from which the call to Talon's office was made is an old and fashionable mansion on Park Avenue. It is inhabited by an eccentric society woman of advanced age. Actually, this old woman is a cog in the plot. Jorgensen hides out in this mansion while he is being taught to control his murderous instincts. He is already lying low when the Secret Squadron agents arrive.

The elderly woman invites the Secret Squadron agents in, and calls all four of them by name. She pretends to be the sister of a man whose life they once saved during one of their many bouts with Ivan Shark. As they talk with her, in the heart of the mansion, she sits in a great stiff-back chair in the gloomy candlelight. They see only a wrinkled aristocratic face and gleaming white hair in the shadows, and they find it almost impossible to believe this charming old woman could have any connection with murder. Although Midnight does not relax his suspicions, he finds it difficult to refuse a request that they stay for tea.

In the kitchen, the old woman orders a tasteless and odorless drug to be dropped in the tea. Summoning a henchman named Slaughter, she tells him, "Send a code to my father. Tell him I have our old enemy Captain Midnight in my power." Thus we learn that the old woman is Fury Shark, and the "Chief" is none other than Ivan Shark himself. But Captain Midnight and the Secret Squadron do not know this.

Unaware but still dubious, Midnight tries to warn Chuck, Ikky, and Joyce not to drink their tea, but they take several gulps of it and promptly black out. Midnight is then surrounded by armed men, who take all four Squadron members to a sub-cellar chamber, where they seal the agents in to die. It looks as though the agents will meet their end in the very heart of New York City. No one will be the wiser, and Fury will have executed her father's principle of inflicting elegant, artful, and suffering death upon their arch enemies. *[Through scores of years, this lesson has been indelibly imprinted upon all master villains worthy of the accolade — including but not limited to Doctor Julius No, Auric Goldfinger, Hugo Drax, Ernst Stavro Blofeld, and Doctor Evil.]*

There is, however, an ancient fireplace in the chamber, and Captain Midnight notices the un-scorched bricks show that in spite of its age the fireplace has never been used. Poking around, he discovers it's a blind without a flue. And when Chuck grabs a loose brick, the youth comes upon a lever that swings the whole structure open. Behind it, in the fashion of such nineteenth-century houses as these, is a hidden staircase. They climb it, and when they reach the third floor, they come upon some peepholes in the wall and stare through them. They see Jorgensen in the midst of a strange tribal ritual. They soon break through the wall into the room, and Jorgensen flees.

Searching for Jorgensen through the great musty mansion, the Squadron agents separate — and suddenly Chuck and Ikky hear Joyce scream, "FA...!" The scream breaks off in the middle, as though she were being strangled! Even before Chuck and Ikky can find Joyce, Captain Midnight has rushed to her aid. He tears Jorgensen's hands away from her throat, and in a life or death struggle, he finally succeeds in overpowering the brutal killer and knocking him unconscious. Carrying their prisoner, the four Secret Squadron agents escape and hurry to the nearest airfield, where they commandeer an army plane and return to Washington.

Aboard the plane, Jorgensen refuses to answer questions, and they lock him in the tail compartment. Finding himself so trapped and bound, Jorgensen goes completely wild, and reverting to the savage animal that he is, he gnaws his way through the ropes that bind him! He breaks into the cabin and finding it empty seizes an automatic pistol and bursts into the flight deck, where all four Secret Squadron agents are planning their next moves. He points the automatic straight at Captain Midnight and pulls the trigger!

Ikky notices that the crazed killer is unfamiliar with automatic firearm mechanisms, and has not disengaged the safety. Ikky and Chuck leap on him, and after a bitter fight recover the upper hand.

THE STRANGE RACE AND THE CHIEF'S MASTER PLAN

In Washington, a bewildered scientist examines Jorgensen and announces that he belongs to no known race of man. Both his physical structure and his linguistics indicate he is a member of an unidentified species. A psychiatrist is called in, and Jorgensen is held under observation in a private hospital.

But Fury, having meanwhile discovered that Jorgensen is gone, summons another of his fellow countrymen. She informs him that Jorgensen must die before he can betray the secret of his origin. Thus Captain Midnight finds his prisoner dead one morning, strangled by a man who has only four fingers on his right hand. Now the Secret Squadron agents know for certain that Jorgensen was only one of a large number of strangers from a strange land — a land of savage murderers.

In the meantime, Ivan Shark travels by "rocket plane" from the mysterious homeland of the Lost People, to his private island some distance off the coast of Maine. The island is the spot from which the trained savages are smuggled to the United States mainland. Shark has set up luxurious headquarters there — fully equipped with gongs, sliding panels, a transmitter, and other favorite paraphernalia. It is here on Nameless Island that Fury joins him. In their discussions, the whole blueprint of Shark's plan is revealed: infiltration of the Lost People into North America, followed by the day of the great attack, and all the rest. But Shark doesn't know that Captain Midnight is heading toward the Maine coast.

The four Secret Squadron agents have reached an impasse with the murder of Jorgensen. The Squadron members ponder the first four-fingered strangulations: the crew members of the *Angela* yacht were choked near the mouth of the Bay of Fundy. The agents also note the significance of some sperm oil that Jorgensen had burned in his idol. They decide that the answer to the mystery lies somewhere in the North Atlantic, perhaps even on Nameless Island.

In a chandler's shop, where fishing supplies are sold, Captain Midnight gets his first clue. The owner happens to mention there are strange goings-on. In certain neighboring villages, even some notoriously poor fishermen have lately been throwing money around with abandon. A townsman then drops in, and he too seems to have plenty of cash. He brags that he has lined up a new job in the next village, and that he's taking his fishing smack down there and going into a more profitable line of business. He says he's never met his new employer, but has an appointment with him that evening at a tavern in the heart of the nearby town.

COUNTERSPYING

The Secret Squadron agents quickly duck out of the shop, and when the garrulous old fisherman reaches his boat, he finds them waiting for him. When he proves to be a pleasant and pliable fellow, they negotiate the purchase of his boat for a generous price — which also includes getting his identification papers. Warning him to stick to fishing, they pay for his boat and then set off. Before long, they land and tie up at a dock of the neighboring village.

While Ikky and Joyce remain aboard the newly acquired boat, Captain Midnight and Chuck slip into the fog-blanketed town and make their way to the tavern. Pretending to be a fisherman and son, the two apply for work with a man named McGrath, who is one of Ivan Shark's lieutenants. From him, they learn what's going on. Shark has hired a whole fleet of fishing smacks to sneak cargoes of Lost People nightly through Coast Guard watches and casual civilian observations. Midnight agrees to smuggle the foreigners on his boat. His plans go awry, though, when an old friend of the fisherman from whom Midnight purchased the boat (and whose identity he assumed) shows up at the tavern. Taking one look at the masquerading Captain Midnight, the man announces he's an impostor.

McGrath and a handful of other men immediately march both Midnight and Chuck down to the docks, intending to rub them out. But thanks to Code-O-Graphs and Locators, Ikky and Joyce learn what's happening and break up the shooting party.

Midnight orders his agents aboard his boat at once. They set out for Nameless Island, still hoping to present themselves to the "Chief" as members of his transport crew. They don't yet know that it is Ivan Shark they're up against.

Late at night, the Secret Squadron agents reach the island. Twenty of Shark's subjects are waiting to be ferried to the mainland. Midnight soon begins taking them on, planning to head for the nearest Coast Guard station. But Shark receives a call from the village, telling him there are federal agents aboard the smack. He sends out one more man after the other twenty — who orders them to mutiny, kill the Secret Squadron agents, and bring the boat back.

The savages launch an attack on the wheelhouse. Most of these lost-race men are armed, and they begin firing up from the deck at the wheelhouse. There is a fierce gun battle, during which Midnight keeps whirling the wheel rapidly back and forth, lurching the boat from side to side. It wrecks the savages' aiming, and throws those who are climbing to the wheelhouse off the ladders. Finally, however, the Secret Squadron agents are outdone by sheer force of numbers and find themselves surrounded. They open the hatch and slip down into the galley, hoping to reach the lifeboat in the stern. But when they step back onto the deck, supersonic shock waves from flying bullets crack around their ears! The agents duck back again, locking themselves in the hold. They are out of ammunition, now, and at the mercy of the gang of ruthless killers.

The four-fingered men allow the smack to crash into a reef. Water floods the hold, and it's either climb out or drown. Midnight orders his agents to go on deck with their hands in the air, hoping to escape somehow from the sinking craft. But Shark has sent another boat after them, and they are carried back to Nameless Island. There, at last, they come face to face with their arch enemy, the international gangster. Sneering at them, Shark boasts of his plan, and that he will soon have a new passage to transport his subjects that will replace his need to hire fishing smacks. (After all, Shark must explain his resourcefulness and skills in order to be appreciated by at least some worthy opponents with high or adequate intelligence.) He still keeps the whereabouts of the savages' homeland secret, though, and then turns the Squadron agents over to the tender mercies of his murderous subjects. The four-fingered ones decide to sacrifice Midnight and his colleagues to their gods at dawn.

In a cell that night, Midnight pulls out the idol that he had taken from Jorgensen's room. In full view of the savage guards, he scoffs at the idol, abuses it, and finally smashes it on the floor of the cell. The guards do exactly what he had hoped. Forgetting civilized weapons in their wrath, they burst in and try to strangle the Secret Squadron agents. In a wild fight, Midnight and his companions best them, and escape from the cell. But they are unable to reach the boat and are stranded on the island. So they head for cover.

While the Secret Squadron agents lie low in a heavy thicket, Shark learns of their escape — and tracking them to the thicket, sets fire to it. The flames drive the agents back, foot by foot, toward the edge of the island. As the week ends, it looks like they must choose between surrender, drowning, or burning.

BID FOR ESCAPE

In his meeting with Midnight, Shark had boasted that he wouldn't need his fleet of fishing smacks to smuggle in his slaves. He said he would have a new passage — one that was evidently safe from the Coast Guard while getting his men to shore. And it is the new passage that gives the Secret Squadron agents hope now. In their desperate predicament, they stumble upon the opening of a tunnel that's being dug under the bay to connect Nameless Island to the mainland. They jump into the tunnel — just in time to escape the flames — and grope their way forward, hoping to get all the way through. But they reach a dead-end, where Shark's slaves have ceased work. And just as they reach this point, the arch criminal's voice comes booming from behind them. It looks as if they are hopelessly trapped under the sea itself.

Narrow-gauge tracks run through the tunnel, and a small car stands at their end. When Shark and his gang climb aboard another car at the shaft's opening and start down, Captain Midnight douses the tunnel lights. The Secret Squadron agents scramble into the car at their end, and move with growing speed on the same track. At the last second, they jump off and the two cars hit head-on. In the resulting tumult, darkness, and confusion, Midnight leads his followers out of the tunnel and into a rainstorm outside.

The Secret Squadron agents race toward hangars at the far-end of Nameless Island, knock out a couple of guards, and seize a small plane. Moments later, Shark reaches the hangars and furiously watches them take off. But one of his henchmen tells him, "Take it easy, Chief, the plane was in here for repairs. It has a loose wing, and in this storm, it won't stay up for more than ten minutes."

Actually, the Secret Squadron agents fly for less than ten minutes, when the billowing storm begins to tear the wing loose. Midnight tries to keep the plane in the air until Ikky can tap out an S.O.S. Then all four bail out and drop into the raging sea. Struggling through giant waves, they finally reach their plane's torn-off wing and hang onto it for dear life.

A Coast Guard station receives the Squadron agents' distress call. The commanding officer knows it's impossible to land an amphibian on such a sea, and he also fears there isn't enough time for a cutter to save the survivors. So he sends out a small helicopter. The pilot locates the four agents clinging to their makeshift raft, but the helicopter has room for only three. Despite their protests, Midnight orders Chuck, Joyce, and Ikky to take the ride back to the Coast Guard station first. "I'll hang on," he says, "until the helicopter can make a return trip."

SECRET SQUADRON'S LOSS

An hour later, Ikky and a Coast Guard pilot come back. They sight some floating plane wreckage, but Midnight is no longer clinging to it! He has disappeared from at least a mile radius, unquestionably beneath the waves. It appears that Captain Midnight is dead!

The early part of the next week is devoted almost entirely to gaining evidence that Captain Midnight is indeed dead. Chuck and Joyce, hearing the news from Ikky upon his return to the Coast Guard station, refuse to believe it and insist on going out themselves to scan the waters.

Other planes from the Secret Squadron join them, and the whole area is culled. Receiving the news, Major Steele radios every government ship in the North Atlantic to keep on the alert. Word comes from a coastal city that a body has been washed up, and Chuck, Joyce and Ikky fly anxiously to the scene to identify it. They are absolutely certain it isn't Midnight. It's there that the press first gets wind of what has happened, and the correspondents crowd around the Squadron agents, demanding to know the truth. Finally, Major Steele has no choice but to make a special announcement over a worldwide hookup that there's little reason to believe the famous Captain Midnight is still alive, and that his death at sea must be assumed to have occurred.

A montage describes various people throughout the world listening to the broadcast in grim silence. The montage ends with Ivan Shark hearing it on Nameless Island and roaring with glee. "Now," he declares, "there is nothing to stop me! We will head straight for the Empire of the Lost People and begin final preparations for the great attack!"

In Major Steele's private office, there is quiet solemnity following the broadcast. After a pause, Chuck, Joyce and Ikky vow to carry on in

Captain Midnight's name and to avenge his death by wiping out Ivan Shark and his whole organization. The agents plan to bomb Nameless Island, but before they can get started, they receive a long-distance telephone call from a rancher in Brazil. His name is da Silva, and he says that a plane has fallen on his estate. It is a strange looking craft, which resembles Ivan Shark's "rocket plane" that he's been reading about in background stories on Captain Midnight's death. The pilot was killed, but in searching the plane, the ranchers found a set of maps and charts in which they felt the Secret Squadron agents would be interested. Ikky, Chuck and Joyce are very excited, because these charts may well show the location of the land from which the savages come. They tell the rancher to deposit the documents at once with the police chief in the nearest city. They will fly to Brazil to get them.

The Secret Squadron agents' guess is correct. A "rocket plane" in Ivan Shark's fleet has crashed, and when he realizes there is a copied set of charts aboard it, he turns back and lands near the wrecked plane. Just as the rancher returns from leaving the papers with the police, Shark seizes him and demands to know where the charts are. The rancher, da Silva, declares that he has outfoxed the great Ivan Shark — whereupon Shark kills him and turns to a member of his gang named Gomez. He tells Gomez, "You will go into the city under this man's name. When the Secret Squadron agents arrive and get the charts, you will introduce yourself as the rancher who telephoned them. Then you will lead them back here to die!"

BRAZIL

The Secret Squadron agents arrive in Brazil, obtain the charts from the police, and pore over them excitedly in their hotel room. Ivan Shark's agent Gomez presents himself, claiming to be da Silva. He says he's seen a picture of Shark in the papers, and believes the dead pilot in the "rocket plane" is Ivan Shark himself. The Secret Squadron agents must come to identify him.

Ikky, Chuck, and Joyce see no reason to doubt the word of the presumed da Silva, so they enter his open car — only to find two armed men sitting there waiting for them. They are taken prisoner and driven to the villa, where Ivan Shark greets them with sardonic laughter. *[Why is it that the villains have most of the laughs?]*

Shark tells the Squadron agents that when they lost their leader, they lost all hope of ever outwitting him. They are putty in his hands, now, and he orders them searched. But even to Ikky's and Joyce's amazement, the charts are not in Chuck's pocket, where he put them when they joined Shark's henchman Gomez! Furious, Shark offers to give them their freedom if they will tell him where the charts are. *[The villains, on the other hand, have the widest mood-swings, too.]*

Shark would not, he assures the Squadron members, offer such a bargain if Captain Midnight were still alive, for Midnight was made of sturdier mettle and would have scorned any such deal.

Chuck asks for a few minutes to think over the offer, and Shark — highly amused at their apparent weakness — has them led to an upstairs room. Upon closing the door to the room, Chuck whispers to his comrades that he stuffed the charts in the upholstery of the car as they climbed in. If they can reach the car, which is standing in the courtyard beneath their window, they'll be in the clear. There's a guard on the balcony, but Ikky sees a Portuguese riding whip hanging on the wall, and they summon the guard in. With one swift flick, Ikky wraps the whip around the guard's wrist and yanks his arm up just as the guard fires. As the other guards come rushing, the Secret Squadron agents leap from the balcony into the open car and drive off — bullets cracking by their ears!

A hot chase ensues. As they drive down the hill, just out of sight of their pursuers, they seize the briefest chance to jump out of the car and let it roll over a precipice. The vehicle plunges down a steep slope and bursts into flames.

Hiding in a thicket, the Secret Squadron agents watch Shark's henchmen jump out of their car and rush down the embankment to see if the Squadron agents have been killed.

While Shark's men are occupied, the Secret Squadron members calmly take the empty car and drive off. They make good their escape, but the only hitch is the charts were in the other car and have been destroyed by the fire. The Squadron agents have at least discovered, however, that the Island of the Lost People is located somewhere in Antarctica. They work feverishly to reconstruct the map from memory, and then radio Major Steele to send them a plane especially equipped for Antarctic flight. Major Steele responds that he will have a Squadron agent bring a properly outfitted plane as soon as possible.

The plane arrives later than anticipated. The agents have been waiting for several hours at the field, and just at the stroke of midnight, the aircraft comes sweeping out of the sky. Ikky, Chuck, and Joyce walk to meet it, regretfully recalling how the late Captain Midnight himself used to arrive exactly in this way, at exactly this hour. But that was in days past.

OUT OF THE DARKNESS

A figure descends from the flight deck of the airplane and removes his goggles. As the week ends — with Ikky staring incredulously and gasping a fervent, "Holy Catfish!" — the pilot is revealed to be none other than Captain Midnight himself! In a scene of jubilant reunion, he explains to them how he was picked out of the water by a Navy submarine before the Coast Guard helicopter could return. He learned from the radio operator aboard the submarine of mysterious signals originating from the Antarctic. The signals did not come from the Byrd expedition; so he had gone into the Antarctic Circle, in search of the hidden transmitter and thinking it might hold the secret to Shark's Lost Race. He hadn't communicated with Major Steele for fear of calling Shark's attention to his presence there. But he had found the Island of the Lost People! And then Chuck, Joyce, and Ikky had left Washington for South America, just an hour before he had returned. He is still keeping his survival a secret, because it will give them a better opportunity to break up the great conspiracy and capture Shark.

TOWARD THE SOUTH POLE

The four Secret Squadron agents, now reunited and guided by Captain Midnight's map, take off for the forbidding land of ice and snow. They refuel at Cape Horn, and follow the route that Lincoln Ellsworth's expedition had taken in 1935.

The Squadron agents fly to the South Shetland Islands, well on the way to the South Pole, when a terrific blizzard builds up ice on their plane's wings and forces the craft down. Upon landing, Midnight says they are only a few miles from the valley that is warmed by the great fires of a volcano and lava rings. This is where the Lost People originated and have lived for untold ages. These people were not even aware they were not the only race of human beings on earth, until Ivan Shark discovered them and proceeded to dominate and mobilize them in his plans for world conquest.

LAND OF THE LOST PEOPLE

While the Secret Squadron agents sit out the blinding blizzard, Captain Midnight shows them some small and hazy aerial photographs he had taken of a fertile Antarctic valley. The valley contains empty wastes of villages and towns under Ivan Shark's domination. The Squadron members note some preparations for the great emigration that Shark will lead.

Finally they get a distant, obscure glimpse of Shark's magnificent headquarters carved into the summit of one of the mountains ringing the valley.

When the blizzard has blown over, Midnight takes off. But the extended subzero conditions have caused fuel mechanisms to malfunction — and the plane sputters, plunges, and cracks up. While the radio remains in working order, they can't get through to the nearest receiver on Cape Horn. So it seems the Secret Squadron members are doomed.

Somehow staving off death for twenty-four hours, the Squadron agents pick up keyed radio signals from an approaching plane. The signals are in Shark's secret code, and Captain Midnight knows the plane must be heading toward the Lost People's valley.

During the period of his alleged death, one of Captain Midnight's accomplishments was to crack Ivan Shark's code, and he now uses that code to send out a distress call to the pilot of the approaching plane. Believing it is one of his comrades in trouble, the pilot drops down to effect rescue, and the Secret Squadron agents ambush him. He is killed in a gunfight, and Midnight and his colleagues take off in Shark's plane, bearing the pilot's body with them. As the week ends, Chuck spots an amazing sight: a green valley in the midst of ice and snow; and looming beyond it, a series of mountain peaks — one of which is carved in the image of the tiny white statue which Jorgensen had kept hidden in his desk drawer.

Midnight's problem is to land in the valley without revealing to Shark that he and his agents are aboard the plane. He solves the quandary by faking a bad landing, taxiing the plane into a patch of brush, and then setting the craft on fire. When one of Shark's stooges investigates, it looks as if the (previously killed) pilot had been burnt to death in the destroyed plane, as this stooge soon reports to the Chief.

Meanwhile, the Secret Squadron agents make their way to what looks like an ancient deserted shrine in the woods outside the villages. They decide to use this as a base of operations. Their object is to capture Shark and Fury, for they know that without them, the Lost People will never leave the valley.

Inside the shrine they encounter a weird, half-mad old priest. He has been banished from the city for protesting against the people's worship of the new god, Shark. The priest speaks crude English, taught by Shark's men. It's been part of Shark's scheme to influence these people most effectively and powerfully. As part of forcibly teaching them English, he had supplanted their religion with unswerving faith in him, and had dominated them with great ease. But the priest was one who had openly rebelled, and had been lucky to escape with his life.

From the priest, Midnight learns much that is valuable, including the whereabouts of Shark's mountain headquarters and that it can be approached only by cable-car.

Meanwhile, one of Shark's lieutenants reports to his master that he suspects some of the Lost People are still clinging to their worship of the old gods. As a test during their next bombing practice — and in preparation for the great attack — Shark orders them to destroy the ancient shrine in the woods.

Thus it is that Midnight and his companions suddenly find themselves and their base the target of a hailstorm of bombs! Luckily, though, Shark's lieutenant was right and the pilots have no intention of risking the wrath of the old gods by destroying the shrine, so they deliberately miss their target. This failure serves only to infuriate Shark, and he orders paratroop maneuvers, with paratroopers to land all over the shrine and wipe it out with grenades and fire.

When the paratroops attack, the old priest rushes out to resist them, and following Shark's orders, they kill him. The attackers are now sure the shrine is empty. But as they approach it, the bells in the tower begin to ring, and the troops beat a hasty retreat. They are certain the gods must be warning them not to attack. Actually, it is Midnight who is ringing the bells, surmising what the reaction of the savages will be. Thus, he and his agents are saved for the moment. But upon being informed of the incident of the bells, Shark knows there must be human beings in the shrine. He calls together a handful of his most trusted and ruthless slaves and commands them to wipe out whomever they find there.

Midnight figures that the shrine will be attacked, but hopes to lie low there until dark and then slip into the city. Shark's gang shows up before dark, though, and there is a bitter gunfight with the Secret Squadron agents using the belfry as a fortress. They kill some of Shark's men, but a few attackers manage to get into the shrine. Standing directly under the belfry, they order the Secret Squadron agents to surrender. Midnight's answer is to cut loose a huge iron bell. It falls through the rotting floor, crushing the men below.

Captain Midnight and his comrades slip out of the shrine and seize the official car, but then Shark's crowd arrives. Keeping their faces hidden, the Squadron agents drive into the city. The car is recognized, and they get an escort all the way up to the foot of the mountain that contains Shark's headquarters. They even manage to climb into the cable-car and start up the long ride to the top of the mountain. But before they get halfway, a scout arrives at the base and informs the guard that all of Sharks agents who were sent out to destroy the shrine have been killed, so the men in the cable-car must be impostors. As the car approaches the gigantic idol's face, which is actually the entrance to Shark's headquarters, Shark himself receives this news.

The arch criminal shouts down demands to know who is in the approaching car, and threatens to cut the cable unless he receives an answer. Midnight orders Ikky to tell the truth. Shark hears that the Secret Squadron agents are thus entering into his own domain. They cannot turn back, and Shark is of course delighted. He has twenty men with machineguns waiting for them at the cable terminal. But only three of the Secret Squadron agents climb out. This is because Shark still thinks Captain Midnight is dead, and so Midnight slips out the rear and dangles unseen from the cable. Shark expects only three agents, of course, and so takes them prisoner and has them led into his office.

As soon as his colleagues have disappeared, Midnight climbs hand-over-hand up the remainder of the cable and sneaks in. Shark, speaking through his public address system, tells the populace that he has captured his enemies and will dispose of them in a public festival. But Captain Midnight, using a mike in another part of the mountain retreat, horns in on the talk and makes a fool of Shark.

The arch criminal is staggered at the knowledge that Captain Midnight is still alive and at liberty somewhere within his own quarters. He locks up Ikky, Joyce, and Chuck and institutes a search. But Midnight seizes a guard's uniform and succeeds in freeing his agents. Just when they're about to make good their escape, though, Fury shows up with a Tommy gun. So once more, they are at Shark's mercy — and this time, it's all four of them.

FATE OF A RACE

Directly across Ivan Shark's headquarters, the smoldering volcano makes its presence felt over the entire week. At the request of his slaves, Shark agrees to dispose of his captives once and for all by flying a helicopter over the volcano — and before the fierce eyes of the entire populace — dropping them one by one into the bubbling crater.

As a special mental torture, the arch criminal has the Squadron agents bound and imprisoned at the top of his quarters. The chamber has two enormous glass windows, which are the eyes of the god's face carved out of the mountain. From there, they can see the cloud of smoke that always hovers above the great volcano. Directly below is a drop of several thousand feet, and the only entrance to the room is a sliding panel, beyond which a number of armed guards stand watch.

It seems that Captain Midnight and his comrades are hopelessly trapped, and now and then the volcano emits thunderous roars that shake the entire valley. It is during one of these bursts that Midnight manages to shatter the glass in one of the windows without attracting the guards'

Ed Prentiss, the voice of radio's Captain Midnight. PHOTOGRAPH: THE WANDER COMPANY

attention. Then he cuts his bonds on a jagged edge of glass and proceeds to free his agents from the cords that bind them. He orders them to pull down the elaborate drapes that Shark had installed for his own private use and tear them into long strips. They tie the strips together to create a makeshift rope. By securing one end to the inside of the idol's nose, Midnight figures it might be possible to drop from there into the mouth. They try it, one after the other, each knowing that one slip will send the person plunging to death below.

After her three comrades have already made the jump, Joyce lands and almost loses her footing. But they grasp her, and the four of them soon prepare to reenter Shark's private chamber. Upon bursting into Shark's chamber, the Squadron agents catch Ivan Shark and Fury completely by surprise and take them prisoner!

Knowing it would be certain death to reenter the valley, Captain Midnight first uses Shark's transmitter to radio Major Steele to send planes. Then he and his agents explore the mountain quarters until they find a narrow passage leading out to a broad plateau beyond the god's head. Shark's helicopter is parked here, ready for any quick getaway that the master criminal might need to make. So it looks as if all the Secret Squadron agents have to do is hustle their prisoners off in the helicopter and try to meet the approaching Secret Squadron planes somewhere in the Antarctic. And thus, Ivan Shark and Fury Shark are at last defeated. And then — a tremendous explosion!

The volcano, which has been huffing and puffing, finally blows its top. Had they been in the valley, the Secret Squadron agents would have died at once, for the burning embers and cinders and sprays of hot lava pour down, and there is no escape for the entire Lost Race! They are soon wiped out.

As for Midnight and the others, they are thrown to the ground by the terrific concussion. Clouds of smoke and dirt blot out the sun! Darkness spreads impenetrably, and by the time Captain Midnight recovers from the overwhelming shock, Shark and Fury are gone.[1] All that can be heard is the sputter of the helicopter's motors in the distance.

ENDNOTES

1 Why wasn't Shark's henchman, Gardo, in this adventure? It was to buffer a cast change that took effect in the next adventure, "Death Deals a Diamond." Gardo's role was taken over by actor Art Hern, while the part of Yates in the next adventure was played by the gravelly-voiced Earl George, who had played Gardo ever since the Skelly Oil sponsored shows from 1938–1940.

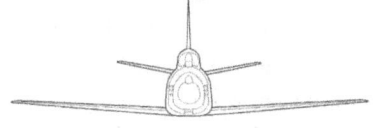

7

Death Deals a Diamond

(1947)

THE STOLEN STAR

The sudden volcano eruption in the forgotten valley of the Lost People enabled Ivan Shark and his daughter to escape from the Secret Squadron agents. When Captain Midnight recovered from the shock of the explosion, he discovered that his prisoners had already regained consciousness and had taken off in the helicopter, which was the only available aircraft. So he and his companions found themselves stranded on a narrow mountain ledge, thousands of feet high, on a remote Antarctic island that was devastated by the volcano.

Meanwhile, in distant British Guiana, a small air-courier company has been entrusted with transporting a mysterious and precious cargo — a cargo that a ruthless gang is endeavoring to steal. At an airfield outside the city of Georgetown, British Guiana, one of the gang members is a man named Yates. He sneaks into the courier company's small plane before it takes off, and mis-calibrates the altimeter. The craft's priceless cargo is contained in a metal case, which the criminal gang is determined to obtain at any cost.

From a safe distance, Yates follows the plane into the night with his own aircraft. When his quarry reaches hills and plateaus over a remote area of the Yucatan Peninsula, it crashes into trees on a plateau, killing the copilot. Yates then lands, kills the surviving pilot, and makes off with the mysterious metal case.

A helicopter piloted by Agent SS-11, otherwise known as Kelly, rescues his Secret Squadron colleagues from the icy Antarctic shelf. Escaping from the forgotten valley, they transfer to a multi-engine aircraft and continue northward. Though Ivan Shark and his daughter have escaped, and the threat of the Lost People has been erased forever, the Secret Squadron's return to the United States is interrupted by developments that will loom large in their lives.

While night-flying over a remote area of the Mexican State of Yucatan, the returning Secret Squadron plane receives a radio message from the capital city of Mérida. The message informs them that a small, two-seat plane has crashed not far from their position. They alter their course and fly over the reported crash site. In the bright moonlight, they spot the remains of a wrecked plane. The Secret Squadron aircraft lands, and the Squadron members investigate and discover the murdered pilot.

Sometime later, in the New Orleans office of a former comrade in arms named Joe Tuttle, the Secret Squadron agents learn the true significance of the Yucatan plane crash. Tuttle tells them the aircraft had been hired by his company to deliver the precious cargo to New Orleans. Inside a metal case to have been delivered was the "Star of Mazaruni," a fabulous diamond thought to be the largest in the world. A gang of vicious criminals has stolen the precious stone in Yucatan; and because of his old friend's request, Captain Midnight agrees to investigate the crime and help retrieve the lost jewel. But Tuttle's private secretary, an attractive young woman named Eleanor Kent, has eavesdropped on the conversation. She quickly telephones a man named D'Arcy, who is the leader of the ruthless thieving gang.

Determined to recover the precious Star of Mazaruni, the Secret Squadron agents, together with their comrade Joe Tuttle, fly back to the isolated area of Yucatan to investigate. But they do not know that Eleanor Kent is a spy, working in Tuttle's own office, and that she has already informed her leader of their plans.

As the Secret Squadron lands their aircraft at a small airport in Yucatan, a man with a machinegun waits in ambush on a high hill above the landing field. Captain Midnight and Ikky climb out of their plane's flight deck — and Chuck, Joyce, and Joe Tuttle also prepare to leave the cabin — when the distant machinegun opens fire.

Because of the attacker's eagerness and distance from the Secret Squadron airplane, he fires prematurely and an initial spray of bullets barely misses Captain Midnight and Ikky. The two quickly scramble back into the aircraft, and Midnight swiftly retrieves a rifle with a telescopic sight. With a steady eye and expert marksmanship, Captain Midnight returns fire, striking the gunman dead. The Secret Squadron agents and Tuttle then emerge unharmed from the aircraft.

Upon inspecting identification on the dead man, they discover he's named Yates, and they also find a substantial check on his body signed by one "Robert D'Arcy." Upon later revisiting the wreckage of the downed small plane, they verify that the metal case is missing, and so Midnight reasons that D'Arcy must be responsible for the theft of the priceless diamond, The Star of Mazaruni.

NEW ORLEANS INTRIGUE

Because Yates had been waiting for them at the Yucatan airfield, Captain Midnight knows that Yates had been informed in advance of their arrival. He believes Tuttle's secretary, Eleanor Kent, is the most likely suspect, and that she's probably a member of the criminal gang.

When the investigative party returns to New Orleans, Captain Midnight quietly pulls Joe Tuttle aside. He suggests that Tuttle direct Miss Kent to follow up on the D'Arcy check to get more information on Robert D'Arcy, in the hope that she would tip her hand. Tuttle asks Miss Kent to do so, and she immediately warns D'Arcy that the Secret Squadron agents are on his trail. The chief criminal reacts in a curious manner. He orders Eleanor Kent to lead Captain Midnight and his companions to his own apartment.

In the apartment of the criminal leader, Robert D'Arcy, the Squadron agents search for the stolen Star of Mazaruni and fail to find it. This is because D'Arcy has sent his chief henchman, a man named Fletcher, to the scene in his place. And Fletcher furtively plucks the big gem from where D'Arcy hid it and slips it into Eleanor Kent's pocket. Captain Midnight remains suspicious of D'Arcy, and arranges to tap his telephone wire. But Eleanor Kent also learns of these plans.

Sometime after eight p.m., in the basement of the apartment building where Robert D'Arcy lives, Captain Midnight waits for information through the tapped phone wire. But D'Arcy has been informed of Midnight's plans by Eleanor Kent. Hence, D'Arcy sets a trap from his apartment by calling the Moon Gardens roadhouse on the outskirts of the city. The Moon Gardens is run by a man named Gleason, who is one of D'Arcy's agents, and D'Arcy orders Gleason over the phone to keep the diamond in the safe at his office. Captain Midnight has no reason to doubt the authenticity of the telephone call, and so acts on it immediately.

Captain Midnight and Chuck leave Joyce and Ikky to watch D'Arcy's apartment, while they head for the Moon Gardens. Upon entering the office of the roadhouse, the Secret Squadron leader and Chuck find two armed men waiting for them. Powerless to resist, they surrender and the two men handcuff their hands behind them. They are then shoved into the backseat of a black sedan and driven along the dark highway.

At nine p.m., in the basement of Robert D'Arcy's apartment building, Ichabod Mudd listens in on the tapped telephone wire. He hears a strangely familiar voice ordering the criminal boss to wait for an important call an hour later about the Star of Mazaruni.

Meanwhile, on a dark road just outside of town, the black sedan takes Captain Midnight and Chuck for a ride from which they will never return. But before long, the sedan encounters a police car at an intersection. While stopped there, Captain Midnight suddenly grimaces and raises his knees and gyrates his body in desperation. His violent body contortions further indicate his hands are bound behind him. This display of alarm and seeming distress attract the officers' attention, and the police car turns to follow the big auto. The sedan speeds up, and one of the henchmen shoots at the squad car. A high-speed chase ensues, with the police firing back. The police shots hit the sedan's rear tires, causing the big black vehicle to swerve and crash.

The police rescue Captain Midnight and Chuck from the hands of Robert D'Arcy's two gunmen. No more than shaken up by the wreck, Midnight and Chuck return to their investigation. They soon speed back in their own car to attempt to arrest the master jewel thief and members of his organization. But a strange turn of events has occurred in the meantime, begun by the telephoned instruction Robert D'Arcy had received at nine p.m.

From the basement of D'Arcy's apartment building, Ikky and Joyce listen on the wire for a telephone call that is to come. At ten o'clock sharp, they hear D'Arcy's phone ring — and to their utter astonishment, they hear the familiar grating voice of none other than Ivan Shark! The international criminal makes an appointment with Robert D'Arcy to purchase the Star of Mazaruni. He instructs D'Arcy to bring the jewel promptly to an apartment house on the west side of New Orleans. Shark promises D'Arcy that he will be unarmed, and demands that D'Arcy do the same. D'Arcy agrees.

D'Arcy leaves for the meeting, and Joyce informs Captain Midnight by Pocket Locator of the meeting address, which is in a run-down neighborhood. Midnight orders Joyce and Ikky to stake out the meeting place. Then he quickly contacts the police, and he and Chuck also head for the apartment house.

The precious Star of Mazaruni can bring immense wealth to Ivan Shark, and thus help finance his grand international schemes — provided he does not have to pay for the stone. Indeed, Shark has no intention of paying. At half-past ten p.m., at the dingy west-side apartment where D'Arcy and Shark meet, the two argue angrily over payment. During the altercation, D'Arcy pulls out a gun and threatens the unarmed Shark. Noting this, Gardo quickly steps out from behind a screen and fires a single shot. The outwitted and shocked Robert D'Arcy falls immobile to

1947 Code-O-Graph Manual, Page 2. PHOTOGRAPH: LEONARD ZANE

the floor, and Shark stands triumphantly over the jewel thief.

The only problem is that Ivan Shark had failed to confirm that Robert D'Arcy had the diamond with him, which he did not. So Shark flies into a tantrum upon finding that D'Arcy is now dead and can tell no tales! And why did Gardo once more have to be so monumentally stupid as to kill D'Arcy!

"But I didn't have time to aim so good in tryin' to save your life, Boss," says Gardo. *[You gotta love these villains.]*

Later, in the shabby room on the New Orleans west side — where they had hoped to trap the international criminal Ivan Shark — the four Secret Squadron agents arrive and find Robert D'Arcy's body. Anticipating correctly that Shark must have gone straight to D'Arcy's apartment after the murder, Captain Midnight leads his companions in rushing across the city. Meanwhile, Shark and Gardo have reached the apartment, and the arch criminal now acts to intimidate D'Arcy's chief agent Fletcher to turn over the diamond.

Upon learning Ivan Shark has murdered his leader that very night, Fletcher fearfully tells Shark he doesn't have the stone, but thinks he has clues to help find where Robert D'Arcy hid it. Fletcher also decides it's wise for him and Eleanor Kent to throw in their lot with Shark. Can't the great criminal genius use a couple more skillful followers to help find the priceless gem and also share in the wealth?

Captain Midnight learns that the arch criminal Shark has joined in the race for the Star of Mazaruni — the most precious diamond in the world. So he decides to have a showdown with Eleanor Kent, whom he knows to be a member of the gang that stole the jewel. But what the Secret Squadron leader does not know is that the girl has already telephoned Shark.

From his lonely cabin in the swampy bayou country outside of New Orleans, Ivan Shark has informed Eleanor Kent that he is well prepared to wipe out any enemies who approach his hideout.

Captain Midnight and Ikky later enter Eleanor Kent's apartment and demand to know where the diamond is hidden. The beautiful spy first tells them she doesn't know, but will try to help locate it. But when it's soon plain that she is found out, she admits the truth. She agrees to lead the Secret Squadron members to the vicinity of Shark's cabin above a river. Before long, however, Captain Midnight catches the treacherous Miss Kent in the act of notifying the arch criminal of their coming.

The Secret Squadron leader decides to push on through the desolate bayou country with Miss Kent, anyway, in the slim hopes of sneaking up on Shark. But in a plane flying overhead, Gardo gets a glimpse of the five figures, and immediately radios their location to his chief. It is then that the criminal mastermind hurries to a hand-operated plunger near his shack — while scarcely containing his laughter.

SHARK'S RIVER TERROR

Determined to wipe out all enemies who might approach his hideout in the heart of the bayou country, Ivan Shark has placed high explosives beneath the river levee. When he learns the Secret Squadron agents have reached the area, he pushes a generator plunger that electrically detonates the explosives. The blast releases a mighty torrent of water that floods every inch of the swampland below.

Thanks to Captain Midnight's caution, however, the Secret Squadron agents are still some distance from the riverbank when the explosion goes off. The agents run ahead of the great wall of rushing water, and by the time it reaches them, much of its force is spent. Nevertheless, the Squadron agents find themselves struggling amid the swirling waves. But where is Eleanor Kent? There is no trace of her in the flowing water.

Amid the billowing torrent, Captain Midnight and his companions manage to pull themselves onto the roof of a half-submerged house which had been torn from its foundations. There remains no sign of Eleanor Kent, as the Secret Squadron agents float swiftly downstream in the gathering dusk. His eyes keen for some means of deliverance, the Secret Squadron leader soon points to a row of lights spanning the river ahead.

Captain Midnight and his agents float downstream to a bridge abutment, and manage to save themselves in the flood-stricken swamplands by scaling the abutment to the bridge above. They then trek to solid ground.

Confident that he has at last gotten rid of the Secret Squadron agents, Ivan Shark takes off with Gardo for New York to make a deal for the precious Star of Mazaruni.

POINTS EAST

After returning to New Orleans, the Squadron members search Eleanor Kent's apartment thoroughly. They come upon evidence pointing to Fletcher's whereabouts in New York City, and that Shark is apparently to meet with Fletcher and another party at Manhattan's Westmont Hotel.

Upon reaching Manhattan, Shark meets his daughter Fury and the gangster Fletcher at the exclusive Westmont Hotel. Fletcher has now secured the diamond, but when he seeks to bargain for it, Ivan Shark forces him at the point of a knife to surrender the precious jewel.

Captain Midnight and his Squadron agents fly their plane to New York, and take rooms at the Westmont Hotel under assumed names. And what of Fletcher? Did he arrange to help Shark sell the jewel through his underworld contacts for a fee? Or did Ivan Shark kill him? Or did he make a discreet retreat and disappear? Despite Fletcher's fate — or perhaps because of it — Shark lies low until the coming nightfall, when he and Fury expect Fletcher's pre-arranged visitor, through whom they hope to sell their diamond prize.

It is now late afternoon. Chuck, Joyce, and Ikky wait tensely in the lobby of the Westmont, while Captain Midnight attempts to discover the room in which the criminal mastermind is quartered — obviously also under a fictitious name. After studying the guest list and check-in times, the Secret Squadron leader believes he has found the answer. Leaving Chuck and Joyce on guard in the lobby, he leads Ikky to an upper floor.

Ascending to the twelfth floor gallery of the Westmont, Midnight and Ikky hope to trap the arch-criminal Ivan Shark before he can dispose of the precious diamond. But Fury gets a glimpse of Ikky in the gallery and warns her father. Taking the stone, Shark and Fury jimmy a door into an adjoining suite. The suite is occupied by an Indian Rajah, the Prince of Chandrapore, but not for long. Learning the prince is preparing to leave the hotel, and to board an ocean liner for a transatlantic trip, Shark kills him. Donning some of the dead man's robes, and taking his identification, Shark and his daughter then flee the hotel undiscovered.

Later in the lobby, Chuck and Joyce see Captain Midnight and Ikky emerge from an elevator. Midnight soon learns that Ivan Shark is disguised as the Prince of Chandrapore, and that he will make an Atlantic crossing aboard the ocean liner, *S.S. Valencia*. Captain Midnight vows he will have the master criminal behind bars in forty-eight hours.

ACTION ON THE ATLANTIC

From a Manhattan police station, the Secret Squadron leader sends a radiogram to the captain of the *S.S. Valencia* to arrest the killer and impostor masquerading as the Prince of Chandrapore. Fury Shark, however, has ingratiated herself with the radio operator, a man named Riggs. She tells Riggs she expects some important messages, and when Captain Midnight's communiqué comes through, she forces Riggs at gunpoint to give her the radiogram. She rings her father in their cabin, and he soon joins her in the radio room. Saying he will sell the diamond and share thousands of dollars of the proceeds with Riggs, Shark bribes the radio operator to ally with him. Later in their stateroom, the international criminal and his daughter wait for their new cohort to carry out their orders.

Ivan Shark succeeds in similarly persuading several crew members of the *S.S. Valencia* to assist him in escaping the vessel. So by the time Captain Midnight and his companions land their large amphibian near the hull of the great liner, the arch criminal — together with Fury and their new followers — have lowered themselves from the main deck in a motor lifeboat and have drawn swiftly away from the vessel. Not until sometime later, when speaking with the ship's captain, does the Secret Squadron leader learn that Ivan Shark has once more eluded him.

The lifeboat cuts northeast through the open sea, and Shark and Fury anxiously scan the sky. Carrying the precious Star of Mazaruni, Shark seeks a more effective means to escape the Secret Squadron's amphibian that has now pursued him halfway across the Atlantic. Just before daybreak, the master criminal and his band hail the tank steamer, *Stormy Petrel*, and climb aboard as stranded refugees — which they are. But then Shark strikes again with his small gang, this time killing the captain and attempting to take over the vessel. The tanker's crew resists, and a violent gunfight breaks out.

The gun battle rages through the night on the *Stormy Petrel*. Finally, by the light of dawn and aboard the searching amphibian, Captain Midnight spots the tanker several miles to the north. The Secret Squadron leader believes the ship is a likely one to which Shark has fled, and he directs Chuck to contact the ship by radio.

Within moments of Captain Midnight's order, Shark's forces win the gun battle, and the international criminal now stands at the ship's wheel. Having decimated the crew of the *Stormy Petrel*, Ivan Shark turns the ship's prow into a heavy fog bank, but not before Joyce Ryan spots the vessel's course into the bank. Midnight quickly formulates a plan.

BOLD GAMBLE

In a swath of heavy fog that blots out all sight of the tanker, Captain Midnight and Ichabod Mudd bail out of the amphibian into the dense mist over the sea. Each wears a life jacket equipped with watertight pouches, and Midnight also bears an inflatable raft. While this is going on, Chuck flies low, soon spotting the steamer amid scattered fog clumps. He lands the plane near the ship's port side, and he and Joyce climb aboard — deliberately letting themselves fall into the arch criminal's hands!

While Ivan Shark relishes capturing Chuck and Joyce, he squints at the nearby amphibian, wondering what Captain Midnight's next move will be. But capturing the two Squadron agents and watching the big seaplane have temporarily distracted the criminal mastermind — and Captain Midnight and Ikky meanwhile stealthily approach from the starboard side and board the ship. Soon after, Midnight and Ikky suddenly appear with drawn guns, ordering Shark and Fury to surrender!

SHARK'S GAMBIT

Ivan Shark and his daughter flee into the ship's hold, now in a desperate bid to outwit the Secret Squadron agents. When Captain Midnight and his colleagues close in, the international criminal calls out from his place of hiding behind some metal drums. Shark warns that the drums are filled with high octane gasoline. He thunders a defiant challenge, threatening to blow up the whole ship unless they surrender to him! Captain Midnight refuses, saying Shark will simply kill the Secret Squadron agents if they surrender. Ivan Shark commends Captain Midnight's insight and

Martin PBM-3D Flying Boat. PHOTOGRAPH: GLMMAM ARCHIVE, WITH SECRET SQUADRON INSIGNIA BY LEONARD ZANE

changes his threat: Allow him and his party safe passage to take the Secret Squadron's flying boat to freedom — or he'll blast the tanker ship and everyone aboard into oblivion!

The Secret Squadron commander and his agents gird themselves, and Captain Midnight challenges Ivan Shark to carry out his threat — or give up immediately! Fury angrily glares at her father. Shark submissively decides that blowing up the ship and dying is not the proper alternative to being captured, so his threat turns out to be a bluff. Shark surrenders, and Captain Midnight arrests the master criminal, his daughter, and their collaborators — along with retrieving the precious Star of Mazaruni. Bearing their captives and the priceless diamond back to Washington, D.C., Captain Midnight and the Secret Squadron end their 1947 summer season.

8

The Devil's Secret

(1947)

ESCAPE

Ivan Shark waits to stand trial in Washington. According to Captain Midnight's associates, the witnesses to crimes Shark has committed would make the trial look like a United Nations delegation meeting. Then Fury Shark suffers a genuine attack of appendicitis. She is removed to a hospital and operated on, where they employ the latest post-operative techniques of encouraging people to walk soon after surgery.

Just two days after Fury's operation, and during her post-op walking procedure, she manages to get her attending nurse — who thinks she is very weak — diverted in such a way that Fury can whack her over the head with a blunt instrument and escape. As soon as Captain Midnight and Major Steele hear the news, they hurry to question the nurse. They find that Fury has taken the nurse's uniform and calmly walked out of the hospital unnoticed. Fury is made of stern stuff.

Sometime after Fury's escape, she reaches a dilapidated old house in Washington that used to be one of Ivan Shark's early hideaways. It belongs to old "Pop" Coster. The Sharks had imposed upon Pop years ago, and with Fury now a fugitive, the old man is very anxious to have her leave. He tells her he's expecting a visitor who, if he guessed Fury were in the house, would certainly report her to the police. But the more Pop argues and explains about the coming visitor, the more curious and determined Fury becomes to stay and see who it is.

[During this 1947 adventure, the Captain Midnight Ovaltine Shake-Up Mug is first offered for an Ovaltine label and twenty-five cents in coin. In 1948, it became fifteen cents in coin.]

Meanwhile Chuck, Joyce, and Ikky are enjoying a summer vacation at a Wisconsin lake resort. But their relaxation is interrupted when they receive a telephone call from Captain Midnight. He informs them that Fury Shark has escaped, and that he will arrive in an amphibian from Washington to pick them up so they can pursue Fury. "Geemaney!" exclaims Joyce, in both frustration and excitement.

Captain Midnight Shake-Up Mug and Ovaltine jar. PHOTOGRAPHS: LEONARD ZANE

The expected visitor arrives at Pop Coster's rundown house in Washington, D.C. He is old Doctor Colt, and Fury Shark is most interested to learn more about him. Despite her weakened condition, Fury exerts her strength of will to browbeat Pop and the old doctor into admitting they have stumbled onto a secret "something," as the doctor puts it. The doctor is afraid to talk about how important this "something" is — which piques Fury's irresistible urge to wheedle more. From Doc Colt, she learns an amazing piece of news that involves a certain brilliant scientist named Professor Pitcairn. After more prying and also veiled threats, the old doctor reluctantly discloses to Fury where the professor might be found.

The Secret Squadron commander's amphibian descends out of the night sky over the Wisconsin resort, to land on the lake at exactly midnight. Chuck, Joyce, and Ikky wait on a short wooden pier, as the amphibian taxis to them. Once they come aboard, Captain Midnight takes off again for Washington so they can try to pick up Fury's trail. At least his agents are able to sleep along the way.

The next morning, Major Steele's office receives an anonymous report that Fury Shark had visited Pop Coster's house in Washington, D.C. The report is based on a telephone call to the FBI by a man refusing to identify himself, and who had hung up quickly to avoid tracing. That man was Doctor Colt, who had called at his earliest opportunity after he had left Pop Coster's place.

Later that day, Captain Midnight and his three agents visit Pop Coster's ramshackle residence, but the place is deserted. They break in and begin searching, when the house suddenly bursts into fiery blazes! Fury had planted incendiary time bombs to destroy any clues. Working against time, the Secret Squadron manages to carry out the contents of a desk and some files, before flames envelop the rickety hovel.

MYSTERIOUS WEAPON

Meanwhile, Fury Shark has lost no time. She is now disguised as a beautiful blonde French girl aboard a plane bound for the Middle West. She is on her way to meet with the professor, whom Pop Coster and Doc Colt had described as a "mad scientist." This professor has developed a mysterious and terrible secret, and before she left Pop and Doc Colt, Fury learned he's also a man who has an inflated sense of self-importance. Having grown up with her father, Fury relates to that better than most anyone on the planet; and over the years, she has honed great skill in manipulating the trait to suit her own ends.

Professor Pitcairn hides himself in — of all places — a remote part of Wisconsin. When Fury meets the man, she is immediately struck by his long red beard, and after talking with him for a while, she comes to understand him easily and knows precisely what to do. For openers — and cunningly playing on Professor Pitcairn's great vanity and arrogance — Fury coaxes him into promising that he will rescue Ivan Shark! The professor seems absolutely sure, that by means of his mysterious secret, he can get the international criminal out of the closely guarded prison. He decides it's a challenge worthy of his powerful discovery and his extensive capabilities.

Meanwhile, Captain Midnight has been looking through the papers that he and his agents rescued from Coster's burning house in Washington.

In one of them he finds a name that interests him above the others. And now, where do they need to go, of all places? He tells Chuck, Joyce, and Ikky they must all return to Wisconsin.

Fury Shark's strength and energy have been growing daily, and she sets about getting together a number of her father's henchmen. She instructs them to make their way as quickly as possible to a secret headquarters in Wisconsin where she will join them. Shortly after telephoning her gangland contacts, Fury witnesses a startling display by Professor Pitcairn. The demonstration completely convinces her that Shark's rescue is not only possible but actually a simple thing. She begins admiring this kindred "madman's" power and ambitions, and by shamelessly flattering and enticing him, she persuades the professor to let her fly to Washington for the rescue attempt. It seems Gardo and her father need not be the only men in Fury's life.

Captain Midnight has discovered Professor Pitcairn's name and general location in the papers that were retrieved from the burning house. So he flies back to Wisconsin with Chuck, Joyce, and Ikky to try to find Pitcairn. After landing at a small airfield outside of Fond du Lac, Captain Midnight questions a few airport officials. To the Squadron's good fortune, the professor's conspicuous crimson beard and flamboyant personality have left memorable traces.

MORE ESCAPING

Although Major Steele has taken every precaution against Ivan Shark's escape, there is one thing he could not foresee, and that is a peculiar gas which Professor Pitcairn has discovered. When released from a small cylinder, the gas spreads with lightning speed and immediately causes everyone within a radius of a quarter-mile to fall into a deep coma.

Accompanied by Gardo and three other henchmen, Fury Shark arrives near the federal penitentiary in Washington, where her father is imprisoned. Swallowing some exotic tablets before proceeding, the gang soon floods the prison and surrounding streets with the professor's gas.

Meanwhile, Captain Midnight and the Secret Squadron have tracked Professor Pitcairn to a Wisconsin roadhouse. The place is called the Golden Horseshoe, and they interview the owner. The Golden Horseshoe's owner reveals the location of Professor Pitcairn's probable retreat in a wooded area, and so the Squadron agents head for it by automobile.

While driving to Professor Pitcairn's reputed hideout, the Squadron agents receive a Pocket Locator message from Major Steele. The message informs them that Steele phoned the prison warden where Shark was held and got no answer. Steele soon learned that everyone in the prison had fallen unconscious, that Ivan Shark had escaped, and that the victims' comatose condition was brought about by some airborne agent.

PURSUIT

Ivan Shark's getaway also makes the terrible new weapon of great importance to *him*, and potentially within his grasp. Such a mysterious and formidable way of overcoming people is also of immediate and overriding concern to the Secret Squadron.

It is getting dark, and instead of continuing toward Professor Pitcairn's hideout, Captain Midnight decides to return to his amphibian. Arriving at their hotel, the Secret Squadron leader gets out of the car and orders Chuck and Joyce to drive back to Pitcairn's hideout. He tells Ikky to remain at the hotel to await further instructions. He then takes the amphibian off into the night for Washington and Ivan Shark's trail.

Later that night, Chuck and Joyce drive deep into the Wisconsin woods and approach a remote lake. There, amid thick groves of trees and shrubbery, they spot dim light filtering through from Professor Pitcairn's hideaway. Leaving the car, they cautiously wind their way through dense scraggly foliage near the house. But despite their attempted stealth, a foreboding voice suddenly bellows at them from the darkness, threatening to shoot if they try to get away. The voice comes from somewhere in the shrubbery to the side, and without warning Chuck and Joyce suddenly fall unconscious!

Several hours later, Ikky anxiously paces back and forth in his hotel room. It is too soon for him to hear from Captain Midnight, and he has been ordered to stay where he is until he does.

Reaching Washington, and conferring with Major Steele, Captain Midnight learns the details of Ivan Shark's escape and appreciates the full extent of that disastrous happening. But he doesn't know that Chuck and Joyce have been captured by the eccentric scientist, Professor Pitcairn — who now calls himself Professor "Sodman," in an effort to obscure his identity and elude tracing.

Meanwhile, chief henchman Gardo drives Fury and Ivan Shark unhurriedly on their way to New York City. Father and daughter converse calmly about their plans in the backseat. *[In addition to Fury's devotion and determination in rescuing Ivan Shark, this is one more indication of the closeness and affection that father and daughter share, and it is shown in various ways throughout the Captain Midnight series. Besides his evident intention to propagate a dynasty to rule his intended empire, Ivan Shark often sincerely calls his daughter, "my dear;" and they usually seem to enjoy each other's company and working intimately together. It's quite extraordinary in this or any era — for the arch villain not only to have a devoted daughter as an esteemed colleague — but also to enjoy a mutually respectful, pleasurable, and loving relationship.]*

The next morning Ikky is even more wracked with worry. He sends a Pocket Locator message to Captain Midnight that Chuck and Joyce have not come back and have not answered his transmissions. Midnight replies that he will return at once to join Ikky and try to locate them.

After arriving in New York City, Ivan Shark has his first conversation with Professor Sodman/Pitcairn, by telephone. Shark is soon outraged by the professor's bragging and bloated opinion of himself. It's a kindred person striking the master criminal too close to home. Meanwhile, Ichabod Mudd waits impatiently for Captain Midnight so they can set out in search of their missing Squadron teammates.

In the professor's hideout, Chuck and Joyce — their hands tied securely behind them — face the professor. He gives them a choice: swear lifelong allegiance to him, which would lead to riches and power, or die.

Captain Midnight joins Ikky. They drive toward the hideout, determined to rescue Chuck and Joyce, even though they know they have no defense against the professor's gas. When their car approaches the private lake near the professor's retreat, they encounter a surprise: men loading large cartons into an amphibian on the lake. From the dock, a man with a long red beard directs the loading. Captain Midnight realizes that besides evacuating his hideaway, the professor is most likely the key to discovering the whereabouts of Chuck and Joyce. Midnight decides the best chance is to follow Pitcairn's plane with the Squadron's amphibian, and therefore, he and Ikky must get back to their own plane as quickly as possible. Captain Midnight stealthily drives the car back to the main road, and then races with Ikky back toward their lakeside hotel.

Captain Midnight and Ikky later fly to the lake where the professor's aircraft was being loaded, but now the plane is gone. They continue their airborne search, with Ikky piloting and Midnight anxiously scanning the skies with binoculars. Finally, in the far distance ahead, the Secret Squadron leader spots an airplane that appears to be an amphibian, and he orders Ikky to overtake it. While Midnight hopes the aircraft will be the professor's, he has not made up his mind about what to do if it is. He suspects Chuck and Joyce may be aboard, so he would not want to shoot the aircraft down, although this would be the otherwise logical action.

Soon, the plane ahead looms large as they gain on it. Captain Midnight recognizes that it is indeed the professor's amphibian, and he takes over the controls from Ikky.

The Secret Squadron leader can easily shoot the professor's amphibian to pieces, but because Chuck and Joyce may be aboard, he tries to force the craft to land on a small lake. The professor fiercely maneuvers his plane very closely in front of the Secret Squadron amphibian — and then looses a cylinder of his mysterious gas right before Midnight's plane! Chuck and Joyce are indeed captives aboard the professor's aircraft, and they watch in horror as Captain Midnight's amphibian tumbles out of control!

Flying right into Professor Pitcairn/Sodman's mysterious gas, both Captain Midnight and Ikky soon slump on their controls. But before completely losing consciousness, the captain manages by some reflex developed over many years of flying, to pull his ship out of its plummeting and set the control on a long upward course. Presently, the plane passes out of the gas-filled skies, and at long last Captain Midnight and Ikky start to shake off the effects of the gas. By this time, though, the professor has escaped.

Landing the Squadron amphibian on the small lake they had recently overflown, Captain Midnight and Ikky resume their journey by automobile. Additionally, Major Steele has given orders that all vehicles within 100 miles of the large and nearby Lake Middleton are to be stopped and searched.

Captain Midnight hasn't yet discovered the professor's ultimate destination, but he learns that Professor Pitcairn now uses the alias of Professor Sodman, and is apparently heading for the Wisconsin town of Fort Middleton. The professor's weapon has enabled him to operate with such increasing impunity that he has also grown more lax — even about being followed — and has become easier to track. It's also conceivable that he might now even be open to some possible communication.

Ivan Shark and Fury have begun to suspect the same thing about the professor's possible communications. They begin to wonder if the professor might betray them to the Secret Squadron. Such a move could not only rid the professor of the notorious Shark fugitives, but also eliminate possibly powerful competition. Such exquisitely paranoid Shark reasoning reflects what he would do in the professor's place, of course. But it is true that Ivan Shark has merely served as Sodman's experiment, only to prove what the professor could do with his gas. And now Shark certainly does covet control of the gas, and to be the professor's chief opponent. Just in case the professor *is* planning to turn him over to his enemies, Shark concocts a surprise of his own.

SHARK'S POWER BID

Ivan Shark has decided to seize the professor the moment they meet. However, Professor Sodman doesn't fall into the master criminal's grasp so easily. Instead of coming to Shark's hideout, he telephones to say he is sending a messenger to speak in his behalf. So Ivan Shark decides to seize the messenger.

It is now one hour later, and Professor Sodman — having first surrounded himself with a cloud of his protective gas — has parked his car outside a barber shop in Fort Middleton. Everybody within a radius of a quarter-mile is soon comatose. The professor's pilot drives Chuck and Joyce in a second car. All in the Sodman party are unaffected by the coma-producing agent, because all have swallowed tablets that immunize against the gas. The professor walks into the barber shop, chuckling to himself.

That evening, Ivan Shark and the professor finally meet at a hotel suite outside of Fort Middleton, both in disguise. Professor Sodman has shaved off his beard and discarded a wonderfully made toupee that he had always worn — and meets Shark as his own messenger. He is sure no one could possibly recognize him as the flamboyant scientist that society is coming to know. But at a half-mile distance from the barber shop, Captain Midnight has observed Sodman through Ikky's pocket telescope!

While discussing the price for Professor Sodman to share his discovery, the professor's ostensible emissary opens a bag and shows the disguised Shark a cylinder of the mysterious gas. The "messenger" snickers that his employer's immunizing agent can also protect any particular individuals they choose — as the bogus messenger toys tauntingly with the cylinder valve. Now alarmed, and with the inhabitants of the entire town of Fort Middleton in comas, Ivan Shark senses foul play at the hands of this "messenger." Shark secretly signals Fury to prick the man with a drug-filled ring.

Fury eases close to the professor, her lips forming a hint of a smile. She softly glides her hand along the professor's arm, and soon after, he collapses unceremoniously to the floor.

Captain Midnight observes that the worst has happened. Fort Middleton, completely surrounded by gas, is isolated from the rest of the country and is now helplessly in the power of Ivan Shark. What Midnight does not know is that Shark has only a very limited supply of Professor Sodman's exotic gas. Unless Shark can find the cylinders which the professor was to bring from his hideout, all of Shark's current plans are in peril.

The master criminal had supposed the supply of gas cylinders would be in the professor's car, but upon searching it, he and Gardo find Chuck and Joyce instead. Drawing a gun on the two Squadron agents, Shark has Gardo tie them up and leaves him behind to guard the pair. Shark then hurries back to his hotel, smiling in grim satisfaction. He will force the professor to tell him where the gas is. But when Shark returns to his hotel suite, he finds that either through an overdose or an allergy to Fury's treacherous drug, the professor is dead! The professor's lifeless face shows an expression of gentle pleasure. But what can Shark rely on in this world!

Frustrated at not obtaining more gas cylinders, Ivan Shark exploits the next opportune thing. With the Fort Middleton inhabitants helpless in their sleep, he has his henchmen systematically plunder the town. In one jewelry store, alone, Fury fills a traveling bag with precious gems: mostly rubies, emeralds, diamonds, and pearls. The Sharks always crave gems.

Captain Midnight works furiously to cut off all possible exits from the city. But in the meantime, Ivan Shark has managed to locate the late professor's cache of gas cylinders. And now, with the very large supply of coma gas at his disposal, Shark feels absolutely confident that he can leave the area at any time. However, the international criminal suddenly remembers Chuck and Joyce. Oh, yes! And he returns to the car where they had been bound. But Chuck and Joyce have been able to extricate themselves from their bonds and escape from Gardo. Once more furious at Gardo's blundering, Shark returns to his hotel to plan his own escape. Must he do *everything* himself!

The master criminal is certain that by this time, Captain Midnight will have every road out of the area covered by roadblocks and artillery. Actually, Captain Midnight has gone further than that. He has arranged for a flight of planes to start circling at dawn, and has given orders that any vehicle attempting to leave the city is to be fired upon at sight!

Three hours before dawn, Shark's hotel lobby is filled with a band of covetous criminals, along with loot worth untold millions that they've plundered from Fort Middleton. With a triumphant grin, Shark addresses his men. He declares that he will soon have enough resources to rebuild his organization back to what it once was.

SCHEMES AND CHASES

By utilizing the late professor's gas, both on the ground and via aircraft — plus protecting his own henchmen with the antidote — Ivan Shark manages to escape with truckloads of his coma gas and his lucrative loot. Later, he orders a network of criminal forces to rendezvous in New York City.

While Ivan Shark has escaped the Fort Middleton area, Captain Midnight and Ikky have reunited with Chuck and Joyce. If only the Secret Squadron could somehow obtain a sample of Professor Sodman's gas, they could then try to have the formula analyzed by one of America's leading chemists.

Ivan Shark reaches New York City and hides his enormous horde of loot. But shortly after he and Fury comfortably situate themselves in Manhattan, something upsets them. A young henchman named Fritz Kramer disobeys orders and makes a daring move. Kramer single-handedly absconds with some jewels and gas, steals a fast car, and escapes. Shark sends Gardo after him, but the word spreads.

Captain Midnight receives information from underworld contacts about Shark's fugitive, who is known outside the gang as "Gray Coat," and who has escaped from Shark's organization with some jewels and gas. So Midnight starts his own pursuit of Gray Coat. If Midnight can get to him first, there's a chance of obtaining a cylinder of Professor Sodman's gas, and possibly an immunizing tablet for potential analysis. As these events unfold, young Fritz Kramer meanwhile travels on a commuter train to Connecticut.

Captain Midnight and his agents trail Shark's renegade henchman, Gray Coat. By nightfall, they track him to a lonely farmhouse in Bridgeport — where a huge, black Great Dane bounds towards them, barking furiously.

A young woman emerges from the farmhouse, restrains the dog, and demands to know who the visitors are and why they have come. Captain Midnight explains they are federal agents who have followed a man known as Gray Coat, who is in possession of a very dangerous gas and stolen jewels. If they can find him, and if he gives himself up before causing harm, the authorities will likely be lenient. The young woman is Fritz Kramer's sweetheart, and she intercedes with Kramer to get him to surrender to the Secret Squadron.

At last, Captain Midnight gets his hand on one tablet of the secret immunizing agent. At this point, however, Gardo and another of Shark's henchmen named Paloff arrive at the farmhouse. Gardo releases some gas from a cylinder he carries. This forces Captain Midnight to swallow the tablet to avoid capture and to protect his agents, the girl, and Kramer. By calling the local fire department, Midnight forces Gardo to run from the farmhouse. But the fire department call also gives Paloff the idea to set the house afire as he and Gardo flee. Much as Midnight would like to, he cannot follow Shark's men. He has to carry Chuck, Joyce, Fritz Kramer and Kramer's girlfriend to safety.

The following day Captain Midnight and his Secret Squadron members formulate plans for their next move in battling the arch criminal and his most dangerous new power. Chuck and Ikky sit at a table across from Captain Midnight; but Joyce is stretched out on the floor — beside the enormous Great Dane.

In making inquiries, Captain Midnight learns that an American scientist at New York University may be capable of the difficult chemical-analysis feat. But Ivan Shark has also decided to analyze the gas and tablets, and believes a Russian-born scientist named Gregory Blattoff is the man to do it. Realizing that Shark also does not know how to manufacture Professor Sodman's secret gas, Captain Midnight foresees the master criminal will need to contact one of America's leading scientists in the New York City area, as well. By a series of brilliantly accurate deductions about Shark's plans, Captain Midnight arrives at the same conclusion about the Russian-born scientist. Captain Midnight feels certain that Ivan Shark would approach either Blattoff or the NYU scientist, and he plans to beat Shark to the punch.

MASQUERADES

Having carefully narrowed the field to the two scientists who know the most in the New York City area about poison gases, Captain Midnight warns them to get in touch with Washington the moment they are approached by anyone who might conceivably be the international criminal. Before long, one of the two scientists, the Russian Mr. Gregory Blattoff (and younger of the two), phones Major Steele in Washington. He says he has made an appointment with a prominent Chinese businessman, Lu Sing, for the following evening. Steele quickly informs Captain Midnight, who is almost certain the Chinese man is really Ivan Shark in disguise. So Captain Midnight arranges to stay with Gregory Blattoff, and to disguise himself as Blattoff for the meeting, which is to be held at Blattoff's own residence. Hoping he can pull the deception off, Midnight decides to let Ivan Shark capture him as Blattoff.

The next morning, the telephone rings at Blattoff's residence. Captain Midnight answers it, pretending to be Gregory Blattoff and speaking in a disguised, Russian-sounding voice. He quickly recognizes the caller's unguarded voice is that of Ivan Shark. The caller identifies himself as Lu Sing, and asks for an earlier appointment than had been arranged. With pretended reluctance, Captain Midnight consents. And from the rooftop of a tall nearby building, Midnight's comrades — Chuck, Joyce, and Ikky — keep watch on Mr. Blattoff's residence through Ikky's "Spy-Scope."

A few hours later, Captain Midnight peers through the front window of Mr. Blattoff's living room, and sees a tall dignified Chinese gentleman come through the entry gate and walk briskly to the front door. A moment

Captain Midnight's 3-4 Power Spy-Scope. This device is a newly offered, 1947 Ovaltine radio premium that has also been used earlier in this adventure. The Spy-Scope is a simple Galilean telescope. Galileans have no exit pupil and are excellent for work in reduced illumination, such as at dusk. While impractical for high-magnification work, the Spy-Scope is very compact and serviceable. PHOTOGRAPH: HAKE'S AUCTION NO. 2272

later, the doorbell rings. Disguised as the Russian Blattoff, Midnight answers the door and allows Shark to kidnap him.

Taken out of New York City by automobile, and pretending to fall in with Shark's plans, the fake Gregory Blattoff agrees to analyze Professor Sodman's mysterious gas for the sum of $100,000. During the long drive to the master criminal's retreat, Shark's car is constantly observed by anxious eyes, all the way into the Adirondack Mountains. Chuck, Joyce, and Ikky stay on Shark's trail from a safe distance, as he drives high in the Adirondacks to his remote "eagle's nest" mansion.

Upon arrival of Ivan Shark's car, Fury Shark has a vague feeling that Mr. Blattoff's face looks familiar. She believes she may have seen him in some newspaper. Her father is not disturbed, but takes no chances, and so locks Captain Midnight in an underground laboratory. While this is going on, Chuck leads Joyce and Ikky to a place of concealment not far from the mansion. Joyce keeps her eye on the building through Ikky's marvelous Spy-Scope. She sees Gardo walking along the hideout's perimeter, while holding a small metal cylinder and turning its valve. Gardo is clearly surrounding the eagle's nest with protective puffs of gas.

SHARK'S REVENGE

The next day, Ivan Shark announces to the bogus Blattoff that he has received information that Gregory Blattoff is actually still in New York City, and Shark will soon find out the truth! He then tells Fury of a new plan he has for humiliating the Secret Squadron. Fury is not sure of the wisdom of her father's decision, but the more she protests, the more he grows firm.

Until Fury can remember why Blattoff's face looks familiar, Shark decides to do nothing with him — at least until returning from the raid he plans against the very Headquarters of the Secret Squadron in Washington! At four o'clock in the afternoon, Shark and Gardo drive their own cars out of the hideaway's gates. Chuck, Joyce, and Ikky spy from their hidden vantage point, and wonder where the cars are headed.

Later on, in the underground laboratory of Shark's eagle's nest, Captain Midnight succeeds in solving the secret of the immunizing tablets![1]

Captain Midnight now desperately seeks a way to escape the dungeon-like chamber where Shark has locked him. Fury also grows closer to recognizing who the ostensible Mr. Blattoff really is. And Ivan Shark and Gardo continue on the way to Washington for their planned raid on Secret Squadron Headquarters.

The morning after arriving in Washington, Ivan Shark and Gardo enjoy a sumptuous breakfast. In the early afternoon, they arrive at the Secret Squadron Headquarters building, and release jets of gas around and inside the facility. They then proceed all through the building absolutely unopposed.

Back at Shark's hideout, Ikky ventures closer in an attempt to contact Captain Midnight, but he is overcome by the gas and is captured. Chuck and Joyce watch helplessly as he is carried inside the hideout. When Ikky is revived by an antidote tablet, he faces Fury. She now realizes it is Captain Midnight who has been masquerading as Blattoff! By clever trickery, Fury also lures Chuck into the eagle's nest as a would-be rescuer, and captures him too.

TRAPPED

Captain Midnight, Ikky, and Chuck are now bound and imprisoned in the laboratory dungeon of Ivan Shark's mountain hideout. Only Joyce remains free.

Meanwhile, Ivan Shark has used the coma gas as a shield, has invaded the Secret Squadron Headquarters, and has escaped unscathed. The raid was not entirely successful, though. For one thing, Major Steele had been absent, and Shark had also been unable to find the hidden vault that stowed the Squadron's Code-O-Graphs and Pocket Locators. Even so, just pulling off the humiliating raid immensely pleases the international criminal. The reason is this Washington excursion, along with sedating the entire city of Fort Middleton — and with only small amounts of Sodman's potent gas — are just preludes to what the dark mastermind is plotting.

Once he analyzes the gas formula and antidote, Ivan Shark has a much grander design for disabling *all* of Washington, D.C., New York City, and other key world centers. By rendering great urban and defense hubs all over the world completely helpless, Ivan Shark's organization will first steal American and foreign aircraft bombers at will. Then he will go on to destroy strategic targets everywhere in his incessant campaign for world dominion.

After telephoning Fury and learning the latest news about her captives, Shark and Gardo head back to their Adirondack retreat. Ivan Shark now feels he's sitting on top of the world — his rightful place, of course, as he sees it. With his enemies now under his power, the criminal mastermind gloats over their impending liquidation and resulting clear pathway to achieve his global ambition.

In the laboratory dungeon Captain Midnight, Ikky, and Chuck struggle against their plight. Eventually, Midnight manages to free Chuck's arms, and then Chuck shortly cuts his two comrades free. The three swallow the antidote. Then they plan to release all of Ivan Shark's remaining stores of gas, thus forcing Shark to try to stop them.

Across the road leading to Shark's eagle's nest, Joyce waits for Shark's cars. She is perched atop a tree, out of range of the master criminal's gas. She rightly believes that Shark's first action, as soon as he returns, will be to eliminate her three Secret Squadron comrades. Fastening Ikky's

Spy-Scope to the top of her rifle, Joyce is determined to shoot Ivan Shark if she possibly can.

RETRIBUTION

Upon Ivan Shark's return, Captain Midnight releases all the remaining coma-producing gas, driving the evil mastermind into a virtual apoplectic rage! Now that the powerful gas is lost forever, the seething Shark schemes to escape to a strange and awesome other hideout. But first he is determined to destroy his three prisoners, exacting the maximum revenge and agony especially on Captain Midnight. But the Secret Squadron leader has warned the arch criminal that he and his agents are not unarmed: In the laboratory, they have manufactured some terrible acid bombs, and if compelled, they will not hesitate to use them. Shark galvanizes his determination to storm the laboratory, but proceeds cautiously.

Captain Midnight and his agents wedge a massive table against the steel door of the laboratory, so the door can be swung only a few inches inward. Some moments later, Shark and his heavily armed henchmen stand at the head of the stairs leading down the passageway to the laboratory.

SLIPPERY SHARK

Infuriated by the standoff, and in a final action of frustrated hatred, Ivan Shark has his men pile furniture and draperies in heaps throughout the house, and sprinkle gasoline all over the combustible piles. He also has Fury collect his immense fortune in jewels and currency. Then the cunning outlaw ignites a raging fire on the floor immediately above the heads of the trapped Secret Squadron agents. But all the gas stores have been released, and are rapidly being consumed by the flames, just as is the outer protective gas shield. So the international criminal and his daughter must also hurry against time before becoming vulnerable to outside threats.

Shark is again up to the challenge. He already has a secret getaway prepared, and orders Fury and his men to bring his collected riches to the entrance of an underground tunnel.

Shark, Fury, and their henchmen make off from the eagle's nest to head for a strange and mysterious hideout that the master criminal has kept secret. Meanwhile, inside the burning building, Captain Midnight uses a laboratory fire hose to spray a huge jet of water, and he and Chuck and

Ikky soon make their escape out of the flaming house. Outside, they are joyously greeted by Joyce and "Lightning," the Great Dane.

Ivan Shark sets off a dynamite charge that completely blocks the escape tunnel's entrance. This thwarts any chance of the Secret Squadron's following him. In the aftermath of the destruction, Ikky suggests a rest. He even eyes a possible feast of hamburgers from Shark's food supplies that have been charred by the fire.

The next morning, Captain Midnight and his agents sit down to a hearty breakfast at an inn nestled amid the many peaks of the splendid Adirondack Mountains. Ivan Shark has escaped, but he is no longer the terrible menace that he was because the Secret Squadron has destroyed all that remained of Professor Pitcairn/Sodman's mysterious gas. Naturally, the members of the Secret Squadron are terribly anxious to get on Shark's trail again. But orders come from Major Steele about a series of baffling attacks and thefts in New York. These felonies must be solved before any attempt is made to recapture the international criminal.

ENDNOTES

1 Analysis was enabled by extensive, post-WWI higher education. Emphasizing undergraduate and graduate-level mathematics and sciences, such education was most valuable to U.S. Army Air Corps intelligence and was government-sponsored over a number of years. This advanced education also accounts for how Captain Midnight's well-developed intellect and knowledge are able to match and sometimes even outdo those of the great Ivan Shark — rather akin to Sherlock Holmes versus Professor Moriarty.

9

The Snow-White Panther

(1947-1948)

SNIPER MENACE

It is now early in the morning, two days after Ivan Shark's escape. Captain Midnight, Chuck, Joyce, and Ikky drive toward the New York suburban home of the French diplomat, Monsieur de la Falois. Ikky sits in the front seat, next to Captain Midnight.

All listen to the Secret Squadron leader speak about Monsieur de la Falois, but as they approach the Frenchman's home, they suddenly hear a shot. Somebody has fired a rifle at M. Falois from the garden. The Secret Squadron members reach the grounds of the house and later carefully search the garden, but discover no clues.

A similar shooting attempt is later made against a world-famous pianist, Peter Kovak, narrowly missing him. The rifle-shot was fired at Mr. Kovak while he was staying at the Oxford Apartment Hotel in Winnetka, New York.

Captain Midnight and Ikky drive to nearby suburban Winnetka, hoping to get information on whoever had made an attempt on Kovak's life. They learn the attack is the work of the so-called "Snow-White Panther." When they visit the Oxford Hotel, Captain Midnight speaks with the manager, Mr. Grayson. Very little useful information seems to come from him, and so the Secret Squadron leader proceeds to study the hotel floor plan and guest list.

Captain Midnight establishes that the shot which almost killed Peter Kovak was definitely fired from the Oxford Apartment Hotel, and Midnight also identifies the shooter's specific apartment, which has been vacant.

DISTURBING PORTENT

Prince Vahlevi, heir apparent to the throne of the oil-rich kingdom of Nyran, is on his way to America for a state visit. It is extremely important to American-Nyranian relations that the visit be both enjoyable and absolutely safe. With the covert Snow-White Panther poised to strike at any important international person, Captain Midnight realizes that the very future of the Secret Squadron is at stake. Any mishaps to Prince Vahlevi will unquestionably mean the Squadron will be disbanded![1]

THE MASTER CRIMINAL RETURNS

There is another hazard facing Captain Midnight that he does not know about: Ivan Shark has decided to offer his services to the Snow-White Panther! In the days that follow, both Captain Midnight and Ivan Shark come to the same conclusion involving a recent and notorious theft of an extremely valuable Italian painting. Only an expert forger could have painted such a nearly exact copy of the Italian masterpiece, which had been substituted for the original that had been stolen by the Snow-White Panther. Both Captain Midnight and Ivan Shark decide to search for this artist, who should be able to lead them to the Snow-White Panther himself.

But Midnight has an additional worry: Prince Vahlevi of Nyran will soon arrive in America on his state visit. Another disturbing fact is that the stolen Italian masterpiece was a painting that Prince Vahlevi had expressed intentions to see and possibly buy.

Both Captain Midnight and Ivan Shark trail the brilliant art forger, Frankie Levis, with Shark determined to meet him before the Secret Squadron leader has a chance. Besides Midnight and Shark, a third person — the Snow-White Panther *herself* — has given orders to contact Frankie, but her orders are much more menacing than the master criminal's or Captain Midnight's. She not only wants Frankie Levis contacted, she wants him liquidated, too.

In an early afternoon, following the unfortunate murder of Frankie Levis, Captain Midnight and Ikky return from police headquarters. Midnight ponders the Snow-White Panther's motives, and concludes they are to make prominent foreign persons and their interests unsafe in the United States. If the Snow-White Panther can accomplish this by thefts and assassinations — at least in major American cities — then rich and famous international persons might be blackmailed in order to escape losses and harm in the United States.

Midnight now believes his only chance of discovering the identity of the mysterious Snow-White Panther is to lure the gang leader into a trap. Toward this aim, he conceives a plan to tempt the Panther to strike at his bait — a fictional East Indian creation that he names the "Maharaja of Pathalmir." Ivan Shark, too, thinks his only link to the strange Snow-White Panther has been destroyed, and so he must devise some temptation as well. The Panther herself is also sure her identity is no longer traceable, now that Frankie Levis has been eliminated. All three of them are wrong. One person has found clues to discovering the Snow-White Panther, and that person is Fury Shark.

Because of clues uncovered by Fury, her father gets a definite lead on the Snow-White Panther. Within a few hours he expects to know where to contact the covert figure. Meanwhile, Captain Midnight proceeds with his plan to trick the Panther into striking at the reputedly wealthy Indian Maharaja (Ikky in disguise), whose sudden arrival in America has been featured in the newspapers.

At a few minutes after twelve o'clock the next night, the Snow-White Panther — a mysterious Madame Vera — has learned that someone has discovered her identity! She wants this immediate danger eliminated before carrying out a plan to disrupt an international conference in Philadelphia. She does not know that the unidentified "someone" is the arch-criminal Ivan Shark — and that when she goes to keep a luncheon appointment with one "A.B. Carstairs," she will meet Shark's daughter Fury.

CATS AND MICE

An intriguing contest proceeds at Pardini's Restaurant in New York City. The Snow-White Panther tries to discover who A.B. Carstairs is without giving away her identity. Instead of going to the Carstairs table, she sits next to it. Fury Shark — disguised as a gray-haired old lady — finds out the person she had come to meet is the woman at the nearby table. So instead of taking her own reserved table — some distance away as she had earlier planned — Fury walks over and sits at the table reserved for A.B. Carstairs. Because the Panther had disobeyed instructions, and is obviously playing a hand of her own, Fury decides on the spur of the moment to change her plans too.

Madame Vera believes the seemingly old woman sitting at the Carstairs table must indeed be A.B. Carstairs, who has arranged the meeting with her, but Madame Vera is suspicious that the lady may not be as old as she seems. Vera orders her henchman Syd to stumble against Fury and try to jerk her presumed wig crooked. But Fury is alert, and as Syd approaches her table, she suddenly rises and strides out to meet her father (the ostensible "A.B. Carstairs") who has arrived in the waiting area. Now sure they have identified the Snow-White Panther and her henchman, Shark and Fury soon outwit Syd and succeed in abducting Madame Vera.

Some opposing groups now gather at the Clayton Towers Hotel. Ikky, disguised as Prince Pathalmir, occupies Suite 14A along with Captain Midnight and Chuck and Joyce. Two stories up, in Suite 16A, are Ivan Shark and Fury, who have forced Madame Vera to accompany them there from Pardini's Restaurant.

Ivan Shark knows Chuck and Joyce are in the hotel, but the Secret Squadron is unaware that the international criminal has returned to New York City and that he is holding the Snow-White Panther prisoner. Instead, the Squadron members prepare for a possible attempt against the phony prince by the Snow-White Panther.

Ivan Shark and the Snow-White Panther (Madame Vera) — although still highly suspicious of each other — actually come to some terms! In return for the two gangs working together to seize some enormous art riches, the master criminal agrees to set Madame Vera free. He and his group will meet her and her colleagues at a designated location off the Hudson River at twelve o'clock midnight. However, Shark has ordered Gardo — who has been waiting in the hotel lobby disguised as a bishop — to trail Madame Vera. As Gardo hurries out of the Clayton Towers Hotel after her, he neglects to disguise his lumbering steps — and Joyce, standing and talking with Chuck, recognizes him.

Learning that the Secret Squadron is pursuing the Snow-White Panther, Madame Vera concocts an idea to bargain with the agents. She will capture Ivan Shark and hand him over to the Secret Squadron in return for their ceasing efforts to apprehend her! After all, wouldn't capturing the international arch-criminal be worth her relatively insignificant freedom in return? The master criminal is also determined to take over Madame Vera's gang — but neither Vera nor Shark realizes how close the Secret Squadron is on their two trails.

Gardo follows Madame Vera to her hideout, but Chuck and Joyce also stealthily follow Gardo by car. They watch Gardo head for a drugstore a couple blocks away; and by Pocket Locator, they contact Captain Midnight and Ikky, and arrange to meet behind a grove of fruit trees near Madame Vera's hideout. When Gardo reaches the drugstore, he uses a payphone to telephone Ivan Shark and tell him the location of Madame Vera's house.

Before Gardo returns — and before either Shark and Fury, or Captain Midnight and Ikky arrive — Madame Vera leaves her hideout by automobile. Chuck and Joyce follow Vera and her gang in their own vehicle, but Madame Vera and her cohorts soon leave her auto and board a speedboat on the Hudson River. Vera's craft roars off on the Hudson — while Chuck and Joyce lose precious time running along several docks, in search of a boat they can use to give pursuit in the dark night.

The double-crossing Ivan Shark and Fury arrive to join Gardo, and they sneak up on Vera's hideout. But Captain Midnight and Ikky have gotten there first, and effect capture of their enemies, except for the more elusive Fury Shark.

Captain Midnight does not know who Madame Vera is, but he receives a Pocket Locator message from Chuck informing him of the pier from which she and her gang left. The fuming Shark knows the meeting place where Vera and her gang are headed — which is where he would have been, had he not decided to double-cross her!

Now seeking revenge, Shark decides to recruit his arch enemy's help, if only temporarily. He tells Captain Midnight the meeting location, a cove some distance along the River. Captain Midnight and Ikky take the criminal mastermind and Gardo along, and engage a boat to head for the Hudson cove. Midnight also sends a Pocket Locator message to Chuck, telling him of the meeting place.

Fury Shark, having eluded the Secret Squadron, follows Captain Midnight and the group into the night with a speedboat. Captain Midnight and his companions continue motoring on the Hudson, toward the cove where the meeting between Ivan Shark and the Snow-White Panther is to take place.

Suddenly, Fury Shark approaches Midnight's boat rapidly from astern in her speedboat. The Secret Squadron's slower craft cannot evade Fury's powerful and maneuverable boat. As both vessels near the meeting cove, Fury once more lives up to her name. At top speed, she brutally rams Captain Midnight's craft! Flying debris from the crash strikes and stuns Midnight, as both boats rapidly take on water and begin to sink! In the chaos, Shark and Gardo plunge into the water, joining Fury to swim for the nearby shore.

In the blackness, the dazed Captain Midnight follows Ikky in tumbling overboard into the deep dark river. Supported by Ikky, Midnight treads water until his senses can clear. Chuck and Joyce arrive in a swift boat of their own, and rescue Midnight and Ikky. But enough time has elapsed for Fury Shark, her father and Gardo to swim to shore. Once ashore, they intend to head for Shark's new hideout in the Bronx, but Madame Vera and her gang wait in ambush. Shark is not the only double-crosser!

From the boat offshore, the Secret Squadron watches in frustration as Madame Vera — now fully revealing herself as the Snow-White Panther — has her gang swiftly capture Ivan Shark and bear him away

Douglas A-26 bomber. PHOTOGRAPH: NATIONAL AIR AND SPACE MUSEUM

with them. Fury and Gardo, however, manage to escape and disappear.

Captain Midnight now knows the Panther is a woman, and he has at least seen her general appearance. For some reason, though, Shark — who tried to mix into her schemes — has been taken prisoner. What Midnight does not know is that Madame Vera has given her partner Syd orders to let himself be bribed by the international criminal. Syd is to help Shark escape and pretend to become a member of Shark's gang. Vera's plot is to use Shark as a scapegoat and hand him over to the Secret Squadron. But Syd has very definite ideas of his own, too; namely, to take Shark's money and then disappear.

The following day is December 30th, and Ivan Shark escapes from Madame Vera as she had planned. At the same time — before either Shark or Vera can carry out their schemes — the famous Maharaja of Pathalmir announces he will fly on New Year's Eve to visit Hollywood. Of course the Maharajah is Ichabod Mudd in disguise, and Captain Midnight makes sure the announcement is widely reported by the press. Since Ivan Shark and Madame Vera do not know the prince's secret identity, both of these notorious characters have the same idea in mind: to capture Prince Pathalmir, seize his highly reputed riches, and do away with him.

The next morning, an old woman enters the hangar from which Prince Pathalmir will depart, and asks Chuck a few questions that make him somewhat suspicious. Too late after she leaves, Chuck realizes this was very likely the Snow-White Panther herself in disguise.

Lockheed P-38 fighter. PHOTOGRAPH: AAF TACTICAL COMMAND, ORLANDO, FL

ROCKY MOUNTAIN INCIDENT

On New Year's Eve, two planes head west across the heavens. What strange feelings must go through the hearts of Chuck, Ikky, Joyce, and Captain Midnight, as they see they are being followed by a fighter plane! It's a P-38, and its pilot turns out to be none other than Ivan Shark!

Upon reaching the skies high over the treacherous Rocky Mountains, a red-hot aerial battle breaks out between the Secret Squadron's A-26 bomber-class aircraft and Ivan Shark's much faster and heavily-armed P-38 Lightning! Shark closes in for the kill on Captain Midnight's airplane, which is nearly 100 mph slower than the P-38 fighter. Then a big strange craft — coated in dark, dull gray paint — swoops down at Shark with a bizarre roaring noise! The interloping aircraft disrupts Shark's attack, and with a fusillade of machinegun fire, drives the P-38 away. Then the phantom aircraft streaks off and disappears. Captain Midnight's A-26 continues on to the West Coast with no further incident.

GRETA HAYDEN

Upon reaching Hollywood, the Secret Squadron agents soon manage to arrange for a stay by the illustrious and bogus Prince Pathalmir, as a guest in the lavish mansion of film star Greta Hayden. But Ivan Shark's gang also quickly arrives in Hollywood, and before long, Gardo succeeds in deceiving the famous movie actress into hiring Fury as a secretary. The newly hired assistant will help Miss Hayden's personal secretary, Mildred, who has had an overly heavy workload. Ivan Shark awaits word from Fury, as he maps out his plot to capture the Maharaja of Pathalmir. However, the disguised Ikky soon sees Fury, and alerts Captain Midnight. The Secret Squadron leader arranges to record calls made from Greta Hayden's home. Every telephone call Fury makes will be recorded.

Chuck joins Captain Midnight in Midnight's room at the Hollywood Plaza Hotel. He brings the first recorded roll of wire from the recorder. But Fury Shark has tricked the Secret Squadron, by speaking a phony message into the recorder about a false visit to Miss Hayden's home to be made by Ivan Shark the following day.

Captain Midnight and his Squadron members plan to capture Ivan Shark at Greta Hayden's home the next day. But that very afternoon, Fury and several of her men break into the home. Fury's gang seizes the disguised Ikky, plus Greta Hayden and Mildred.

When the movie star's abduction story breaks in the papers, it creates such a sensation that Major Steele angrily telephones Captain Midnight from Washington. Upset that the Secret Squadron was unable to protect the famous film star and Ikky from being kidnapped, Steele warns Captain Midnight that he has just forty-eight hours to clean up the case!

Several hours after Midnight receives the call from Major Steele, Ikky (as Prince Pathalmir) and Greta Hayden and Mildred find themselves imprisoned in a dark damp hold of Shark's floating headquarters. Anchored miles off the Southern California Coast, it's an old rundown gambling ship named *The Black Car*.

UNMASKED

Ivan Shark soon discovers that the true identity of the Maharaja of Pathalmir is none other than Ichabod Mudd. But his rage and hunger for revenge are disrupted by a sudden storm that sweeps in from the Pacific. The storm drives gambling visitors off the unsteady old boat in panic and upsets all of Shark's plans, not to mention his ship. In an amazingly short time, the furious elements buffet and dangerously waterlog the shabby old craft.

Putting wisdom before valor, Shark decides to disembark, as did his visitors earlier. But one of his crew dashes this plan with news that the crew is seasick and in no condition to do anything. Soon after this, the boat is a scene of bedlam. Even the beams begin to bend, crack, and fail under the weight of the monstrous waves, as the gale rips into the superstructure. Even below decks, every man has to tie himself down. Ivan Shark himself cries out in frustration and nausea.

SECURITY BREACH

When the raging storm finally dissipates, Ivan Shark searches Ikky for a Pocket Locator and Secret Squadron Code-O-Graph, but finds none. He then tries to intimidate Greta Hayden and her secretary into admitting that there *were* a Pocket Locator and a Code-O-Graph. But Greta Hayden does not disclose that the Pocket Locator and Code-O-Graph are actually hanging out a porthole. Instead, she says Ikky left the Locator in her home, hanging on a wall behind a certain picture.

That very night, Captain Midnight — playing a hunch by Chuck — almost captures a mysterious person in Greta Hayden's home. The intruder escapes, but Midnight does get a fine batch of fingerprints on a picture frame.

The monstrous gale has damaged *The Black Car* ship severely — now a bent and broken hulk that no one any longer wants to visit. Ikky, Greta Hayden, and Mildred remain forlorn captives in the ship's dank brig. They now feel not only imprisoned, but semi-buried in a dark, clammy ship of horror. Fury returns aboard the eerie derelict, after a disastrous trip to Greta Hayden's home.

The next morning, Chuck and Joyce receive an unexpected Pocket Locator message from Ikky. The coded message says Ikky has escaped from Shark, knows his hideout location, and to meet at a vacant roadhouse on a hilltop in Los Valiz Pass, at twelve o'clock midnight. The message ends with the words, "I am famished." Since they've never heard Ikky use a word like "famished," their suspicions mount that both the Code-O-Graph and Pocket Locator have been captured by Shark. In fact, Ikky has been knocked out by one of Shark's men, and Shark triumphantly announces to his henchmen that he has captured Mudd's Code-O-Graph and has sent a message to Captain Midnight via the Secret Squadron Pocket Locator.

Captain Midnight receives the Pocket Locator message while at the Hollywood Police Station. After analysis, the police crime lab reports the fingerprints on the picture frame in Greta Hayden's home are those of Fury Shark.

Captain Midnight departs for the rendezvous at the hilltop roadhouse in Los Angeles. After Midnight heads out, Chuck sends a message to Ikky. One that reads: "Hope you will be back in time for your birthday next Friday." The message puzzles Joyce, as she and Chuck wait impatiently for an answer in their rooms at the Hollywood Plaza Hotel. No reply comes, and Chuck pulls out an unopened envelope he had received that afternoon from Secret Squadron Headquarters. Upon opening the envelope and reading the document inside, he and Joyce immediately leave the hotel.

Chuck and Joyce overtake Captain Midnight's car, on his way to Los Valiz Pass, where he is supposed to meet Ikky. They tell him the Pocket Locator and Code-O-Graph had fallen into enemy hands, but that a new Code-O-Graph is available to replace the 1947 model! Captain Midnight immediately orders the old Code-O-Graph scrapped, and telephones Washington to get the new Code-O-Graph — an improved 1948 model — issued at once to all Secret Squadron members.

MIDNIGHT CONFRONTATION

Now forewarned, Captain Midnight, Chuck and Joyce proceed to the top of Los Valiz Pass in their two cars. They sneak up on foot to the abandoned roadhouse, but instead of approaching a dimly lighted portion, they slip to the back where the inside is dark. Captain Midnight and Chuck wait and listen, while Joyce silently heads back to hide her car behind a clump of trees. She then stealthily returns to rejoin Captain Midnight and Chuck, telling them where she has hidden the vehicle. Midnight orders her to get back to her car and wait there.

Shark is now alone in the roadhouse, and only a few feet separate these bitter enemies. Captain Midnight and Chuck suddenly burst into the dark back room and seize Ivan Shark. Chuck quickly tricks Shark into revealing that it was Shark who had sent the message signed with Ikky's name. But Shark retorts that he is holding Ikky hostage, and unless Captain Midnight resigns as head of the Secret Squadron, Ikky will be liquidated. He had wanted to tell Captain Midnight that to his face.

The leader of the Secret Squadron knows Shark will inevitably double-cross him. The only way to save Ikky, Greta Hayden, and her secretary is to discover the location of Ikky's prison. He discusses the matter with Chuck, whereupon Midnight decides firmly not to resign — but to let Shark go — with the promise that he and Chuck will leave first and not follow him. Shark cackles with satisfaction, and taunts Midnight that he had better keep in touch by Code-O-Graph and Pocket Locator — which are safely at Shark's base. He adds that Midnight had also better reconsider resigning soon — before Shark grows tired of holding the hostages and disposes of them!

Captain Midnight and Chuck leave the roadhouse, but Midnight hurriedly stops by Joyce's car and tells her Shark does not have the Pocket Locator and Code-O-Graph with him. She is to follow Shark as secretly as she can, in an effort to track him all the way to his destination. Captain Midnight and Chuck then drive off in the car that Midnight had brought. A half-hour later, Shark leaves the roadhouse and drives away, and Joyce follows him stealthily from a safe distance.

Joyce trails Shark to docks along the oceanfront and watches him depart on a launch from a slip belonging to *The Black Car*. Joyce hurriedly risks a Pocket Locator message, before Shark reaches the boat, informing Captain Midnight of Shark's offshore hideout. No longer chancing compromised code and radio communications, Midnight orders Joyce back to the hotel to wait by the phone, while he and Chuck pursue Shark.

At last knowing about Shark's boat, Captain Midnight heads for a small airport where he can arrange to get a helicopter. Aboard the ship, Ivan Shark realizes that another storm is brewing, and that the craft is no longer safe in such weather. So he plans to set it afire and cast it adrift, leaving Ikky aboard, but taking Greta Hayden and her secretary with him as hostages. In the meantime, he will hang on until the storm grows a little more violent and also wait for Gardo's return.

In her Hollywood hotel room, Joyce hears two things simultaneously: a knock on her door and her ringing phone. She opens the door. It's Chuck. Then she answers the phone. It's Captain Midnight. He tells her he has secured a helicopter and will head out to Shark's boat and notify Shark that he is trapped. Midnight will tell Shark that if he frees the hostages, he will be allowed safe passage to escape. In the meantime, Joyce should call the police and Coast Guard and have them standing by to arrest Shark — either at the ship or when he comes ashore — depending on the outcome of the negotiation. After making the calls, Joyce and Chuck should get to the docks as fast as they can.

RESCUE OR DISASTER

Captain Midnight flies a helicopter out to *The Black Car* amid the increasingly violent storm. Hovering over the ship, Midnight announces his terms over a loudspeaker for rescuing the hostages. The response is quick and violent. Gardo fires machinegun bursts at Captain Midnight's helicopter! The bullets damage the engine, and the sputtering craft drops to the churning sea!

Chuck and Joyce have commandeered a speedboat and rush toward the ship. In the howling winds and pounding rain, the mastermind Shark is elated at the sudden victory over his arch foe. He orders Fury and Gardo to carry the hoard of jewels, as he leads them in descending to the launch and abandoning ship. Several timed, incendiary grenades then explode that turn the vessel into a blazing inferno! Ivan Shark and his party speed away in the launch, toward a desolate northerly shore, while the arch criminal's laughter pierces the winds and downpour as they go.

Chuck and Joyce rescue Captain Midnight from the raging sea. Without delay, Midnight leads them into the blazing ship, where they rescue Ikky, Greta Hayden, and Mildred. The international criminal has escaped. But Greta Hayden had overheard Ivan Shark argue heatedly with his daughter about something the day before. The film star tells Captain Midnight that Shark had insisted to Fury that while the "Island of the Lost People" had been destroyed, the nearby "Land Which Time Forgot" was still a safe haven. Fury didn't like the idea one bit, and had strongly protested.

Hearing Greta Hayden's information, Captain Midnight wants to resume chasing Shark; but upon returning with Chuck and Joyce to the Hollywood Plaza Hotel, Midnight receives a telephone call from Major Steele. The Major congratulates the Secret Squadron agents for rescuing Ikky, Greta Hayden, and her secretary — but he now orders Captain Midnight and his Squadron members to return to Washington immediately. The Secret Squadron must begin a new mission that concerns a sudden and alarming threat to American national security.

ENDNOTES

1   Captain Midnight's startling conclusion about potential disbanding — declared in November of 1947 — is the first explicit utterance that the Secret Squadron's radio-adventure days may be numbered. That portent was not exactly shocking to kids in those days, either. The 1947 plastic Code-O-Graph was most commonly considered with contempt. Captain Midnight — who always used all metal or mostly metal decoders had fallen to plastic! How pitiful and discouraging — especially to devoted youths — that radio's Secret Squadron would probably not last indefinitely. But near the end of 1947, hope still burned. Maybe Captain Midnight would return to robust metal Code-O-Graphs and save the future of the Secret Squadron. It turned out that hope came true for two more years.

10

Faster than Sound

(1948)

STRANGE SIGHTING

It is late the next morning. Captain Midnight, Chuck, Joyce, and Ikky sit in Major Barry Steele's Washington office and finish debriefing the Major on their last mission. After listening and getting answers to his questions, Steele moves on to his urgent matter. He informs them of a potential new danger to United States security.

A strange and unidentified plane has for some reason of its own, flashed across America from coast to coast. It left the East Coast at seven a.m. Eastern Standard Time and arrived over the West Coast at seven a.m. Pacific Standard Time! With a three-hour time difference, and a coast-to-coast distance of about 3,000 miles, the plane had traveled at the stunning speed of 1,000 miles per hour! Such a highly faster-than-sound aircraft does not belong to any American armed forces, and there is little doubt it is the fastest airplane in the world in early 1948.[1]

This one action — with the phantom aircraft having flown across North America in only three hours — has made obsolete every combat airplane in the American Air Force. Captain Midnight and the Secret Squadron are ordered to track it down at once. The Secret Squadron therefore flies to "a great American airbase" (Muroc Dry Lake), where the armed forces are experimenting in supersonic flight. Captain Midnight is told that it may be months before America has a plane ready to take the great plunge, not only through the dangerous barrier of sound, but well beyond and over a great distance, as had been observed with the mysterious craft.

For several days there is no move, no sight, and no trace of the unidentified new plane. Then word comes that flashing north from

Mexico, the craft has ranged at incredible speed — as far as the Canadian border — and back south again to disappear somewhere across the Panama Canal in South America. All South American countries deny possessing such an aircraft, and are as alarmed as Washington at the threatening possibilities. It seems almost impossible to believe, but Captain Midnight is soon forced to accept that the strange plane

Top: Bell X-1. *Bottom:* **North American F-86 Sabre Jet.** PHOTOGRAPHS: NACA, NATIONAL MUSEUM OF THE USAF

has evidently been built by some private individual or group. If this private source turns out to be a renegade against society, there's no knowing what tragedy may follow.

Captain Midnight decides the plane must be operating out of a secret base somewhere in the remote South American wilds. He organizes a massive radar hunt to get an approximate idea of where the plane's base might be located.

One night, a coded message reports the aircraft has crossed the Mexican border again, this time headed along the U.S. West Coast and apparently toward San Francisco. Based on its longitudinal flight paths — and also disappearing south of Panama — Captain Midnight concludes the mysterious aircraft probably originates from a South American country that borders the Pacific Coast — therefore, Colombia, Ecuador, Peru, or Chile.

The 1948 Captain Midnight "Mirro-Magic" Code-O-Graph uses the most diverse materials ever employed in a Code-O-Graph: brass, aluminum, steel, and plastic. Its circular brass housing is 1.95 inches in diameter and 0.20 inches deep. Within it are the cryptological elements: two aluminum disks, one with a number scale and one with a cipher alphabet, mounted on a shaft connected to a knob external to the housing. Two round windows on the housing reveal the numbers and the letters, one pair at a time (the number disk has holes through it so that the letters can be read through the number disk). Cipher settings are achieved by using a pointer on the letters disk, pointing to any of twenty-six numbers on the back of the larger numbers disk. The Code-O-Graph back is of red vinyl, with a large inset and exposed metal mirror. PHOTOGRAPH: LEONARD ZANE

ENCOUNTER

In the speediest fighter plane available (an F-86 Sabre Jet, at 685 mph maximum speed) Captain Midnight flies to meet the phantom craft. But the unidentified jet is so fast that (as the Secret Squadron leader afterward described it) he was left behind as if he were a sagebrush passed by a wild stallion. Captain Midnight demands that an American supersonic plane being built be rushed to completion. The usual safety tests must be bypassed. A man and a country have to take a big chance.

AN EVIL GENIUS' DESTINY

While the mystery of the exotic supersonic aircraft deepens, the seeming fate of the master criminal, Ivan Shark, is revealed. When last heard of, he was headed for a secret, awe-inspiring hideout at an Antarctic island that he called "The Land Which Time Forgot."[2] Shark's party had arrived on the island, which is a huge crater rising tall and steep above the sea — with sole access to the interior through a long, winding tunnel, entered high up the mountainside. Fury and Gardo had detested the idea of this island base for a number of reasons, not the least of which was the stifling weather: round-the-clock, ninety-plus-degree heat and unrelenting, oppressive humidity! Shark had been adamant, however, and they had been forced to accompany him. No sooner were they all safely inside the crater, though, than a terrible rumbling started: It was an earthquake that sealed the exit tunnel under millions of tons of rock and debris. There, Ivan Shark and his gang could swelter forever and a day — cut off from the world with their ill-gotten and now useless jewels.

THE MYSTERY PLANE ATTACKS

Meanwhile, news has flashed to Washington that the mystery aircraft has at last revealed some intentions. It has attacked a U.S. B-36 bomber, flashing around it with blurring velocity, and sending the bomber crashing to the ground. With a top speed of 418 mph, the huge B-36 had been child's play for the phantom jet.

Captain Midnight calls a Secret Squadron meeting. The renegade plane's hidden base has been narrowed down to an unexplored spot in western South America — an area inhabited by a tribe of ferocious headhunters. The American supersonic plane is being pushed to completion, with workers laboring around the clock. But the Secret Squadron cannot sit still doing nothing, waiting for the craft to be completed. For one thing, the plane may develop some unexpected fatal flaw. For another, the Secret Squadron has always been at its best when keeping after an enemy — attacking, not standing still and waiting. Captain Midnight decides to take an aircraft over the unexplored South American region, where the hideout is believed to be, and bail out. He will somehow contact the local Indians and try to get them to guide him to the base. Chuck, Joyce, and Ikky will follow.

Convair B-36 bomber. PHOTOGRAPH: NATIONAL MUSEUM OF THE USAF

Before long, a second Army plane is shot down, and a first glimpse is also revealed of the supersonic renegade leader. He's a soft-spoken little man, with a shade of a foreign accent that's almost indistinguishable. Instead of giving orders, he politely makes suggestions. And then, suddenly, the quiet gentle voice says some phrase such as, "May I suggest, my dear Patro, that he be liquidated without delay? And I think, if you don't mind my saying so, that it could be done in a peculiarly horrible manner by our friends the headhunters. Also, if I may say so — at once!" Steel glints in that "at once!" and shows the man's cruelty and ruthlessness, but the motives underlying his sudden attacks on America remain shrouded.

PETER POLINOFF

Peter Polinoff is a representative of "some foreign power" (the U.S. and the Soviet Union are now superpower opponents). He has orders to contact the owner of the mysterious plane and negotiate whatever it takes — anything at all — to obtain the plans of the aircraft and the right to build it. Polinoff is to be flown to South America, and is instructed to use any means to reach the interior where the secret base is hidden.

Inquiries by Captain Midnight and other members of the Secret Squadron uncover information about a tough old explorer named Brock Butterfield. He's an Englishman, educated at Oxford, but also an American citizen for the last fifteen years, and a man who knows as much about South America as any one person can. He speaks several Indian dialects and is now far up the Amazon at a small native village where he makes his headquarters. The Secret Squadron is to meet him there.

Despite Captain Midnight's excellent flying skills, he seeks a local pilot who is familiar with the obscure location of the village where Brock Butterfield lives. So the Secret Squadron members fly to a South American coastal city, where they are to pick up a small amphibian and a flier who knows the country. From there, the pilot will immediately fly them to the interior and to Brock's headquarters.

Peter Polinoff also learns of Brock Butterfield's knowledge of the interior and his explorations there. So he tries to find an amphibian to fly him to Brock's village. He contacts the very pilot who has been retained to fly the Secret Squadron, and by astute questioning, he realizes America is wasting no time. He must act quickly if he is to win the contest.

Before Midnight and his agents reach the South American coast, Peter Polinoff ruthlessly kills the young pilot the Secret Squadron was to meet. He then steals the amphibian and continues up the Amazon to the interior.

When the Secret Squadron members arrive at the coastal city, they are at a loss to account for the strange disappearance of their pilot and his amphibian plane. A day is lost while they wait for his return. Following that, they get a map of the rough whereabouts of Brock's headquarters. They commandeer an amphibian of their own and finally set out.

The owner of the mysterious high-speed plane is a very wealthy man named Ito Gobi. He heads a small Japanese colony and refuses to accept that the war between the Allied and Axis powers is over. He also controls a tribe of savage Indians who believe him to be a god. Long before the outbreak of World War II, and expecting it would be inevitable, he had founded the hidden South American colony. A brilliant scientist and aeronautical engineer, he has for the last ten years been experimenting in fabricating his extraordinary jet plane. Now that it is a tested success, he is building a fleet of fifty of the supersonic monsters, and is determined to wipe out the U.S. capital city of Washington. He believes he will then end the war successfully for his emperor god.

Meanwhile, Peter Polinoff has not had too much difficulty finding Brock. When Brock hears the amphibian approaching his headquarters, he thinks it is Captain Midnight and the Secret Squadron, and he lights a signal fire.

At first, Polinoff tries to bribe Brock into taking him deeper into the interior. When Brock indignantly refuses, Polinoff concocts a clever strategy, since he too can speak English with an Oxford accent. Because Brock is known to be quite reclusive and an avid detester of civilization, it is most likely that Captain Midnight has never seen Brock. So Polinoff decides he will kill Brock, dispose of the body, drive the natives from the village into the surrounding forests, and pretend to be Brock. Carrying out the plan will also be an ironic and satisfying twist for an emissary of his country. He will use the Secret Squadron to help him find the aircraft source they, too, are looking for.

The first part of Polinoff's plan works almost without a hitch. He does manage to kill Brock Butterfield, but in the battle is shot through the arm. He drives the natives from the village and disposes of Brock's body.

It is not long before the Secret Squadron arrives, and just as Brock had done for him, Polinoff signals the Squadron's amphibian for a landing and then meets the agents. He explains to Captain Midnight that for some unknown reason, his natives had gone berserk and tried to kill him. When their attempt failed, they fled into the forest. Captain Midnight is at first deceived, and seeing how awkwardly Polinoff's wound has been bandaged, his concern mounts, and he insists on doing it over.

Polinoff has made a serious mistake, because Indians of the wilderness do not possess revolvers. If they were attacking, they would use blowpipe darts, or bows and arrows, or lances. But Polinoff's wound is obviously caused by a bullet. Midnight's suspicions are aroused, but he says nothing. He wanders through the village and sees no signs of any extensive battle — only what seems to be hasty abandonment. He returns and questions Polinoff, who explains that he had one personal bodyguard whom he had armed with a pistol — and then suffered the unfortunate consequences of misplaced trust. This, of course, could possibly explain the shooting, and for the moment Captain Midnight pretends to accept it, but he shares his suspicions with Chuck and Ikky. He shortly sends them out to do a little local exploring, while he and Joyce keep the supposed "Brock" busy discussing plans.

Before long, Polinoff senses he has slipped up and isn't going to get away with his scheme. He seizes a brief moment toward the end of the day when he is unobserved. Hurrying to the river, he boards the amphibian that brought the Secret Squadron and takes off in a desperate attempt to reach the owner of the supersonic plane first. Captain Midnight and Joyce note the takeoff with alarm — just as Chuck and Ikky rush up to report a discovery. In a hidden backwater channel, they have found the amphibian that was to be waiting for the Secret Squadron at the coastal starting point. It is now clear that the man claiming to be Brock is an impostor who had stolen that plane, and now he has also stolen the amphibian the Secret Squadron had obtained.

It is now after sunset, and although Captain Midnight's first instinct is to take off after Polinoff, he decides that only by the blindest luck would he come anywhere near the destination during the hours of darkness. Common sense says to delay a departure until dawn.

Later that night, Captain Midnight radios Washington. He learns the mysterious jet plane is daily growing bolder and more reckless. Its breathtaking speed makes it unbeatable by any American craft now able to take to the air. The experimental, American supersonic airplane is being rushed to completion. But without a series of thorough tests, it may be suicide for the first man who attempts to fly it through the extremely dense barrier of sound, and then hurtle well beyond that into the mysteries of supersonic flight.

Dawn at last comes — along with a tropical downpour. The Secret Squadron takes off despite the foul weather and heads in the direction where they believe the hidden base to be. By noon, there is still no trace of an airfield or unknown colony.

After hours of flying over a sea of impenetrable forest, the searching Secret Squadron finds a stretch of more or less open country. Captain Midnight sets the amphibian down on a small lake, deciding to try to contact some of the local Indians. Taxiing around the lake, Midnight comes to a small village. It seems deserted, or all its inhabitants have fled at the first approach of the plane.

An old man moves to the water's edge. He beckons them ashore and into a hut. A little girl lies inside the hut, her body perspiring, her face flushed, her dazed eyes only partly open. The old man can speak a few English words, indicating at least some exposure to the outside world. He keeps repeating, "Fever, fever." Captain Midnight gets some quinine from the medicine chest. The old Indian knows at once what it is and is effusively grateful.

Captain Midnight is also most grateful at this twist of fate — sensing the old man can help him if the Secret Squadron can succeed in adequately communicating. Midnight takes out a pad and begins sketching.

He draws a plane, and shows by gestures that it is many times more than the size of the drawing. He points to his amphibian and imitates a takeoff with his hands. The old man understands, and points nervously in a northerly direction. Then he builds little hills in the sand. Midnight gathers he is to fly north to a range of hills or mountains. Noting and appreciating these directions, the Secret Squadron members hastily climb aboard their aircraft and once more take to the air.

Peter Polinoff has flown recklessly throughout the night and into the day, when he hears a larger plane approaching him. A burst of machine-gun fire sends his craft tumbling down, and he desperately parachutes out. Sometime later, perhaps hours — he has no way of knowing — he wakes up on a couch. A short, gray-haired Japanese man silently stares at him with cold searching eyes.

An hour later, fed and bathed, Polinoff is cross-examined. Boldly, he declares his mission.

Ito Gobi replies in soft, high tones, "I should consider your offer, because I have already thought about requesting certain foreign aid, should I need it. However, you have wasted both time and effort in tracking me down, and it is I who will do the approaching, should the time come when I consider it necessary. You have also, my dear sir, wasted a valuable servant of your country — I mean yourself! I want no outsider to live more than a few hours, after once entering my little Eden here. So sorry. So terribly sorry. Patro, take him away."

Polinoff shouts that he has valuable information, pleading with Gobi that the Secret Squadron is close on his trail. Ito thanks him politely, says he will exercise all necessary precautions, and just as politely sends him out to his death.

SECRET SQUADRON ON THE TRAIL

The Secret Squadron flies low over the thickening tropical forest that stretches like an endless ocean in all directions. The amphibian runs into another tropical storm, and its motors start to miss. There is only one thing to do: bail out, one by one — with Midnight last and also bearing the plane's portable radio repeater, for which he had originally arranged with the pilot Polinoff had killed. They jump into the unseen jungle below. Ikky is caught up in a high tree. Captain Midnight lands in a swamp, and the bulky radio repeater almost drags him under. But he works his way to solid ground, and the watertight repeater and sturdy, waterproof Pocket Locator remain in working order. Chuck and Joyce are luckier than Midnight and Ikky, falling close together in a small forest clearing. Although separated, all soon contact each other with their Locators, and the repeater can relay signals over a much longer range. It takes time, but they all regroup.

The Squadron members stumble upon a stream and decide to follow it. Suddenly, in the distance, they hear the sound of a jet plane taking off! The hideout cannot be far away. Perhaps the luckiest thing that has happened to them was being forced to bail out. It may mean they can reach their destination unobserved.

Captain Midnight and his agents struggle through the forest. Presently, they find the land rises steeply, and after a time, they reach a hilltop. Midnight climbs a tall tree to look around. In the distance lies a valley — obviously inhabited by civilized people — and there's more: a group of large hangars! A big hollow in the side of another hill looks as though it might be a launching site for the new type of jet-propelled plane. There is no doubt in Captain Midnight's mind that the Secret Squadron has found its destination. Then an enormous aircraft streaks overhead, and moments later, Midnight hears a BOOM and then the roar of the craft's engines.

Captain Midnight hurriedly climbs down and tells the others what he has seen and what the concussive sound meant. Plans must be made. There are a number of guards at the base, but apparently because of its remoteness from civilization, not too many of them. At nightfall, the Secret Squadron will move out to spy the terrain.

HIDDEN BASE

At his base within the valley, Ito Gobi receives reports and gives orders. The jet plane will fly in widening circles around the base and shoot any approaching aircraft out of the sky. He also sends a small group of his Indians to search the forest. And these natives have a very developed skill: Like dogs, they can smell out and track human scent.

Meanwhile, Captain Midnight decides the safest place for the Secret Squadron to pass the remaining hours of the day is high up in the trees, and Joyce spots a tall one in a cluster that's closest to the base. Descending alongside a narrow brook, the Squadron agents reach the tree. It's large and broad-limbed. Thick vines cover its multiple trunks, also making it fairly easy to climb. They haul themselves up. And only moments later, a file of Indians — sniffing actively like canines — comes into view. From the sudden excited chattering, Captain Midnight realizes these jungle men sense they are in the vicinity. However, the natives do not look upwards, and so slipping silently like dark brown shadows, they disappear into the forest. Nothing again stirs until just before nightfall — when the Indian group returns and silently files back toward the hidden base.

It is exactly twelve o'clock, when Captain Midnight — buoyed by his traditionally fortuitous hour — whispers to Ikky to follow him down the tree. Chuck and Joyce are to stay behind. If Midnight and Ikky are taken prisoners, the two younger agents are to contact Washington on their Pocket Locators, make a detailed report, and ask for aid.

Captain Midnight and Ikky silently ease through the undergrowth, and eventually reach the forest's edge. The hidden enclave does not stir. Only an occasional light glints in the utter darkness. Midnight points to the nearest hangar. He will go on ahead and reconnoiter. Ikky will stay until he gets a Pocket Locator signal to follow. With all his senses alert, Captain Midnight creeps like a shadow. By the side of a huge building, he notices a guard standing near a small door. Occasionally, the guard walks to the front of the building and disappears for a few moments, checking the other side of the structure.

Timing himself exactly, Midnight races to the corner, and as the guard returns around it, the Squadron leader knocks him cold with one smashing blow. The guard's rifle, however, clatters to the ground. For a moment, the Secret Squadron leader stands tense. No one approaches, and no voice challenges him. He steals back to the small side door, cautiously opens it, and slips inside. Suddenly, brilliant lights turn on. Momentarily blinded, Midnight is surrounded and seized. Then a soft mocking voice says in a gentle, sinister manner, "Captain Midnight, I presume?"

A taut confrontation follows. Captain Midnight deliberately taunts Ito Gobi about his rashness and foolishness into thinking that he alone can defeat America. Ito counters by announcing that a fleet of planes in the hangar buildings will soon be completed. Then these aircraft will wipe the city of Washington off the map, as merely a beginning. "There is not a plane in America fast enough to stop them," declares Gobi.

Captain Midnight continues to sneer and laugh in disbelief. In a sudden rage, Ito Gobi gives an order: The supersonic plane will take a quick trip to Washington and back, with Ito at the controls. While over Washington, Captain Midnight will be hurled out over the city, as a gesture of Ito's contempt and warning of what is to come. *[As another diabolical and megalomaniacal artist, Ito would prove his supremacy by humiliating a worthy, but ultimately dishonored and destroyed enemy.]*

GRAY PREDATOR

At once, Captain Midnight is hauled to the launching site on the hillside and dragged aboard a strange dark plane. It is one of the most wicked-looking airplanes he has ever seen. And now he grimly recalls the encounter over the Rockies. The time when Ivan Shark's P-38 fighter attacked Midnight's slower A-26 bomber — and a menacing, dark gray

Mystery Jet — Did Bob Burtt anticipate Rockwell's B-1 bomber, twenty-six years before its first flight — even to its gray color? PHOTOGRAPH: U.S. AIR FORCE

aircraft swooped down to overwhelm the P-38 with speed and firepower that drove Shark into hasty retreat. This monstrous jet, inside the gut of which he is now a prisoner, was that gray aircraft. And now it blasts out a frightening roar of sound as it takes off.

Back at his place of concealment, not far from the hangar where Midnight was seized, Ikky contacts Chuck and Joyce. He reports what he has seen of the Squadron leader's capture, and that Captain Midnight was apparently rushed off to the supersonic plane. Ikky anxiously says he'll rejoin them to plan their next moves.

Aboard the mysterious gray aircraft, Captain Midnight is thrust into the smallest compartment and the hatch locked. Cramped and curled up, he racks his brain for some means of escape. Using his Pocket Locator, he first contacts Major Steele and then Chuck. He tells Chuck how dire things are. He will try to escape from the plane, but at the moment, it looks impossible. He doesn't even have a parachute, and even if he did, trying to exit the plane at 1,000 mph would tear him apart.

ICHABOD MUDD'S SCHEME

Chuck, Joyce, and Ikky agonize over the situation — and suddenly, Ikky has a brainstorm! He'll start a forest fire and burn the whole secret base off the map! Quickly, he outlines what he has in mind: With the capture of Captain Midnight, the people at the hidden base probably think themselves secure. So the three Squadron agents will sneak down, steal some cans of fuel, and creep well back into the forest and start such a fire as this part of the world has never seen!

Making off with cans of fuel, Ikky and Chuck fell a sentry and wound another — then race back into the forest — as the camp comes to life with shouts of alarm and confusion.

Sherman Marks as Ichabod Mudd. PHOTOGRAPH: PHOTOFEST

Chuck, Joyce, and Ikky soon start the fire blazing in the encircling forest. The centuries-old growth of enormous trees catches fire faster than any of them would have dreamed! The conflagration causes consternation in the camp.

Meanwhile, as Ito Gobi's plane nears Washington, Gobi sends Patro back for Captain Midnight. Patro unlocks the compartment that imprisons the Secret Squadron leader, and Midnight slowly raises his hands in submission. This distracts Patro from Midnight's feet, and a sudden kick by the captain causes Patro to fall. One blow from Midnight's hard fist and Patro is out cold. The Secret Squadron leader seizes Patro's gun and parachute.

Ito — not knowing this has happened — slows the jet craft over the heart of Washington, in preparation for hurling Captain Midnight from the plane. But Captain Midnight now doesn't need to be forced. He jerks open an escape hatch, leaps from the plane, and billows out into the night.

Not long after, Major Steele — who has vainly tried to contact Captain Midnight — hears a knock on his office door. The door opens, and Midnight himself enters. Midnight says he will explain later and asks one question: Is the American supersonic aircraft anywhere near finished? Steele telephones the field out West. Only a madman would take a chance to fly it. "I am good and mad!" declares Midnight, "It's our only chance!"

The Douglas D-558-II Skyrocket was a rocket and jet-powered supersonic research aircraft. Fifty-eight percent of its fuel was rocket fuel, and earlier D-558 models even employed RATO (Rocket-Assisted Take Off) boosters until a more powerful jet engine was installed. The first flight of the D-558-II was on 4 February 1948. That date meshed amazingly with Captain Midnight's final episode of "Faster than Sound" on 5 March 1948. On 20 November 1953, Scott Crossfield piloted the Skyrocket to Mach 2, or more than 1,290 mph (2,076 km/h). It was the first announcement that *any* aircraft had exceeded twice the speed of sound. The 1954-1956 *Captain Midnight* television series based the Captain's "Silver Dart" aircraft on the D-558-II, with an expanded cockpit. PHOTOGRAPH: NASA, WITH SECRET SQUADRON INSIGNIA BY LEONARD ZANE

SKYROCKET

Captain Midnight is swiftly flown to California — at least on the Pacific coast, as is his ultimate destination in South America. The recently finished, quite untested plane is rolled out. It's a combination rocket and jet-propelled aircraft. Midnight climbs aboard and goes through the checkout procedure. Then, with a heart-frightening roar, he is airborne.

Faster, he pushes the plane. Faster…faster, he reaches the sound barrier. The plane trembles like a leaf in a storm! Faster…faster…he's through! His still accelerating speed is terrifying in its possibilities! And now, the plane flies as smooth as a bullet, as it bores through the stratosphere.

SHOWDOWN

Now, Captain Midnight finally has a supersonic aircraft that can match the performance of Ito Gobi's predator plane, if not best it. But the "Silver Dart"-type Skyrocket's reliability is precarious and unproven. So the Secret Squadron leader must use all his skill and instincts to hold the combination jet/rocket plane together, and then engage it in combat!

Captain Midnight streaks in the Dart/Skyrocket — finally catching and challenging Ito Gobi over the blazing land inferno that Ikky, Chuck, and Joyce had ignited. On the flaming terrain below, the raging forest fire is incinerating Gobi's South American airbase. This time Ito cannot prey on a disadvantaged craft, and he must fight on equal terms. In a terrifying air battle between Captain Midnight and Ito, it is the latter who now pays disastrously for his misdeeds and arrogance! Riddled with Captain Midnight's deadly Skyrocket fire, Ito's jet plummets to the valley floor and explodes in a huge, booming cloud of crimson flames and black billows!

Witnessing Ito Gobi's destruction, Captain Midnight hurriedly lands the Dart/Skyrocket on a lone portion of Ito's strip that will soon also be consumed by fire.

There's just enough time to rescue Chuck, Joyce, and Ikky — stuffing them into what is normally an ample cockpit for up to two crew. With all of them crammed in, Captain Midnight takes off again to escape the area — this time flying a lot slower than sound.

ENDNOTES

1 U.S. Air Force test pilot Chuck Yeager was first to break the sound barrier, only months before on 14 October 1947, flying the Bell X-1 (true) rocket plane. Yeager flew at Mach 1, at 45,000 feet over Muroc Dry Lake in California. That was more than 300 mph slower than the mysterious coast-to-coast plane.

2 This was actually a reflection of Edgar Rice Burroughs's similarly-named tale, in many ways. See Appendix 5.

11

The Jewels of the Queen of Sheba

(1948)

ASAR BUBASTIS

Major Steele has a new adventure for the Secret Squadron, which he believes will be a rather enjoyable diversion. The Emperor of Abyssinia wants American scientists and the American free-enterprise system to search for and develop uranium deposits. These deposits might be found in the unexplored hinterland of that African empire. The Squadron youths and Ikky are very excited at the prospect. It looks like an interesting and fairly peaceful month is ahead for them. But this is not to be, for in the portion of Abyssinia they are to explore — mostly by helicopter — another group of men will cause them great trouble. They too are exploring, but oddly not for uranium deposits reported in that part of the country. They are searching for a crumbling black marble pyramid, said to be the tomb of the ancient Queen of Sheba — a tomb containing a fabulous collection of jewels buried with her at her death. This group of cutthroats is headed by an international criminal named Asar Bubastis — also known as "The Pharaoh" — because of his emaciated appearance and odd, square-shaped beard. "The Pharaoh" operates a front business in the capital city of Addis Ababa — a guide service for travelers who wish to journey into the interior.

Asar Bubastis and his confederates know the Sheba jewels will be priceless archaeological finds that would never be allowed out of Abyssinia. The artifacts are sure to be considered the property of the nation. As Asar puts it, the treasured jewels and precious metals will be "shut up in some gloomy museums or palaces to gather dust." He believes the gem value, alone, will run into many millions of dollars, and he intends to break up the wonderful gold and silver settings and sell the jewels and precious metals separately.

It is now *Tseday*, or spring in eastern Africa, and Asar and his men fly a helicopter over an unexplored mountainous portion of Abyssinia named the East African Rift. They carefully scan the vast and precipitous mountain ranges and valleys below, keenly searching for a particular land feature — but what? Of all things, a triangular mountain plateau that appears pure white in the spring. At least, that is what a very old story in Abyssinian folklore tells. According to the legend, said to be handed down since Biblical times, a certain high and triangular-shaped plateau in Abyssinia will turn white during only one week in the spring. The ancient tale does not identify which week, so Asar must repeatedly search throughout the entire Abyssinia spring. The spring months span from September through November, and the East African Rift spans over a thousand miles. So Asar's quest is challenging and daunting in the extreme.

Captain Midnight and the Secret Squadron know nothing of Asar's expedition. And neither does Asar know that Midnight's secret expedition is going to comb the very territory in which he is so interested — but for an entirely different reason.

PHONY ZOOLOGISTS

Captain Midnight and his Secret Squadron agents fly their own helicopter into Addis Ababa, pretending to be a zoological expedition seeking guides into the wilderness. Midnight has chosen this cover-up after learning of a rumor that reached the capital city of Addis Ababa. The rumor tells of a mythical white gorilla, somewhere in a great Abyssinian mountain range. The ostensible zoologists would like to find this rare beast. Upon making inquiries, Midnight learns of the explorer called "The Pharaoh," who might be able to assist his party.

Captain Midnight soon meets Asar Bubastis, who quickly admits that he too would like to find the extraordinary mountain animal. Actually, he has never heard of it. Asar's hasty statement arouses some degree of wariness in Captain Midnight; but Asar says he even has some current business in the rumored location, and as a courtesy he could point out some areas to the zoologists. The two men then agree to fly their aircraft to meet at a prearranged destination.

At a charming valley that is high in the mountainous interior, two helicopters fly in and their occupants meet. As a matter of fact, the Secret Squadron would indeed like to capture the unique white gorilla if it does exist. "An albino gorilla is a possibility," Midnight says to Bubastis, "and it would be a priceless gift to make to some American zoo." Asar has difficulty suppressing his contempt for what he considers such triviality, and his feigned interest wears thin enough to where Captain Midnight is no longer deceived. While Midnight does not know what Asar is really after, his first suspicion is that some foreign power has gotten wind of the potentially rich uranium deposits and is trying to find and exploit them before America can make the discovery.

Captain Midnight casually looks over Asar's craft, and it appears to be without guns. Midnight's party, however, has stowed plenty of powerful weaponry in their helicopter; so the Secret Squadron leader feels moderately safe for the moment. Before long, Bubastis shows the masquerading Squadron agents some spots on a map and also points to various mountain ranges in the area where the rare gorilla might be sought. Evening shortly arrives, and Asar suggests both groups bed down for the night and take off for their destinations in the morning. Midnight and his companions concur.

ANCIENT TOMB MYSTERY

Following his growing suspicions, Captain Midnight sneaks up behind Bubastis' tent and eavesdrops on a low-toned conversation between Asar and his men. Midnight hears them talk of some hidden plateau in the mountains. The plateau is triangular-shaped, and according to an ancient legend, for one week out of the year in the spring, the top of it turns white. This is because the plateau is said to become covered by millions of calla lilies. So many white lilies smother this plateau, that from the air, it will look like a recent snowstorm has laid a white carpet over its apparently smooth surface. Rising from amid this scent-laden, mountainous platform is supposedly the black marble pyramid — and that pyramid is the lost tomb of the Queen of Sheba! Inside the tomb is said to be a treasure of jewels that will stagger the imagination!

Asar explains that as a prized gift, King Solomon of Israel had his artisans make a signet ring for the Queen of Sheba. And this ring has always carried with it a secret. Only the queen's signet ring is able to show when the spring week arrives, during which the calla lilies on the hidden triangular plateau will bloom. During that week, and only during that week, the capstone on the Queen of Sheba's ring will sparkle green! Asar tells his men that he has traced this ring to a remote tribe that is reported to be somewhere in this region, and that he must find the tribe and seize the ring in time! Hearing all this, Captain Midnight steals back to rejoin his colleagues.

ENEMY

Early the next morning, Asar Bubastis wishes the masquerading Squadron members disingenuous good luck and takes off with his men. As his helicopter rises into the air, "The Pharaoh" Asar waves a most imperious and florid farewell to the party on the ground.

Captain Midnight immediately yells to his companions: "Down! Flatten your faces, now!" Asar has dropped a bomb, and a tremendous explosion suddenly booms! The bomb completely destroys the Secret Squadron's helicopter, but the four Squadron agents escape harm.

Asar at once flies back to his headquarters in Addis Ababa, with the news that another expedition is exploring deep in the wilds of Abyssinia. Although that expedition insists it is on a scientific safari, he is sure they are after the mythical hoard of jewels that once belonged to the beautiful Biblical queen. Now accelerating his plans, he will add more men and a second helicopter to double the strength of his group. "If it comes to war," Asar declares, "we must be strong enough to wipe out all traces of the other expedition!"

Meanwhile, Captain Midnight decides they must make their way to the nearest lake and contact civilization. A second helicopter will probably take too long to get, so they use their Pocket Locators to order an amphibian flown to them. It will be flown from the United States to Cairo, and from there in hops totaling over 1,500 miles south to Addis Ababa. Fortunately, Captain Midnight knows that his close friend Andrew Maxon is in Egypt, flying sightseeing parties up the Nile in his own small amphibian, and Midnight plans to ask his help.

Secret Squadron Headquarters in Washington contacts Maxon, and Captain Midnight soon receives word that Andy would be delighted to set out on an expedition like this anytime. Following delivery of the larger, longer-range Secret Squadron amphibian to Cairo, Andy will fly it from there in a series of refueling stops to Addis Ababa. By that time, Joyce and Ikky will have secured ground transportation to meet him at the Abyssinian capital. Under Joyce's and Ikky's directions, the three will then proceed to an as yet undetermined lake in the remote region to join

Captain Midnight and Chuck. For speed, the amphibian will fly rings around the helicopter; and because they now have a ruthless enemy to battle, this extra speed may be critical.

NEW THREAT

In order to get a better look at the surrounding country, the isolated members of the Secret Squadron toil up a mountain slope. As they make their way, Joyce remarks how completely lovely the countryside is. But she fails to notice the insidious danger that lurks. Every footstep is tracked by stealthy, black-skinned figures that silently watch them; and though hidden from view, these phantoms keep them completely surrounded.

Captain Midnight is uneasy. He senses what feels like unseen presences and keeps glancing sharply in all directions. But the native trackers have generations of jungle skills, and even his sharp eyes do not see their flittering bodies, nor do his ears hear their feathery-treading feet. Nonetheless, he gives strict orders that the four of them must stick close together and never be separated by more than a few yards.

It is nearing dusk when the first sign of any human beings appears. It is an enormous, grotesque stone idol that towers in a clearing. A huge pile of ashes — the residue of countless fires by generations of worshippers — surrounds the massive idol. Augmenting the stone figure's

Fleetwings Seabird — Andy Maxon's type of amphibian. PHOTOGRAPH: ORANGE COUNTY PARKS

terrifying impression are deep, sighing moans coming in bursts through its leering lips. Even Captain Midnight is momentarily taken aback, as this dreadful sound echoes across the clearing to where they stand. The four Squadron agents draw their pistols.

Captain Midnight soon senses that the wind, flowing in wisps out of the idol's mouth, must be flying through primitive pipes set in the hollow stone head. He speculates that some ancient reed-maker realized that every evening at a certain time, a cold wind blew down from the snow-clad mountaintops. And this artisan had the imagination to give the ancient idol a deep, otherworldly voice. But Midnight's musings are suddenly broken off, when out of the encircling jungle charge hundreds of dark-skinned savages — all armed with bows, arrows, and spears — to surround them completely! A deep powerful voice rings out, in amazingly good English, "Stand where you are! At the first shot, you will be riddled with a thousand arrows!"

The Secret Squadron agents stand as if turned to stone. Captain Midnight tells them to drop their guns as a sign of peaceful intentions. An enormous Negro man, almost eight feet tall and with a lion skin over his shoulders, strides through the ring of warriors. He stares at the Squadron members for a moment, saying nothing. Then he asks, "Who are you? What do you want, here?"

"I am Captain Midnight of the Secret Squadron," the captain begins.

"Who?" the man responds.

"Captain Midnight."

Suddenly, the huge black man starts to laugh, his mighty voice roaring throughout the clearing.

"Why are you laughing?" Midnight asks. "Have you heard of me?"

The huge Negro chief tells them an extraordinary story. He is in fact an extremely well educated American black man. Disgusted with civilization's seemingly interminable wars, he sailed for Africa and struck out for the interior, determined to live a simple primeval life. He has been here just over three years. His size, strength, and superior education have earned him a place — even in this wild and inaccessible spot. His American name is Mark, and he is now acting chief of a tribe that calls itself the "Hooda-Wijis" — the Lion-Killers.

Captain Midnight is about to explain his predicament, when the chief interrupts him. He tells Midnight that although he is acting chief, his powers are limited by custom and tradition. If the members of the Secret Squadron are able to escape with their lives, there is only one chance for them.

"What is that?" Captain Midnight asks.

TRIAL BY ORDEAL

"You will have to fight a lion, single-handed, with your only weapon a hunting knife," Mark says. "By ancient laws, no stranger is allowed to mingle freely with the Lion Killers, who has not himself earned the right by killing a lion."

"What about my friends, here?" Midnight asks.

"I will tell my people they are your slaves," Mark answers. "But if the lion kills you, they will also be killed — to accompany your spirit into the other world."

Midnight murmurs, "Needs must, when the Devil drives." (That is, when forced into desperation, you must do things you normally would not.) "I'll face your lion as soon as you can arrange it; but I hope you'll give me some pointers! Fighting a lion was not one of the courses I took in college."

Meanwhile, Asar Bubastis carries on his operations at a wilderness camp. He learns — as Midnight had already suspected — that it will take at least two weeks and perhaps longer to procure a second helicopter. Then, too, he gets the idea of finding a mountain lake to use as a base, and to arrange by "radiotelephone" to buy or hire an amphibian. He gives orders to his headquarters in Addis Ababa to make the necessary arrangements that night.

The lion fight is to take place the next day at noon. Midnight contacts the Secret Squadron base in Cairo, giving orders for someone to get ahold of Andrew Maxon as soon as possible and to have him stand by. He explains his fantastic situation. If he survives the coming battle, he'll get Mark to guide them to a lake, and will send its exact location to Cairo. If he doesn't — well, Andy can continue his pleasure flights up the Nile.

That evening, Mark explains to Captain Midnight how he had managed to kill a lion when he first got to this part of the country. As he was led into the arena, he had charged the lion immediately, and as he charged, he scooped up a handful of sand. When the lion reared up to strike him with its claws, he had momentarily blinded the beast with sand. This slight advantage, combined with Mark's enormous strength, had proven enough for him to win the victory. Then suddenly chuckling to himself, he utters, "But I've got an idea that may give you an advantage." However, he refuses to say more. The week ends with Captain Midnight waiting at the arena gates, as they slowly open.

Chuck, Joyce, and Ikky are securely bound at one end of the arena where they await the outcome. Separated from Captain Midnight during the fight, they are treated as the common slaves that Mark had told his tribesmen they are. They have no idea what Mark has up his sleeve to make Captain Midnight's coming battle easier than it appears to be. They stand tense, as the doors of the arena are opened — and a huge, black-maned lion leaps out and savagely roars.

Captain Midnight quickly stoops to pick up a handful of dirt, then runs toward the terrifying animal. As the beast rears back to meet his charge, Midnight flings the dirt in the lion's eyes. With a bellow of fury, the animal rolls over, snarling and pawing at its eyes. Captain Midnight plunges his hunting knife deep in the lion's side. The beast struggles up, leaps at him, and knocks him down. It looks like the end of Captain Midnight. But suddenly, the lion gives a convulsive shudder — and rolls over dead! Captain Midnight staggers from beneath the enormous carcass.

Joyce, Chuck, and Ikky are almost speechless with relief. But instead of showing their feelings, they maintain their roles as slaves, bowing gravely before their "Master."

How did Captain Midnight survive? The advantage that Mark had chuckled about was coating Midnight's blade with a fast-acting poison.

Following Captain Midnight's passing the deadly ordeal, he is initiated into the elaborate Rite of Hooda-Wij, confirming his acceptance by the lion tribe.

THE RING'S SECRET

That night in a talk with Mark, Captain Midnight explains his real mission. He tells Mark of his expedition to find uranium in cooperation with the Emperor of Abyssinia, and that Asar Bubastis' criminal band may be looking for the same uranium deposits that he's been commissioned to find. Mark has some valuable information of his own to impart. He doesn't know what the other expedition is looking for, but he does know of a traditionally forbidden place that may be what Midnight's group is trying to find. He knows its general direction, and tells Captain Midnight of a taboo legend about its mountainous location.

Mark describes a triangular plateau — that for one week every year, when the moon is in its fourth phase — is "covered with snow." He believes such a plateau does exist, but it is absolutely forbidden to his people, and therefore to himself. Mark does not know that the white carpet is a mass of calla lilies that blooms at the same time every spring. But he does speak of the plateau's "black crown" that is visible only during this brief period in the snow. He says if that is the spot Asar Bubastis is looking for, then it is the place the Secret Squadron must find first.

Captain Midnight remains silent, as Mark continues. From a pouch beneath his chief's lion cloak, Mark furtively pulls out a small and ornately-carved wooden case. Opening the case, he shows Midnight a beautifully fashioned gold ring with a large, sparkling orange gem on

Emulation of the "Original" Queen of Sheba signet ring by Leonard Zane.
PHOTOGRAPH: LEONARD ZANE

top. He explains the ancient legend told that this was a great queen's ring. Over the ages, much blood was spilled and tragedies suffered — and empires rose and fell — because of it. However, the legend also said that destroying the ring would loose an unspeakable curse. And so it became part of the taboo that the Lion-Killers have guarded and have sworn to keep secret over countless centuries. But now that Asar Bubastis is likely to try to hunt down his tribe and slaughter them, he will trust Captain Midnight to take the ring and deliver it to the Emperor of Abyssinia. Struck by the ring's strange story, the danger to Mark and his tribe — and how the ring may be the key to uranium deposits, as well as ancient treasure — Midnight promises to carry out Mark's wishes. Mark closes the case, hands it to Captain Midnight, and Midnight tucks it in his flight jacket.

The next morning, Chief Mark leads the Secret Squadron quite some way out of the territory over which he rules to a remote mountain lake called Lake Tohiba. He does not want civilization interfering in any way with his simple people, and he bids the Secret Squadron farewell.

ASSAULTS

Back in so-called "civilization," Asar Bubastis learns through his underworld connections that Andrew Maxon is leaving on a secretive trip to the wilds of Abyssinia. He concludes it is a trip to rescue the group, which he has now learned is Captain Midnight's Secret Squadron. He gives orders that Maxon is to be prevented from leaving Cairo at all costs.

Republic RC-3 Seabee amphibian. The twin-bladed "pusher-prop" Seabee was introduced in mid-1946. It was especially noted for making extremely short takeoffs and landings on small lakes. PHOTOGRAPH: ALAN HUNT

Later that same day at twilight — while Andy Maxon's private amphibian lies parked by a dirt airstrip at Cairo's outskirts — a fast, low-winged plane swoops out of the sky and strafes his little plane to pieces! The phantom attacking aircraft swiftly escapes, and Maxon later arrives to find his amphibian destroyed beyond repair.

But Captain Midnight's earlier Pocket Locator message to the Cairo Secret Squadron base had at least alerted the agents there. So when the larger, Secret Squadron amphibian aircraft reaches Cairo from the United States, both the plane and Andy Maxon are kept under heavy guard until he is able to leave for Addis Ababa. And this plane is armed with machineguns.

Learning of the second amphibian, and of the heavy security, Asar's next order is to have Maxon followed and shot down enroute. But Maxon departs clandestinely at midnight, catching Asar's pursuers mostly unawares — but only mostly. In the darkness, an unidentified pursuing aircraft manages to pump some machinegun bullets into the amphibian and disable its weapons system! In a desperate effort, Andy Maxon turns off all his plane's lights and manages to lose the other aircraft in some clouds. Fortunately, none of the hits are critical to flying the plane, and Maxon continues on his way to Abyssinia.

When Andy Maxon arrives in Addis Ababa in the morning, Joyce and Ikky are there to join him. They check the bullet hits and make a few scant repairs, but there's no quick fixing the gun controls. They then refuel the amphibian and take off for the remote Lake Tohiba, where Captain Midnight and Chuck await them. But with the daylight, Asar Bubastis' best pilot now follows them in a speedy aircraft from Addis Ababa. The aviator is an ex-Nazi named Wolfgang — an extremely skilled ex-fighter pilot with impressive World War II combat kills to his credit. *[In fact, a transcript of the 26 March 1948 Captain Midnight broadcast that follows shows a post-WWII shift in attitude toward a former U.S. wartime enemy. Now, there is at least unabashed technical admiration of someone who is now an "ex-Nazi" aviator. Such praising comments regarding the German's excellent piloting skill include Chuck Ramsay's statement: "Wow! What a beautiful display of flying that guy is putting up, even though he is hit!"]*

Eying the pursuing aircraft, Joyce sends a Pocket Locator message to Captain Midnight, asking if they should turn back to Addis Ababa.

RETURN, NOW, TO THOSE THRILLING DAYS OF YESTERYEAR!

The adventure continues, from Captain Midnight's exciting radio broadcast of 26 March 1948, "The Jewels of the Queen of Sheba:"

ANNOUNCER *[Tom Moore]:* And now, on with the action packed adventure, "The Jewels of the Queen of Sheba," with Captain Midnight and the Secret Squadron. Yesterday, Captain Midnight — by means of the Pocket Locator — ordered Ikky, Joyce, and Andy Maxon to continue toward Lake Tohiba, in spite of the mysterious plane that was following them. But he asked them to keep him posted every few minutes. Now they're nearing Lake Tohiba, and Andy Maxon at the controls is trying evasive tactics again. Listen:

SFX: *Two buzzing airplanes.*

ANDY MAXON: I'll give that boy credit.

ICHABOD MUDD: And I'd give my left arm to know who's at the controls! Wait — maybe it's Sans Souci, Andy. No, no, no, that sly old fool couldn't fly a kite. But it could be the other one. The face in the window — the one who posed as a chauffeur.

ANDY MAXON: Yeah.

ICHABOD MUDD: But whoever it is, Andy, I bet one thing: It has some connection with Asar Bubastis!

ANDY MAXON: If I ever find out if that's the guy who shot-up my nice little amphib at Cairo, I'll fix his clock good!

ICHABOD MUDD: Not with this plane, you won't Andy. We're more or less at his mercy. The only armor we got is our pistols.

ANDY MAXON: And ah know it. He's got more speed than we got, too, and there's nothin' I can do about it. If we had some clouds — but in this country, there just ain't such a thing as clouds.

ICHABOD MUDD: Well, it won't be long, now. Accordin' to my calculations, we should be seein' Lake Tohiba any time, now.

ANNOUNCER: Precious minutes pass, and as the plane nears Lake Tohiba, Captain Midnight and Chuck wait anxiously along the shore.

CHUCK RAMSAY: It ought to be due any time, Captain.

CAPTAIN MIDNIGHT: Well, they might have struck a slight headwind. No need to worry, yet, Chuck. We heard from them just a few minutes ago on the Pocket Locator.

CHUCK RAMSAY: Gosh, it sure will be good to see Ikky and Joyce again!

CAPTAIN MIDNIGHT *(chuckling slightly):* Yeah.

CHUCK RAMSAY: This is the longest we've been separated in quite a while.

CAPTAIN MIDNIGHT: Yes it is, at that.

CHUCK RAMSAY: Uh, Captain?

CAPTAIN MIDNIGHT: Yes, Chuck?

CHUCK RAMSAY: That ring — do you mind if — if I look at it?

CAPTAIN MIDNIGHT: Why, no, of course not.

CHUCK RAMSAY: I got a glimpse of it before, but not a good one. I — well, it has such a fabulous history that I've almost been afraid to ask.

CAPTAIN MIDNIGHT: Yes, I know what you mean. It is a fabulous ring. You *feel* that the instant you look at it.

CHUCK RAMSAY: Are you going to turn it over to the Emperor of Abyssinia, eventually — after you capture Bubastis and find the jewels of the Queen o' Sheba?

CAPTAIN MIDNIGHT: Yes, I believe the Emperor is its rightful owner. Here — I'll take it out of its case…Okay — here is the original ring that King Solomon gave the Queen of Sheba. A ring that's caused bloodshed and suffering, triumph and disaster. A ring that's as fabulous as the Queen o' Sheba herself was.[1]

CHUCK RAMSAY: Gosh — what a beauty! Uh, what's that cut in the top, Captain?

CAPTAIN MIDNIGHT: Oh, that's the Hebrew letter "S," Chuck, and I suppose stands for Sheba, because this is her signet ring.

CHUCK RAMSAY: Boy, I'd like to have a ring like that!

CAPTAIN MIDNIGHT: Hm, hm!

CHUCK RAMSAY: Captain, do you believe the story about the hidden plateau, snow-capped once a year, crowned with a black crown?

CAPTAIN MIDNIGHT: Strangely enough, Chuck, I do. I was of course very skeptical when I first overheard Bubastis talking that night in his camp. But later, when we got tangled up with Mark and those Hooda-Wijis, and he told me almost the very same story — well, then I began to take this legend seriously. I'm quite convinced, now, that Asar Bubastis is crazy — like a fox. Those jewels *must* exist, Chuck, and that plateau must also be an important key to the location of the Queen o' Sheba's tomb. Now, see, here's another clue.

CHUCK RAMSAY: Oh, what's that, sir?

CAPTAIN MIDNIGHT: The surface of this top stone. Notice anything peculiar about it?

CHUCK RAMSAY: Nothing, except that it's — it's got a triangular carving on it.

CAPTAIN MIDNIGHT: Yes — so is the hidden plateau supposed to be triangular, remember?

CHUCK RAMSAY: By gosh, you're right, sir! Gee, that's a beautiful ring!

SFX: *Aircraft sounds.*

CAPTAIN MIDNIGHT: Oh, oh, that sounds familiar.

CHUCK RAMSAY: And wonderful! It's them, they're coming!

CAPTAIN MIDNIGHT: There they are, coming in from the southwest.

CHUCK RAMSAY: Yes, you can just barely see a speck against the blue sky. Boy, oh boy, will I be glad to see them.

CAPTAIN MIDNIGHT: And there's that other plane. Hey! Look! The second plane has made a dive on them. They're going to it!

SFX: *Buzzing planes and machine gun fire.*

ANNOUNCER: Yes, in less time than it takes to tell, a furious battle takes shape, high in the skies over Lake Tohiba. Andy Maxon's bewildered at first, but he rapidly recovers.

SFX: *More buzzing and shooting.*

ANDY MAXON: Well, wha'd he wait all this time for? I don't get it!

ICHABOD MUDD: I don't either. But this is no time for us to worry about that!

ANDY MAXON: Oh, I'll burn the feathers offa his tail!

ICHABOD MUDD: Hey! Atta boy, Andy, you almost clipped him that time!

ANDY MAXON: I will the next time.

ICHABOD MUDD: Look out! Here he comes at us again from above! Comin' in at high noon!

SFX: *Buzzing and machine gun fire.*

ANDY MAXON: Ohhhh! They got me!

ICHABOD MUDD: Joyce! Andy's been hit! Grab the controls, Joyce! Take her down! Take her down quick! Land it on the water! I can see the Captain and Chuck! Take it easy, Andy, we'll be down in just a second.

ANDY MAXON: Ohhh, I'm all right.

ICHABOD MUDD: Easy, boy.

ANDY MAXON: Oh, my leg!

ICHABOD MUDD: Easy, boy.

ANDY MAXON: Go back and get that rat, Ikky! Don't let 'im get away.

ICHABOD MUDD: Aw, don't worry. We got no intentions o' lettin' 'im get away!

ANNOUNCER: Swiftly, expertly, Joyce brings the Seabee into a perfect glide along the water. She pulls up to the shore, and Ikky calls out:

ICHABOD MUDD: Cap'n! Cap'n! Andy's been hit in the leg!

CAPTAIN MIDNIGHT: All right. Hand him out. Easy, there. Grab him, Chuck.

CHUCK RAMSAY *(grunting):* Okay!

ANDY MAXON: Cappy — it's good — to see you again.

CAPTAIN MIDNIGHT *(good natured):* Never mind the talk, you crazy idiot. Close your eyes and relax.

ANDY MAXON: Go get 'im, Cappy! Don't let that buzzard get away.

CAPTAIN MIDNIGHT *(resolute):* I don't intend to. Now, the two of you get out, you need a rest. Chuck, you stay here with the others. I'm going up and bring that vulture down if I can!

ICHABOD MUDD: He's got a machinegun — a portable machine-gun, Cap'n — you won't stand a chance.

CAPTAIN MIDNIGHT: We'll stand less of a chance if we stay down here and make a perfect target. Come on, now make it snappy!

CHUCK RAMSAY: Hey! Hey, he's makin' a run on us! Duck, everybody!

ICHABOD MUDD: Hit the dirt!

SFX: *The attacking plane buzzes low, firing its machine gun, then swoops back up.*

CAPTAIN MIDNIGHT: Everybody all right? Nobody else hit? Good. Joyce, do what you can for Andy's leg. Here I go!

CHUCK RAMSAY: Good luck, sir!

ICHABOD MUDD: Good luck, Cap'n!

CHUCK RAMSAY: Give 'em the works, Captain Midnight!

SFX: *Captain Midnight takes the plane off.*

ANNOUNCER: Captain Midnight climbs straight up,[2] and the ex-Nazi fighter pilot's there waiting for him. There ensues the most vicious dogfight that the Secret Squadron has seen since the war! A grinding, grueling dogfight, in which Wolfgang the ex-Nazi pits his evil skill against the matchless skill of Captain Midnight! But it's an uneven battle.

SFX: *Airplane buzzing, machine gun fire, pistol shots.*

ANNOUNCER: Captain Midnight's able to get in only a few random shots from his pistol, at close range, against the machine-gun of Wolfgang! But then — Wolfgang runs out of ammunition! Captain Midnight realizes it instantly and becomes more daring. He can afford to take chances now, and he does.

SFX: *Airplane buzzing and pistol shots.*

ANNOUNCER: Closer, closer the two planes come together, both men firing repeated pistol-fire through the glass of their cockpits. And then:

ICHABOD MUDD: Joyce! Chuck! The Cap'n got 'im! He got 'im! I can see smoke streakin' from the other plane! Hey, look, he's goin' into a dive and the Cap'n's right on top of 'im!

CHUCK RAMSAY: Wow! What a beautiful display of flying that guy is putting up, even though he *is* hit!

ANDY MAXON: Well, how is it goin' kids? Who's winnin'?

ICHABOD MUDD: Aw, you just relax, Andy, everything'll be all right! Yes, sir, everything's gonna be all right!

CHUCK RAMSAY: See — that other plane is running off into the distance, smoking to beat the band!

ICHABOD MUDD: Yeah, but Chuck, what's the Skipper comin' back for! Why don't he follow up the advantage!

CHUCK RAMSAY: Well, we'll know in a minute, because he's coming in fast!

SFX: *Midnight's plane swiftly descends, lands on the lake, revs and then cuts the engine. The cabin door opens and closes.*

CHUCK RAMSAY: What happened, sir?

CAPTAIN MIDNIGHT: Engine's been acting up. Was afraid to trust it. How're you feelin' now, Andy?

ANDY MAXON: Cappy, you ol' codger. If this ain't one on me, comin' in as a cripple, when I had it in mind to be of assistance to you.

CAPTAIN MIDNIGHT: Ha, ha, ha. You'll be plenty of assistance, Andy. It's doggone good to lay eyes on your ugly frame again after all these years.

ANDY MAXON: Too many years, eh Cappy? By golly, you ain't changed a bit.

CAPTAIN MIDNIGHT: Thanks, Andy, and the same goes for you, but come on, now, lie back and let me look at that leg o' yours. That's the first order o' business.

ANNOUNCER: Captain Midnight examines the wound, finds that the bullet has gone completely through the fleshy part of Andy Maxon's calf. While painful, the wound is not serious. And later that evening, after both groups have caught up on all the news, Captain Midnight gets to another order of business — that of the precious ring of the Queen of Sheba.

CAPTAIN MIDNIGHT: And that's the story of this ring that I'm about to show you. I want you to see it, because after seeing it, you'll be as impressed as Chuck and I, who were just as skeptical as you probably are now.

ANDY MAXON: Doggone, Cappy, that's the craziest story I ever heard.

ICHABOD MUDD: I ain't skeptical, Cap'n, but I'm dyin' to see the ring.

CAPTAIN MIDNIGHT: Well, here it is. There — feast your eyes on that!

ICHABOD MUDD: Wow!

ANDY MAXON: Say!

ICHABOD MUDD: One look at that ring, and you can understand why the Queen o' Sheba treasured it so much.

CHUCK RAMSAY: Captain, do you know what? I think that ring — I mean a reasonable copy of it — would make a wonderful souvenir for all the members of the Secret Squadron!

CAPTAIN MIDNIGHT: Hmmm. Say, that's not a bad suggestion, Chuck. In fact, it's a mighty good one.

CHUCK RAMSAY: Do you really think so?

CAPTAIN MIDNIGHT: Um, hm.

CHUCK RAMSAY: Boy, I can see right now how thousands of faces would light up if they could have a ring something like this!

CAPTAIN MIDNIGHT: As a matter of fact, Chuck, the more I think of it, the more I like the idea. Not merely for its sentimental value, but — for other reasons.

CHUCK RAMSAY: Oh, what do you mean, sir?

CAPTAIN MIDNIGHT: Well, I can't explain, now, but I'll keep that suggestion in mind, Chuck. In fact, I promise to give it lots of thought. Now look: it's getting dark. I want you all to notice something. Remember my telling you that the hidden plateau would turn white one week out of the year?

CHUCK RAMSAY: Yes.

CAPTAIN MIDNIGHT: And that week would come in the springtime, the moon would be in its fourth phase, and according to the legend, the ring would at that one week of the year — emit a greenish glow?

ICHABOD MUDD: Yeah?

CAPTAIN MIDNIGHT: Well, are my eyes deceiving me, or is that ring sparkling green right now?

ANDY MAXON: Wow!

CHUCK RAMSAY: Loopin' loops!

ICHABOD MUDD: Leapin' sawfish!

MAXON: Well, I'll be dogged. It does have a greenish sparkle to it.

CAPTAIN MIDNIGHT: I didn't notice until this afternoon. A couple o' days ago, its sparkle was of another color, entirely. Fellas, this means that the time has come that the hidden plateau can be plainly seen from the air. 'Twill be entirely white for one short week.

CHUCK RAMSAY: And that's why Asar Bubastis needed the ring so much. So he could tell just when the hidden plateau would be easily visible from the air.

CAPTAIN MIDNIGHT: Yes, but we haven't any time to lose. If that plane got back to Addis Ababa or any place from where the pilot could contact Asar Bubastis, we'll have that gang o' cutthroats on our trail in no time. Even if he doesn't make it, we haven't much time. We've got to get our plane repaired so we can get up in the air and find that plateau before that week is up! And there, we'll find the tomb of the Queen o' Sheba!

ANNOUNCER: Success at hand! But time is one element, Asar Bubastis is another! Will the legend of the ring prove to be true? Will the Secret Squadron actually find the hidden white-capped plateau? Don't miss Monday's thrill packed adventure, "The Double Cross!"

ANNOUNCER *(continuing):* Now tonight, we have a thrilling secret code message from Captain Midnight in the new 1948 secret code. And every Secret Squadron member who has that swell new 1948 Mirro-Magic Code-O-Graph can work it out in a hurry! Now here's tonight's message — an exciting clue about Monday's adventure — in Master Code 19:

5-19-26-21-15-11-3-12-20-26
26-21-11-16-1-6-15-11

M-Y-S-T-E-R-I-O-U-S
S-T-R-A-N-G-E-R

Announcer Tom Moore. PHOTOGRAPH: PHOTOFEST

ANNOUNCER *(continuing):* Tune in Monday, same time, same station to Captain Midnight! Stay tuned now for Tom Mix, which follows in just a moment! Until Monday, this is your Ovaltine announcer, Tom Moore, saying goodbye, and *Haaaaapppyy Landiiiiinnngs!*

Working against time, the Secret Squadron repairs the amphibian — including its previously damaged weapons control system — thanks to Ikky's masterful skill. Captain Midnight soon takes off in search of the Queen of Sheba's white-capped plateau. Ikky and Andy Maxon are left behind to guard the base camp, while Chuck and Joyce do some exploring.

Before long, Chuck and Joyce actually do come to see the white gorilla! It is not, however, as Midnight supposes, an albino. It is an extremely old male that for some unknown reason has survived long beyond the normal lifespan. It isn't exactly white, but a grizzled grayish-white — and still a terrifying sight, with its enormous arms and red-rimmed eyes. Joyce barely escapes its charge by jumping from a bluff into the icy lake water.

Meanwhile, Asar Bubastis realizes something has happened to the plane that was to intercept Andrew Maxon. This setback, however, is offset by two events: First, his search party — using a newly acquired helicopter — has not only discovered the plateau of the lilies, but has even briefly landed and surveyed the black pyramid. Second, he has been approached by a secretive individual (the "Mysterious Stranger" of the Code-O-Graph message in the 26 March 1948 "Secret Squadron Signal Session"). This person has offered him the use of three heavily armed, long-range fighting amphibians as protection. Calling himself "Mr. Z," this man explains he represents a foreign power. Its intelligence knows what Asar is after and will help him any way it can. It wants none of the jewels and artifacts that Asar is looking for, but it does want Captain Midnight killed and all further exploration discouraged. He refuses to explain further (although he of course represents the USSR in a uranium contest with the USA). At first, Asar is suspicious, but eventually he thankfully accepts the proffered help.

Meanwhile, Captain Midnight, too, has glimpsed the hidden plateau. The roughly triangular-shaped land mass is ensconced inside the crater of an extinct or dormant volcano! This is why the flower-covered plateau was concealed from ground-level view, and could be seen only from above. A dense growth of shoulder-high calla lilies stretches from edge to edge of the great plateau. And centered near the broadest portion of the triangle, a craggy black pyramid protrudes amidst the white!

Because of the high, thick foliage, Midnight sees it will not be feasible to land the amphibian, so he decides to go back for his colleagues and employ a new plan. When they return over the crater, four Secret Squadron members will parachute onto the plateau: Captain Midnight, Chuck, Joyce, and Ikky. Andy Maxon will fly back to civilization, and do whatever it takes to get a helicopter to come back and pick them up.

Extinct volcano caldera, containing a triangular plateau, in Ethiopia's Simien Mountain Range along the East African Rift. And what is the rising, roughly pyramidal shape in the plateau's foreground? Again, Robert M. Burtt did his research. PHOTOGRAPH: JOHN SEACH

THE BLACK PYRAMID

Later that afternoon, the Secret Squadron takes off in great excitement and flies directly over the triangular plateau. Then suddenly — out of the setting sun — two strange, heavily armed foreign planes attack! Midnight puts up a terrific battle, but when a third plane comes to rescue the other two, he realizes the situation is hopeless and gives orders to abandon the crippled plane. The wounded Andy Maxon, Chuck, Joyce, Ikky, and Captain Midnight parachute down just in time. As Midnight descends, he sees they're about a mile from the black pyramid amid the flowers below.

Night soon falls, and Captain Midnight decides not to wait till morning because morning will doubtless bring the foreign planes back and perhaps even reinforcements. He therefore directs his Squadron team to head for the pyramid and to begin exploring it right away. He orders Joyce to contact Secret Squadron headquarters at once, to tell them what has happened and to ask for help. Via her Locator, Joyce does so, as the party sets out for the pyramid.

The black pyramid is bigger than Captain Midnight had supposed, and especially awe-inspiring and eerie amid the white flowers by night. They struggle through the shoulder-high lily plants, which are already rapidly losing their blossoms. Soil and weather conditions at this plateau make the calla lilies both grow and wither very quickly.

Midnight realizes what an impregnable fort the pyramid would make, if they could only find the entrance and get inside. As the Secret Squadron members draw close, something suddenly startles them. Through what is apparently a crevice on one side — about halfway up to the top — a huge cloud of bats pours out. Hundreds of thousands of them! "There," says Midnight, "is where the entrance must be!"

Andy Maxon's leg wound grows more painful, and the Secret Squadron agents pause by the base of the pyramid to try to make him more comfortable. Then they clamber up the side of the pyramid, with Chuck helping Andy. It is at once apparent that the bats are streaming out of what must be the originally sealed entrance. Through the centuries, it has crumbled away, leaving a partly open portal. It is therefore not too difficult to pry away several square slabs of black marble — and to squeeze into a dark, echoing passageway. The squeaking bats still pour out, and Joyce shudders as their flapping wings stir the air against her.

Leaving Andy Maxon to keep watch by the entry, the rest of the Squadron team moves down a steep, twisting and turning corridor. At last, they find themselves in a huge chamber. A tomb of white marble rests on a massive square platform surrounded by twelve smaller tombs and stone chests. The lid of one chest has slipped partly to one side, and Ikky shines his flashlight inside. He gasps and calls to the others. It is heaped with jeweled ornaments of every size, color, and description! Whether the stones are semiprecious or precious, here is a fortune — besides archaeological value — that's beyond estimation!

Because powerful foreign planes have attacked, Captain Midnight concludes there must be a good deal more to this plateau than a forgotten tomb, however precious its loot. Perhaps uranium deposits are here, too. But at this moment, they are interrupted by Andy Maxon calling from near the entrance, and they hurry back to him. Andy's face is flushed and he's in pain, but that's not why he called. He points outside.

Asar Bubastis must have figured the delay was too risky for him — and at least fifty men are parachuting out of the night sky to surround the black pyramid!

DARING ACTIONS

Because of the thick and high growth of lily stalks, Captain Midnight says, "We can remain here for weeks without their catching a glimpse of us. What happens next, of course, is up to chance. If necessary, we can pick them off, one by one." Others agree, and Chuck, Ikky and Captain Midnight slip out onto the black surface of the pyramid. They then crawl as silently as possible down to its base. In the distance, they hear men shouting, and so are able to avoid stumbling into the hands of the enemy. Overhearing various cries, they learn the men have orders to gather at a certain corner of the pyramid and wait for daylight. They also find out the men are to clear a landing strip the next day. With fifty new invaders and only the tall growth of lily plants to mow down, Midnight realizes it shouldn't take very long!

At dawn, the men immediately begin working. By noon, the first plane lands. It's a swift, twin-engine foreign fighter, and two helmeted figures get out, followed by Asar Bubastis.

Midnight has an idea. Whispering to Chuck and Ikky to follow him, he stealthily makes for the runway below. Crouching and creeping quietly, they reach a point above the far end of the improvised runway and peer down. They see Asar and his group get to the pyramid and start to climb the face.

Inside the pyramid, they realize Andy Maxon's wound must have been much worse than any of them knew. Now he cries out in a fever, half-delirious, and Joyce suddenly finds herself alone to defend their adopted fortress. As the first person's head appears in the portal, she fires a warning shot and follows it with a burst of machinegun fire — as if she were not there by herself.

On hearing the shooting, Captain Midnight exclaims in a sharp but muted voice, "Got to capture that plane!" Most of the calla lily blossoms are now withered and fallen away. But Midnight, Chuck, and Ikky crawl down and through the tall stalks along the side of the runway until they come near the aircraft. The guard walking around it is very alert, taking no chances. Captain Midnight picks up a small rock and hurls it over the craft to the other side. The guard turns to look at what caused the noise, and Midnight and Ikky are on him in a flash. A terrific blow from

Midnight's fist, and he is out cold. Quickly, they scramble into the plane and hastily take off, but at this moment two more fighter planes come swooping down!

The Secret Squadron leader realizes his disadvantage in a strange plane with stranger armament, but he dives to the attack! The battle that follows is one of the fiercest that Captain Midnight has ever fought. After a vicious dogfight, he manages to force one plane down — and it crashes into the crater with a huge explosion! It had carried bombs. The other plane shoots out Midnight's left engine, and it looks as if he will be lucky even to crash-land. And worse: he goes into a spin. But this is a deliberate tactic because following this, Captain Midnight suddenly zooms his amphibian up below the enemy plane, fires his machineguns, and sends it crashing into the caldera! Another aircraft bomb-blast goes off!

TREASURE AND URANIUM

Captain Midnight immediately flies low toward the pyramid. Another burst of his machineguns sends the ground attackers scattering. By repeated bursts, Captain Midnight herds most of them onto the runway. At this point, a whole *flight* of helicopter reinforcements that Joyce had called for arrives! Facing this, the ground troops throw down their arms, and the Secret Squadron reinforcements quickly take over.

It is later found there *are* uranium ore deposits, not on the plateau itself, but in the valley below it. The jewels — which may or may not belong to the ancient queen who visited King Solomon — are of course the property of the Abyssinian government. But Joyce is given a beautiful ring from the queen's tomb as a memento. It is made of gold, with small flawless emeralds surrounded by a cone of rubies on the top, forming the shape of a calla lily.

It is no wonder that this *Captain Midnight* adventure is called "The Jewels of the Queen of Sheba," rather than "The Abyssinian Uranium Expedition."

HOW THE QUEEN OF SHEBA'S RING STONE WORKED

Radio scripting for this adventure purported that the Queen of Sheba's ring stone glowed in reaction to radioactivity from nearby uranium deposits, but that would have meant that even radium watch dials (which were very common in the 1940s) would have caused the stone to sparkle![3]

Secondly, such a claim would not explain the sparkling during only one, consistent spring week out of the year. Thirdly, the uranium deposits were in the valley below, not in the triangular plateau from which the calla lilies grew.

The radio program thus did not reveal this actual, fascinating secret:

(1) The Biblical tale of Sheba's visit to Solomon's court is purported to have taken place around 970 BC, and the queen brought both gem and flora gifts.

(2) Calla lilies are native to Southern Africa (Bob Burtt did his research, again).

Among the "spices of great store"[4] that the queen brought were vessels of fragrant nectar extracted from calla lilies. She had intended the offerings as perfume. The resourceful king, however, went on to surprise the queen with a crafted gem as part of his fabulous ring gift to her.

Leonard Zane's emulated Sheba ring stone and mirror-image-set gold Hebrew "S." The extension on one tail of the "S" signifies a "Sh" pronunciation. PHOTOGRAPH: LEONARD ZANE

(3) Solomon had his artisans boil down some of Sheba's aromatic and syrupy nectar to a colored concentrate. They then poured a bit of the thick concentrate into a specially crafted gem mold that contained a sculpted triangular relief. They also fashioned a gold Hebrew letter "S," signifying Sheba, to be set in the molded triangular recess. After baking and hardening the molded substance to amber-like consistency, the king's jewelers polished the casting to sparkling gemlike luster.

(4) Solomon's jewelers then set the gold Hebrew "S" in the cast capstone, and mounted the finished signet onto an artful gold ring that included lily symbols in relief on the band.

(5) Royal signet seals from those days have been found impressed in clay.

(6) It was not necessary for King Solomon to know the secret of when Sheba's white flowers bloomed. But enough symbolism was known to make the triangular recess on the stone's surface, which then impressed a raised triangular object around a recessed Hebrew "S."

(7) During one particular spring week, airborne sex hormones from the blooming lilies' pollen reacted with the hardened pistil nectar, causing the gem on the queen's ring to sparkle green.

(8) The queen and her priestesses knew the sparkling phenomenon, but they kept their knowledge secret for later situating and consecrating Sheba's tomb on the hidden triangular plateau.

FATE OF THE QUEEN OF SHEBA'S TOMB AND JEWELS

What happened to the hidden triangular plateau in Abyssinia, and to the Queen of Sheba's precious jewels, other than the queen's signet ring and the other ring given to Joyce? Why have there been no popular excursions to the queen's fabulous black pyramid? The following speculations into the mystery are based on what the serial adventure presented and also omitted. Supplementing what was told in the radio scripts and broadcasts:

(1) In the vicious air battle, above the dormant volcano hiding the Queen of Sheba's black pyramid, Captain Midnight shot down two attacking

planes that crashed and exploded in the great caldera surrounding the triangular plateau.

(2) The bomb explosions had somewhat delayed effects on the stability of the long-dormant rock strata and magma below the volcano's cone. By the time Secret Squadron helicopters and manpower arrived, frightening earth tremors had begun to shake the whole caldera. The terrifying tremors increased in magnitude, swaying and crumbling the Queen of Sheba's fabulous black pyramid! Storms of bats fled the pyramid in great torrents!

(3) The arriving Secret Squadron aircraft removed everybody barely in time, because what followed was a tremendously violent and focused earthquake! The massive temblor shook the caldera, its triangular plateau and the pyramid apart — roaring with deep, ripping and widening fissures that made the huge crater collapse inward upon its cavity.

(4) All remains of the crater, the mysterious plateau, and the black pyramid it had once concealed were crumbled and buried under a mound of rubble. The awesome event thus interred the Queen's disintegrated pyramid, her tomb, and artifacts under millions of tons of massive rock slabs, boulders, and earth.

(5) The Emperor of Abyssinia deemed the cataclysm an omen of the great Queen of Sheba's will. He ordered all records and accounts of the spot eliminated, and consigned all traces of its annals to neglected and forgotten mysteries of the land. Not one calla lily has ever grown there since.

ENDNOTES

1 According to Wikipedia, the *Kebra Nagast* account of Abyssinian folk tales dates back at least 700 years, and tells that King Solomon gave Queen Makeda (the Queen of Sheba) a ring. This ring was both for her and also to identify their son Menelik to King Solomon, once Menelik had grown to manhood. The ring could prove Menelik the rightful heir to the throne and to all the material and mystic treasures of Israel.

2 "Straight up" is an exaggeration for the amphibian. Captain Midnight simply climbs to meet the ex-Nazi fighter pilot.

3 See Wikipedia in regard to Radium Dials.

4 Kings 10:10: "And she gave the king…of spices of very great store, and precious stones: there came no more such abundance of spices as these which the queen of Sheba gave to King Solomon."

CAPTAIN MIDNIGHT'S INITIAL STAMPING RING

Captain Midnight turned over the Queen of Sheba's fabulous ring to the Emperor of Abyssinia. The Squadron leader then went on to develop the 1948 "'Printing' Initial Ring," as a radio-premium souvenir of the Queen of Sheba adventure, for Secret Squadron members.

Instead of using a Hebrew letter "S," a Secret Squadron member ordered a custom English letter. The polymer stamp was pushed inside the brass ring-cap, which held a small inkpad, and so the ring could stamp the inked letter onto a flat surface.

Captain Midnight's 1948 "'Printing' Initial Ring." PHOTOGRAPH: LEONARD ZANE

"'Printing' Initial Ring" leaflet. PHOTOGRAPHS: LEONARD ZANE

12

Piracy on the High Seas

(1948)

MARAUDING HELICOPTER

"Modern Piracy on the High Seas!" cry U.S. newspaper headlines from coast to coast. It's "modern" piracy because the means employed are very technologically advanced. A new type of jet-propelled helicopter, extraordinarily large and fast, has been robbing ships in international waters.

The first ship to be plundered was a British transatlantic liner, the *Queen Anne*. The huge marauding aircraft had overtaken the liner on the Atlantic and dropped two bombs across her bow, forcing her to heave to. It then hung over the ship, immediately threatening to send her to the bottom with a third bomb, unless orders were strictly obeyed. A long silken ladder was lowered from the hovering point to the top deck. A dozen masked men swiftly climbed down. The ship's captain, fearful for the lives of the women and children under his care, was forced to open the craft's safe and hand over the money and jewels kept there for safekeeping. This first haul had netted the pirates over a million dollars. The huge helicopter then disappeared at incredible speed.

In three days, five passenger liners in far flung parts of the world were forced to submit to the same treatment. There is absolutely no clue about the pirate helicopter's base. Unless there are several craft of this type, her range seems to be worldwide. After the first assaults, it was twice seen over the Atlantic, and then the Pacific. She swooped on a helpless passenger liner in the Indian Ocean, and the next day held up another off the coast of Madagascar.

The value of the loot the big copter accumulated was enormous. Then, just as abruptly as these acts of piracy had begun, they ceased. It looked as if whoever was the guiding intelligence had decided on just one series of quick coups to gain an immense fortune, and then had planned to retire from crime to enjoy the wickedly gotten gains. Captain Midnight, having recently returned from the Secret Squadron's mission in Africa, does not believe this. "Thieves always fall out," he says. "The attacks will sometime be repeated."

GENERAL PERCIVAL DRAKE CROMWELL

At a hidden base in the New Mexico wilderness, it looks very much as if Captain Midnight's words are already proving true. A man with the rather highfalutin name of General Percival Drake Cromwell addresses four of his lieutenants. "The General," as he's called, has a strange soft voice and a precise way of talking that is definitely ominous. His lieutenants wish the spoils to be split up immediately. The General is adamant: There will be no split for six months. Even then, it is the General who will dispense the booty. He will take no chances. He knows a safe way to do this, so that the stolen goods can never be traced back to any member of his gang. After the looted goods have been safely disposed of, he will divide the money that has been received from them. He points out that a delay of six months will be well worth it, because they will be extremely rich men. The lieutenants are apparently persuaded, and they disperse.

The thieving lieutenants later get together, however, and discuss the whole affair. They do not trust the General. One of them suggests a plan: They will steal the huge helicopter and make three raids on their own. Then they will kill the General.

The conspirators are shortly surprised at the ease with which they are able to steal the giant helicopter. They think, for once, that the General has slipped up, and they anticipate three easy acts of piracy.

The lieutenants, however, have not reckoned on the General's cleverness. By a recording device he had installed in their wooden hut, he had overheard their plans, and now chuckling to himself, takes quick action. By shortwave radio, he transmits a widespread Morse code announcement that the *S.S. Plutonia* will be attacked at a certain hour the next day.

At first, Captain Midnight believes the General's shortwave warning to be a phony, but Major Steele authorizes the Secret Squadron to make sure. In a supersonic jet airplane (again the Silver Dart/Skyrocket model) the Secret Squadron leader takes off to intercept the helicopter, should it really put in an appearance.

Meanwhile, the General — accompanied by his beautiful French niece — destroys all traces of his headquarters by burning it to the ground. They then set out for "civilization" to carry out a long-developed plan.

Captain Midnight discovers the piracy tip-off concerning the *S.S. Plutonia* is genuine. He intercepts the big marauding helicopter, shoots it down, and drops a rubber life raft for any survivors. One man is rescued. He is bitter. He says he knows little about the leader, who is called the General and is a smart guy. He says the General has two great ambitions: money and power. Now he has accomplished the first, and the rescued man says he's glad to squeal on his former chief. He admits the gang had run out on the General, and says authorities will find the hideout near Santa Rosa, New Mexico.

INVESTIGATION

Captain Midnight sends Ichabod Mudd, Chuck Ramsay, and Joyce Ryan to investigate the New Mexico piracy hideout, cautioning them to watch their step. Later, he receives word that their search has been in vain. The camp has been burned out, and whoever was there has flown the coop. Midnight orders the Secret Squadron agents to remain in the area, and to ask around various neighboring towns to see if they can pick up any information.

Captain Midnight receives a message from Major Steele that large amounts of high explosives, guns, planes, and oil are being shipped out of the country. Bills of lading are being falsified. And once sold, the materials are apparently put aboard certain ships and sent outside the United States. Midnight orders Ikky to follow out these shipments. Ikky does this by being boarded up in a huge box marked "Explosives." Air vents and sufficient food, water and sanitation are provided to him, and he begins a long baffling trip. What Ikky will do for his country!

Meanwhile, Chuck and Joyce have been hanging around a New Mexico town, and one afternoon they listen in on a group of fliers talking. The pilots are debating whether to take an unknown person's offer to hire fliers. They show Chuck and Joyce an advertisement in the paper:

"WANTED: FLIERS. Opportunity, adventure, high wages. Wire Box 12, Santa Rosa, New Mexico."

Chuck and Joyce send a telegram, and are promptly visited by a stranger who offers them a huge sum to sign contracts to pilot for a certain "Señor Miguel," for one year. It looks fishy to the young Squadron agents, and they send a report to Captain Midnight. The Secret Squadron leader orders them to accept it, on the surface. They do, and are whisked off by plane to a destination they are told nothing about.

The two Squadron agents are flown to the Caribbean island Kingdom of Caraguela. This is supposed to be a sleepy, backward nation, but Chuck and Joyce are surprised at the hustle and bustle of the place. The airfield is twice the size the country needs. Police and military troops wear fine uniforms and bear the most modern firearms. The citizens seem to be very fond of this man, Señor Miguel, whom they consider rather a national benefactor — even dubbing him the "Santa Claus" of Caraguela. He is for everything that everybody wants. And now, after a long visit elsewhere for his health, Señor Miguel is coming home. Chuck and Joyce are puzzled. Something big is going on here, and they advise Captain Midnight that he'd better come down.

Meanwhile, Ikky takes his long sea voyage in the box of "Explosives." Based on the weather getting warmer, and on his hearing the sailors' rough talk, he judges they are somewhere in the Gulf of Mexico. Upon arrival, his crate is loaded onto a dock and taken far inland. At night, he cuts his way out of the box and hikes back along a narrow road to town. After inquiring, he finds he is on the island of Caraguela. By Pocket Locator, he learns Chuck and Joyce are also on the island, and he heads for the airport to meet them.

General Drake Cromwell has arrived secretly at the island kingdom. His henchmen have been working quietly on his account for six months, sowing seeds of popularity in his behalf. Now the General — with the pirated fortune at his command — can finance a revolution that he has long wanted to stage. He has two special reasons for wanting to rule Caraguela: First, he feels that it rather belongs to him, because a family legend states that one of his early ancestors discovered the island; and second, he seeks power after falling from grace in his home country of England. So he therefore hates the English. He also hates the Americans, because the Americans fought on England's side in the last war.

General Cromwell wants to discredit both Great Britain and the United States. If he could rule Caraguela, he knows the little nation would be of excellent strategic value in the future, in the event an enemy country would wish to strike America. After setting up rule in Caraguela, he is also ambitious to create a league of American enemy nations in South America. This league would consist of countries that pretend friendship with the United States, but will really throw the dagger into America's soft underbelly if and when the time comes to fight.

Cromwell's henchmen have been doing an effective job. With several million dollars to distribute, they have been winning friends and adherents everywhere. Guns and planes and other weapons are now flowing in, too — piling up to be ready when the word goes out to effect a coup.

Cromwell tells the poor he will take from all the rich and give to the poor. He tells the rich that he will make them richer. He buys the army fine new uniforms and equipment, buys out the army leaders, bribes the police, and convinces many people that his revolution will be for the good of the country.

Nobody knows how really sinister General Drake Cromwell is, except his niece and a handful of his most trusted henchmen. In fact, one of his biggest arguments to win over the conservatives is that he wants to ensure friendly relations with America and that he has inside connections with American government officials. He declares he is "a great friend of America."

Ikky meets Joyce and Chuck in the capital city of Caraguela, and they have a grand reunion. But Ikky is suspicious of the setup, and especially of this so-called "Señor Miguel, the friend of the people." Chuck and Joyce, however, have actually been favorably impressed by the propaganda and the people's goodwill toward the man.

In a speech to Caraguela's citizens, Señor Miguel (General Cromwell) gives a glowing picture of the good the people can do. A bright future is coming to the country, and all should remember their patriotic allegiance because great happenings may start at any time. The General's niece, Gabrielle, also gives a speech. She enchants her audience with her beauty, her vivacity, and charming personality. Ikky is still suspicious and refuses to be taken in. Chuck and Joyce accuse him of being grumpy because he had such a long and uncomfortable ride in the "Explosives" box. Ikky does feel grumpy and behaves as though he is ready to explode, himself, at any time.

Captain Midnight arrives, catches up on the situation, and tries to see the famous Señor Miguel, but it is impossible for a stranger to get near the man. Midnight visits the president of the existing government, who is supposedly an unfriendly fellow who resists progress. He is indeed a rough, gruff, dyspeptic old man — but far from the villain the propaganda has made him out to be. Captain Midnight decides the president is more or less okay, and therefore the smooth-talking, artful Señor Miguel is the one to investigate.

Captain Midnight goes along with Ikky's suspicions, but the question is how to see this Señor Miguel? The Secret Squadron leader flies his plane in an amazing aerobatic exhibition over the Señor's country estate, ending up buzzing the house. Two of Miguel's best fliers are sent up to force him down, but he outmaneuvers them. When he lands, Midnight is arrested and whisked off to Señor Miguel.

Far from being displeased, Miguel is greatly impressed. This is the kind of flier he has been looking for. He asks Midnight to lead his group of pilots, to train them for combat, and to have them ready for any eventuality by the first of the month. That's only two weeks away. Midnight pretends to accept and shakes hands on the deal with Miguel, but Miguel is surprised and rather annoyed that Midnight shakes hands with a glove on. Midnight apologizes, saying he's injured his hand and must wear a glove for a few days. Actually, the glove is coated with a fine, barely perceptible wax that records all of Miguel's fingerprints.

Captain Midnight dispatches Ikky back to Washington, where the prints are checked and also compared with those found on various spots on the rail of the *Queen Anne* — the first ship robbed by the pirate helicopter. Sure enough, a match is found. This "Señor Miguel" is none other than the leader of the sky pirates — none other than the notorious General Percival Drake Cromwell. So Midnight develops a plan, and Ikky returns to Caraguela to join the effort.

REVOLUTION

The poor unsuspecting natives of Caraguela are much too sold on Miguel by now to change their allegiance from his nefarious cause. And pilots — many of them American — have been treated so well and are enjoying themselves so much that Midnight is afraid he can't change their minds. There are also many South American pilots whose allegiance he can't count on. So Midnight plans that on Zero Hour of "R-Day" (Revolution Day), he will on some pretext lead the squadron of planes to another country. He will notify the lawful Caraguelan president and his personal state guard, which will arrest Señor Miguel and take him to America. There, the Secret Squadron officials and Major Steele will be waiting to arrest him for his crime of robbing the *Queen Anne*. Suddenly, however, Captain Midnight himself is arrested!

A renegade American pilot, jealous of Midnight's ability, had recognized him and told Miguel he was sure this expert pilot is the famous leader of the Secret Squadron. Midnight is whisked off to a country prison and kept under heavy guard. The rest of the Secret Squadron agents are also arrested, except for Chuck Ramsay.

Having escaped his pursuers, Chuck hides out in a Caraguela airport hangar and dons a disguise. He decides to stay around the airport, where it is obvious that things are brewing.

Infuriated by the near-sabotage of his revolution, Miguel decides to strike without further delay. He pronounces "R-Day" as the following day, starting at 06:00. Hearing this, Chuck boldly enters the barracks that houses the American fliers. In a stirring speech, he makes them realize that Señor Miguel is nothing more than an international bandit and renegade who has no interest in the people, and who is financing this revolution with stolen money. Chuck convinces the Americans how they've been duped and what fools they've been.

The American fliers commandeer two Jeeps and go roaring into the countryside. Miguel's men pursue them, and both groups do battle along the way. The fliers successfully reach their prison destination, overcome the guards, and rescue Captain Midnight, Ikky, and Joyce.

Back at the capital, Miguel organizes the pilots who have remained with him. He tells them he will personally lead them to victory. They will take off in the morning and bomb any building and plantation that offers resistance — and not to worry about killing women and children. The existing government will be blamed.

CAPTAIN MIDNIGHT'S SURPRISE

Miguel's forces take over the radio station, and broadcast two bulletins about tomorrow's being the big day. The situation will settle into a battle between two groups: Miguel's fliers, who have control of the airport and the radio station, and the loyalist Americans under Captain Midnight. Midnight's strategy is to unite with the lawful government forces that are already fighting in the suburbs, and to do this in the middle of the night. Midnight knows that radical measures will have to be taken, and so he decides to spring a surprise that he has carried with him ever since he suspected Miguel was their man.

Captain Midnight has several hundred new-type bombs. They are of a kind perfected since the war, and are intended to impede, temporarily, but not to harm life. They are fog bombs. Midnight and his forces must sneak through the enemy lines, and set off the noiseless bombs at a dozen different points in the capital city. They must do this at night, because the fog will not draw attention in the dark. By doing this, the loyalists can assure that dawn simply will not come!

06:00 arrives and visibility is almost nil! The fog has also been greatly thickening, so no one is sure who will join whom. The capital seems like a dead city. All normal community life is suspended, and the revolution cannot start!

But before long, *real* explosive bombs suddenly begin dropping from the sky! They are concussive, devastating bombs that begin taking a heavy toll on life.

Midnight is furious. He realizes some of the rebel planes must have gotten off the ground, or else they got outside help. His main goal now is to capture Miguel, to get a confession from him, and to make him call off the revolution over the Caraguela radio station. This is the only way to stop the violence now. Otherwise, the revolutionaries will start fighting as soon as the fog clears — and the fog bombs will remain effective for only a few more hours.

The heavy explosive bombing compels Captain Midnight to abandon his idea of capturing Miguel. He now tries to find the bloodthirsty fiends who are ruthlessly dropping bombs on the fog-ridden city. Groping his way to the airport, he finds a plane and takes off by instruments and instincts. But there is an unseen incursion: a large transport plane that had been abandoned on the runway in the fog, and Midnight's aircraft grazes the top of the plane, losing its wheels! Then, when his craft rises above the fog, he encounters three combat airplanes. The planes indiscriminately drop bombs, as though the operation is a big game.

DOGFIGHT

Captain Midnight attacks instantly, and during the melee, he recognizes his prize — Señor Miguel himself. Señor Miguel — alias General Percival Drake Cromwell — is simply a demented, arrogant, and disgraced Britisher. A hectic air battle ensues. Midnight downs the first two planes, and then goes after the General, who is no mean flier himself.

Captain Midnight pulls a peculiar tactic: He out-flies the General, but does not go in for the kill. Instead, he continually forces him down into the fog — a nerve-wracking experience for the General. For once in the fog, it is absolutely impossible to know where he is going. Midnight does this repeatedly, and sees his tactic is driving the General frantic. The General tries to turn tail, and then abandons his retreat, as both he and Midnight realize he doesn't have enough fuel to get very far. Finally, Captain Midnight rams the General's plane in midair, and they both have to parachute out.

CHOICE

Captain Midnight jumps right next to Cromwell, so that they go down side-by-side. It is a terrifying experience for both men — as they shoot at each other from a distance of thirty yards! But Midnight's aim is the more accurate. As they near the ground, Midnight hears a scream from the other and realizes he has shot him.

Both men land, with the General gravely wounded and near death. Midnight finds him and gives him a choice: He can make a full confession over the Caraguela radio station, and call off the revolution — and Midnight will get him medical aid, which he must have to survive — or he can let the revolution go on and die without medical attention. Of course, Captain Midnight tells him that if he chooses the first action, he will immediately be placed under arrest in America and will probably spend the rest of his life in prison. The General chooses medical care and life. He makes a full confession over the radio, the revolution is called off, and the country is saved.

13

The Sky Rustler

(1948)

CIRCLEVILLE

Old Pete Wister, a friend Captain Midnight has not seen since 1921, telephones to ask Midnight to come to the great cattle range area of the Southwest. Pete lives in the rural Texas town of Circleville, not far from Austin. He had once nursed Captain Midnight back to health after a nasty crash in the pilot's early flying career. Pete says he's in bad trouble, and Midnight and the Secret Squadron take off at once for Pete's small ranch. Upon arriving, they find that Pete clams up and won't say a word about his trouble. Something has happened in the meantime to make him change his mind. But what it is, Captain Midnight cannot find out.

Pete is a small cattle-rancher, seems to be in good health, and hasn't had great financial worries. What is it that's bothering him now? His daughter, Linda, asks Captain Midnight if her father has told him about the "Sky Rustler." Midnight says no, he hasn't told him anything. Linda immediately clams up, too.

There seems to be curious tension — a great secrecy that is mystifying and unexplainable in this land of rugged individualists proud of their freedom. The mystery seems to be indicated one night, as some kids walk along this mid-Texas range. By moonlight, the youths see a huge cargo plane swoop down and perform a remarkable operation. The mighty cargo ship lands, its tailgates open some twenty yards ahead of a herd of frightened cattle, and a number of the cattle are driven into the plane. As this operation is going on, the youths attract the attention of the Secret Squadron agents who had driven out and stopped to scout the area.

The squatting plane is too far away for Captain Midnight and his agents to hear the conversation between a man with a peg-leg and a ranch-owner. The Secret Squadron would find this conversation most interesting.

SHAKEDOWN

"Remember," warns the peg-legged man, "one word out of you, and every cattleman in the *country* will suffer for your indiscretion. You can well appreciate that ten percent of your herd per year isn't much to pay for the kind of protection I'm giving you. Don't you agree?"

The rancher fearfully agrees.

The peg-legged man adds, "I'll be back next month at this time. See to it that your choice steers are separated out from the rest, so I won't have to waste time picking them out, as we did this time."

Then the cargo ship takes off, leaving Midnight and his Squadron agents quite intrigued. When they reach the ranch, Pete Wister has learned they have seen the curious event. Pete is terrified and asks Midnight not to repeat a word of it to anyone. It is obvious, Midnight realizes, that ranchers are in the thick of some shakedown. When fine men like Pete Wister refuse to talk, it must be big and bad. Several more times, Midnight tries to inveigle the truth out of Wister but without result. Pete finally says he would appreciate it if Midnight pulled up stakes and left. His presence is causing talk.

Undaunted, Captain Midnight visits the rancher who was intimidated the night before. The man is completely taciturn, uncooperative, and sullen. He warns Midnight to mind his own business. Texas ranchers can take care of themselves.

More puzzled than ever, but not giving up, Midnight and the Secret Squadron stick around. In the next week, they see the cargo plane pay three more night visits to surrounding ranches — some large, some small — and each time the plane collects more cattle.

Midnight meets with the Texas Rangers, who say they can do nothing, since nobody has asked for their help. If the ranchers want to transfer or relocate parts of their herds, it is after all within their right. Captain Midnight gets angry. "Somebody has a terrific whammy on these cattlemen!" And Midnight is determined to get to the bottom of it, if it takes him all summer.

Meanwhile, just south of the Mexican border, at a derelict ranch of adobe buildings, a man experiments with viruses. He is the same peg-legged fellow who has been raiding the cattle in the United States. His assistants call him "Doctor," and a successful doctor he seems to be. Just now, he is exultant because he has perfected an extremely rapid way of spreading a certain very deadly virus infection. To prove its effectiveness, he tries it out on one of the healthy steers brought in recently from America. The beast dies in just a few hours, and the doctor is delighted. In its new form, the virus can be dusted on ranges of cattle, just as one would dust crops with DDT (dichlorodiphenyltrichloroethane insecticide) from a low-flying airplane.

Who is this evil doctor? During the course of a conversation at his hideout, it is revealed that his license to practice medicine north of the border has been revoked. As a result, he hates America and all for which it stands. He has vowed vengeance, and is in a position to wreak such havoc throughout the United States as has never been seen before. In a few days, he can infect great herds of American cattle with a deadly virus disease that acts too quickly to stop. In a few months' time, he can wipe out most of the cattle in the entire United States!

Captain Midnight persists in his efforts to get the ranchers to talk, and this time he visits several big ranch owners. They admit to being extorted, but say they'd rather be shaken down than take the consequences. But what these consequences are, they will not say. At this, Midnight gives up. What's the use, with such a bunch of men who are totally uncooperative? He packs up, getting ready to leave, when Pete Wister and a few other small ranchers come to see him.

Wister and his group realize their position is untenable. Even with the danger as great as it is, they can't afford to carry on with the threatening doctor's setup. They confess everything. This doctor is taking ten percent of the herds, large and small, over a year's time. Larger ranchers can afford to kick in ten percent; but for the small ranchers, *seven* percent is the margin that separates them from ruin. They can't go on giving ten percent of their best cattle to this monstrous man. "If we don't kick in with the ten percent," they continue, "the doctor will wipe out all our stock by sneaking cattle infected with foot-and-mouth disease into our herds. There's no way of stopping him and no way of telling which animal has it unless you examine each cow and steer one-by-one. When we have thousands of cattle, this takes time. By the time we discover the terrible disease, hundreds of others will have caught it."

NATIONWIDE THREAT

The peg-legged doctor has isolated and perfected the virus, so all he has to do is drop small powder bombs in the midst of the herds. These bombs contain enough of the dreaded foot-and-mouth disease to kill millions of cattle, and he is said to have perfected an even faster way than that. Pete tells Captain Midnight that the doctor claims he can dust the range with his germs, "just as we dust our crops with small planes."

"How do you know he really has this germ in such a form?" asks Midnight.

"Oh, he has it all right. He's shown us by killing off Andy Lockson's entire herd over at Bueno Nuevo Ranch."

Midnight now fully appreciates the gravity of the situation and its even nationwide menace. He knows he must proceed with extreme caution. First, he asks the small ranchers to describe this doctor.

According to the cattlemen, the doctor is a meticulous dresser, educated in manners and speech, cold, ruthless, polite, but sarcastic when crossed. He has no emotions, no weak spots.

"Baloney!" says Midnight. "Every man has a weak spot."

They call attention to the doctor's wooden leg. Also, he never wears a gun. He is afraid of guns. He accidentally shot his own leg so seriously that he lost it, and has had an uncommon fear of firearms ever since.

Captain Midnight ponders the situation, wondering how a doctor could've so easily lost his own leg. Finally, he decides on a course of action. He gets the small ranchers to prevail upon a big rancher to go off to a cattle convention in Houston. While he is gone, and with the rest of the cowpunchers' cooperation, Midnight takes over the ranch. Midnight pretends to be the new owner, who has just bought the ranch and knows nothing about the shakedown racket.

When the doctor's cargo plane pays its fortnightly visit, Midnight comes out and objects because of ignorance. The doctor politely explains every detail, while Chuck and Ikky record the whole conversation with a wire recorder. When through, Midnight pretends to be greatly impressed by the doctor's ability and brains. The doctor is in turn flattered. Midnight sees the doctor's weak spot is his vanity, and so he flatters him even more. Captain Midnight's strategy is to ply information from the doctor, to discover his hideout, and to detain him as long as possible; that is, long enough for a flight of Secret Squadron planes to make a lightning-fast raid.

Midnight pretends to dislike America also. "Why don't we throw in together?" he asks. "I'll take my cattle south, and we can extort millions of dollars — not just from independent ranchers, but from the American government itself!"

The doctor is impressed with Midnight's acumen, his imagination, and his organizing ability. "But even so," says the doctor, I would want to double-cross America only after extorting as much from the nation as possible — and then wipe out all American cattle with my deadly virus!"

"Fine!" says Captain Midnight. "We see eye-to-eye on everything. But now, the thing to do is to find a spot in the United States from which to operate. Now, I know of a ghost town not far from here that would be ideal. We could insist that the American Department of Agriculture send a plane to the Southwest with three million dollars in cash. When it nears the area, we could direct it to the ghost town and instruct it to land. In a matter of minutes, the money could be turned over to us, and we could then take *their* plane and escape across the border!"

The doctor likes this plan very much.

"But the thing to do now," says Midnight, "is to go and look over this ghost town. I can drive you there in three hours."

At this point, the doctor gets worried. He says he must get back. Besides, if he doesn't return by dawn, his men will start their merciless infecting of American herds!

DISCOVERY

Captain Midnight's efforts to detain the doctor without attracting his suspicions seem to have failed — when suddenly a worse blow strikes. The real ranch owner unexpectedly returns, and unwittingly tips off the doctor that a trick has been played on him!

Enraged, the doctor threatens to wipe out this rancher's entire herd immediately! Midnight draws out a gun, levels it at the doctor, and tells him who he is.

"Okay," says the doctor, "Captain Midnight can have his own way. But if I don't get back to headquarters by dawn, you will see the most awful cattle devastation imaginable!"

Faced with this threat, Midnight gives in. The doctor hurries out and takes off, but Midnight takes off after him.

Seeing he is pursued, the doctor drops his cargo of twenty cattle, one-by-one, to lighten his plane and increase his speed. Midnight stays on his tail. The doctor fearfully and clumsily lands at his headquarters, seriously damaging his big craft, but he escapes and hurries into the house as fast as his peg-leg can move.

RUSES AND HARM

Captain Midnight also lands, and soon sees a pilot rush out from the house and warm up a small plane with two open cockpits. Obviously, the doctor is going to "run" for it, in a manner of speaking. Midnight sneaks up, knocks out the pilot, and puts on the pilot's helmet and goggles. Then he sits in the front cockpit, waiting for the doctor.

The doctor exits the house, carrying a flask. He moves to the small plane and climbs into the rear cockpit. Once seated, he instructs the masked Captain Midnight to fly south. Instead, Midnight flies north toward the U.S. border, and he pulls a gun on the doctor. But the doctor calmly raises his wooden peg-leg and shoots Captain Midnight with a pistol concealed in the leg!

The doctor's phobia of guns is pure bunk. Captain Midnight is painfully injured, and a wild struggle ensues in the plane. The deadly virus flask is upset and spills over Midnight. But in the battle, Midnight manages to knock the doctor out of the aircraft — and the doctor falls to his death.

Captain Midnight jumps with his chute, as the plane crashes into the Gulf of Mexico. By maneuvering the shroud lines, he barely manages to side-slip to shore. Although painfully injured, Midnight's first order is that he be disinfected before being brought back to the United States.

The injured Captain Midnight requires a long summer's recuperation of thirteen weeks before he can resume his Secret Squadron missions.

14

Death Has Four Faces

(1948)

SMUGGLING ALIENS

After the summer, Captain Midnight brings everybody back to Secret Squadron Headquarters, announcing he has returned from a meeting behind the Iron Curtain. Major Steele has told him of a series of strange killings — murders that he believes are somehow related to a gang that is smuggling foreigners into the United States. Each murder victim has been stabbed through the heart with a broad, razor-sharp, two-edged blade.[1]

An ominous telephone conversation takes place between a man in Maine and a cryptic, disguised voice in California. The discussion concerns still one more murder to be committed. The Californian's voice belongs to a man calling himself "The Sword."

Some hours later, Captain Midnight and his Secret Squadron agents — Chuck, Joyce, and Ikky — are in a plane flying east. Their destination is a fishing village on Long Island Sound, named Port Flemington. The Secret Squadron is on the trail of what Captain Midnight believes to be a gang of saboteurs smuggled into America by a foreign country. There have been four mysterious murders, all committed the same way. Victims were stabbed through the heart by a broad, razor-sharp, two-edged blade. The strangest thing is there is no clue to each victim's identity. Each seemed to have "dropped from the skies." The latest body was discovered just outside Port Flemington.

Captain Midnight believes there is a connection between the fishing village murder and two others like it by a gang of alien smugglers.

Although he does not know it yet, there is. Across the continent in Hollywood, a mysterious foreign-born person who calls himself "The Sword That Hangs over America" — or "The Sword," for short — heads the covert organization.[2]

THE SECRET 4

Captain Midnight uncovers confirming evidence that an alien smuggling band is involved with the sinister Sword's murders. The ring is possibly sneaking a group of highly trained and dangerous saboteurs into the United States.

Meanwhile, a clandestine underworld group called "The Secret 3" learns from its "Sword That Hangs over America" boss that a fourth member will be added to their number, so that from now on, they are to be "The Secret 4." The new member is referred to by the code name "The Rock." The Sword also informs them that Captain Midnight's Secret Squadron is now investigating the alien deaths. And because of this turn of events, Captain Midnight is to be considered Enemy Number One. He must be eliminated as quickly as possible, and at all costs.

LIVE SABOTEUR

One of the smuggled aliens is soon captured alive in Port Flemington and held at the local prison. His name is Peter Barko, and Captain Midnight visits the prison to interview him. Staring into the prison cell that confines the illegal alien, Midnight is struck by the taut and stern expression on the man's face. A guard admits Midnight into the cell, and the Secret Squadron leader speaks quietly with the prisoner. As the conversation progresses, the man eventually makes an admission. During a delay in his assignment, he had discovered for himself that America is a more just and benevolent country than he had been led to believe.

In remorse, the alien goes on to confess fully that he was in the United States as a spy and saboteur. He tells Captain Midnight that he was eventually to receive his orders from an unidentified person he was supposed to meet at a New York City restaurant called "The Bottle of Ink." Barko was to identify himself by the password: "What is the pen mightier than?" With the imprisoned alien's cooperation, Captain Midnight spends hours with him — learning about his background, his friends, his relatives, and so on — so that Midnight can take his place.

Meanwhile, across the continent in Hollywood, two men talk in an apartment living room. One is named Carl Masterling, who is the brother-in-law of a famous scientist. The other man is an unidentified member of The Secret 4, who is attempting to blackmail Masterling into stealing a valuable scientific paper from the scientist. Masterling resists the threat, much to the other man's frustration and anger.

Captain Midnight is going to impersonate the captured saboteur, Peter Barko, in hopes of discovering who the ringleader of the smuggling gang is. In the meantime, The Secret 4 ring has sent out orders from California that Captain Midnight is to be eliminated. The extraordinary efficiency of this band is demonstrated by the fact that Captain Midnight's flight to Port Flemington on the Jersey Coast had been learned. And an attempt to sabotage his plane had already been made — although discovered by the Secret Squadron and foiled.

Carl Masterling expresses worry to a friend of his — a frail old Chinese man named Sing Lo, whose hobby is breeding singing canaries. Because Masterling has refused to steal the scientific paper, he fears being targeted for assassination, and he is right. Due to the failure to blackmail Masterling, The Secret 4 group has decided to liquidate him as quickly as possible. One of its four executives, The Rock, will personally carry out the brutal deed.

Captain Midnight is all set to take the place of the captured saboteur, and to head for a furtive rendezvous at The Bottle of Ink restaurant in New York City. He is now operating under an assumed identity that temporarily loses his would-be killers. However, news comes of another broad, two-edged blade murder in California. This time, the slain man is known, and he was not a recently smuggled alien. His name was Carl Masterling.

Captain Midnight decides to arrange the rendezvous at The Bottle of Ink at a later date and fly now to California. But this move re-exposes him to his deadly pursuers.

The Secret 4 band possesses an airbase hidden away in the grim vastness of Death Valley. No one in the organization, or anyone else, can use this airfield without advance written permission from The Sword. From either there, or perhaps from Hollywood — it is not known for sure — the strange character who calls himself The Sword bristles with fury that Captain Midnight had thwarted their sabotage attempt and eluded pursuit. In a disguised voice, he telephones each of his lieutenants and vents his rage.

Captain Midnight battles the ferocity of a sudden storm, as he and Joyce Ryan fly high over Ohio on their way to California. Two members of The Secret 4 — The Sword and The Rock — learn of his flight, and they plot to shoot down his plane. A lone, well-armed airplane soon flies east from California. Its pilot is the newest member of The Secret 4, the man known as The Rock. He heads for Cheyenne, where he thinks there is only a one in ten thousand chance that he might intercept Captain Midnight's plane and shoot it down over the Rockies. However, it turns out this tiny chance becomes very likely to materialize, because Captain Midnight casually decides to stop over briefly at the Cheyenne Airport.

Meanwhile, Ichabod Mudd and Chuck Ramsay have managed to turn up some information on the mysterious Secret 4 organization and the pervasive underworld network through which it operates. Tracing a lead to Chicago, they learn of a suspicious man there named Richard Partridge, and they get his address. Ikky and Chuck have reason to believe this Richard Partridge might be connected with a gang of saboteurs in California. They soon locate and confront Partridge, and manage to uncover what appears to be a link to this California gang that calls itself The Secret 4.

THE ROCK'S ATTACK

The Needle and The Dagger stay in close communication with The Sword and The Rock. As Captain Midnight flies westward, these menacing four carry out their plan against him.

The Rock locates Captain Midnight, and he has only one idea in mind: to sneak up on Midnight's aircraft and shoot it down over the Rockies. Captain Midnight, flying west with Joyce, suspects someone is trying to keep track of his flight. Later enroute, Joyce notices another plane is following and nearing their XP-46, but at this moment her Pocket Locator flashes, and she starts to take down the message.

Without warning, The Rock closes on the plane in which Captain Midnight and Joyce are flying, and blasts it with a barrage of machinegun fire! While there is plenty of rear cockpit armor to protect Midnight and Joyce, their XP-46 is mortally hit, and it plunges headlong toward the snow-covered Rocky Mountains below. At less than a thousand feet above a white-capped peak, Captain Midnight manages to pull out of the dive long enough for Joyce and him to parachute out. Fortunately for them, the snow below camouflages their white parachutes, and The Rock fails to see them. What he does see, and with no small satisfaction, is the XP-46 crash into a mountain and explode.

Upon landing on a mountainside, Captain Midnight and Joyce find shelter under a large snow-covered crag. Joyce immediately contacts Chuck and Ikky via Pocket Locator. Requesting emergency helicopter rescue, she transmits approximate coordinates — and says she will send Pocket Locator homing signals, and also use the 1948 Code-O-Graph signal mirror upon sighting a rescue helicopter.

Curtiss XP-46. PHOTOGRAPH: NATIONAL MUSEUM OF THE USAF

THE SWORD'S SECRET

By radio messages, the clandestine character known as The Sword breaks a strange piece of news to his four lieutenants. He is, so to speak, "living a double life." For he is not only the voice heard via electronic communications — that they have always known as The Sword That Hangs over America — he is also one of his own lieutenants! In other words: he is either The Blackjack, The Dagger, The Needle, or The Rock. He slips away at intervals and doubles as the voice of The Sword. He keeps secret which one he is, because he wants the lieutenants to be suspicious of one another — always on the alert, always wary. And in this way, he also feels sure they will always be loyal to him.

COUNTERMOVES

From where they were downed on a mountain in the Rockies, Ikky rescues Captain Midnight and Joyce by helicopter, while Chuck flies behind in an A-26. Captain Midnight and Joyce are reported killed in the

XP-46 plane crash. Upon landing both aircraft at a small nearby airfield, they all transfer to the A-26 and fly to Los Angeles.

In Los Angeles, Captain Midnight disguises himself as a man named Dr. Brody, and he discreetly proceeds to investigate the death of Carl Masterling. In Chinatown, he meets with the aged and fascinating philosopher Sing Lo. The elder Chinese says he had talked to Carl Masterling

Los Angeles Chinatown. PHOTOGRAPH: LEONARD ZANE

just before Masterling was murdered. In speaking with Sing Lo, Midnight is most impressed by the philosopher's great calm and stoic fearlessness. He also learns of Sing Lo's love of canaries and how the elder man can imitate their singing by whistling.

Meanwhile, Chuck and Joyce discover that someone has been watching Sing Lo's house, and Midnight suspects it is one of the gang of saboteurs. Since the false announcement of Captain Midnight's death in the plane crash, The Secret 4 band — just as Captain Midnight had hoped — has relaxed its extreme alertness. Its members now feel safer, because of believing the Secret Squadron leader no longer dogs their trail. But as two of them — The Needle and The Blackjack — discuss Captain Midnight's death, another matter arises that causes them considerable concern.

A strange day of unforeseen events upsets the agents of the Secret Squadron. In the first place, The Bottle of Ink restaurant — used as a rendezvous by saboteurs in New York City — is destroyed by fire. In the second place, Sing Lo — the old Chinese philosopher, who was the last known person to see Carl Masterling alive — is suddenly kidnapped by The Rock. Captain Midnight had counted on using Sing Lo to draw one of The Secret 4 into a police net that he was planning to throw around Sing Lo's house. But now, a police sergeant telephones him the news. The Secret 4 gang has struck first.

SECRET SQUADRON OFFENSIVE

Captain Midnight — disguised as Dr. Brody — starts organizing many in Chinatown to hunt for Sing Lo. He stresses that the ancient Chinese philosopher has one extremely skilled accomplishment: He can whistle exactly like a singing canary. Because the old man has a very frail voice, Captain Midnight believes he will use this method to attract attention to where he is held captive — whistling his canary song in hopes that someone will discover him.

Reflecting on his earlier conversation with The Blackjack, The Needle is anxious to learn how much old Sing Lo may know about The Secret 4's operation and to whom he might have disclosed such information. The Sword shares The Needle's concern, and directs The Secret 4 to exercise whatever torture is necessary to get Sing Lo to talk. But because of Sing Lo's frailty, The Sword soon amends his orders to take care not to kill the old man.

Because Sing Lo is extremely astute, as well as completely unafraid of death, Captain Midnight is sure the old philosopher will risk some means of leaving a clue or attracting attention to the hideout where he has been taken. And events prove Midnight right. Before long, one of the searchers recruited in Chinatown follows a lead to a mansion in Hollywood, where old Sing Lo may have been taken. The searcher reports this to Captain Midnight, alias Dr. Brody. But The Needle, of the sinister Secret 4, has also learned of the Chinatown recruits directed by the mysterious Dr. Brody. He radios some of his henchmen and issues orders.

Captain Midnight decides that since The Secret 4 organization has been striking so quickly and effectively, he must do something to start leading events instead of only reacting to them. He therefore leaves Chuck, Joyce, and Ikky in Los Angeles to shadow the Hollywood mansion — where Sing Lo is believed to be imprisoned — while he flies back to New York City. Disguised as the saboteur, Peter Barko, he will visit the charred remains of The Bottle of Ink restaurant, and try to see if he can meet any members of the sabotage organization.

Outside the fire-blackened ruin of The Bottle of Ink in Manhattan, Captain Midnight — masquerading as Peter Barko — is approached by an extremely secretive girl. She swiftly leads him to a parked car. She then hurriedly drives him north, leaving the city and speeding along the Merritt Parkway.

As the saboteur, Peter Barko, Captain Midnight is accepted by the vicious spy ring as a belatedly arrived member. His first assignment is to destroy a bridge "somewhere in the Middle West."

Meanwhile, Joyce Ryan is close on the trail of The Needle. While Chuck maintains surveillance of the Hollywood mansion, where they believe Sing Lo might be held, Joyce and Ikky keep watch near an elite Los Angeles fruit market. They have learned this market might be patronized by one of the leaders of the sinister Secret 4. They do not know that his code name is The Needle, but they have managed to obtain a fairly accurate description of him. He's a short, stocky man with absurdly small feet, and wears highly polished patent leather shoes. However, the Squadron agents' stakeout by the market is fruitless. They spot no one fitting the description of this underworld character. One reason they fail to detect The Needle is that he publicly disguises his petite feet with specially-fitted oversize footwear, and similarly confines his patent leather preference to more private settings.

Captain Midnight, alias Peter Barko, is being taken to some unknown destination in the Midwest with orders to blow up a bridge. Meanwhile, Ikky and Joyce rejoin Chuck to watch the Hollywood mansion where they believe Sing Lo is imprisoned. So far, Sing Lo has resisted torture and has not divulged anything of value to The Secret 4. And then the three Squadron agents hear what sounds like canary chirping.

Later that afternoon, the Squadron agents lead a detail of police to raid the place. They rescue Sing Lo, but find no one who fits the description of The Needle. They do not know that The Needle is actually in a small nearby house reached by a secret tunnel. While the raid and rescue action proceeds, The Sword also sits in the neighboring house, talking with his mother.

Disguised as the alien saboteur, Captain Midnight is on his way to the unidentified Midwest destination. He is driven along by a bodyguard named Ed, who is extremely nervous, because the sabotage organization is testing Ed's discipline and reliability too. The bodyguard drives fast, and when rounding a curve at excessive speed, he loses control of the car. In a flash, Midnight strongly braces himself before the car crashes. Dazed and bruised, Midnight emerges from the wreck — but Ed is killed. Captain Midnight realizes there is only one thing to do now: return to the gang's eastern headquarters and report the mishap.

Meanwhile, Sing Lo tells the Secret Squadron agents and police that through a small window, he had seen one of his captors walk into the little nearby house two days before. So that night, the agents and the police go to the small house with a search warrant, but before they can enter the dwelling, a sudden fiery blast envelops the house in flames! In the blazing fury and confusion, only a brief glimpse is seen of a black car zooming out of a back alley and disappearing into the night. The Sword, his mother, and his lieutenants have made good their escape.

CAPTAIN MIDNIGHT'S PERIL

The disguised Captain Midnight still does not know what bridge he was supposed to destroy. Nor does he know why. He feels it is urgent to discover at least one of these two things. But his cold reception upon returning to the gang's eastern headquarters, and explaining the events, shows that he will be told nothing. The spy ring suspects he might have caused the accident that killed Ed. However, the ring decides to give him one more chance to destroy a bridge, somewhere in the Midwest. This time he is to be heavily guarded, and shot if he fails to carry out the assignment. Midnight realizes he must at least pass this crucial examination if he is to learn anything at all from the group.

Taking separate commercial flights, three bodyguards from the spy ring and Midnight meet at an airport in the Middle West. From there, the bodyguards join a fourth ring member, who drives them all into a remote area.

In the late afternoon, Midnight's sabotage party drives up to a Midwest cabin to spend the night. Because of his ominous predicament, Captain Midnight senses that he dare not wait any longer. He decides he must somehow contact Major Steele by Pocket Locator, and have the four men who are guarding him seized. Midnight knows that in the process, he himself has a very good chance of being killed, but he feels the time has come for him to take that risk. The guards never relax their vigilance over him for a minute, sometimes even brandishing a drawn revolver or two at him. But that night, under the blanket of his bed, Captain

Midnight — pretending restlessness — manages to send a coded message to Major Steele in Washington.

Just hours later, Major Steele has the saboteurs' cabin stealthily surrounded by army soldiers. Steele gives orders that the detail of soldiers is to wait until morning. When Captain Midnight and his guards step out of the cabin to go to their car, the soldiers are to act and act fast!

Meanwhile, The Sword and his lieutenants are transferring more of their field operations to the Southwest. They now plan a terrible, devastating blow against the little city of Mashowgan that is situated by a small lake. The Secret 4 will use a revolutionary new weapon that only The Sword knows about.

The Secret Squadron finally makes a breakthrough! Thanks to Captain Midnight's courage and the superb marksmanship of U.S. Army sharpshooters, the four saboteurs are overcome! A surviving saboteur, in terror for his life, promises to tell all he knows. The agent says that some horrible attack is being planned by The Secret 4 against the town of Mashowgan. The agent also reveals the code names of The Secret 4 executives: The Blackjack, The Dagger, The Needle, and The Rock. He says that one of these men is also the mysterious "Sword That Hangs over America," a foreigner who leads the organization. But no one knows which one he is. Beyond this, the saboteur has no idea of how or when the attack will be carried out.[3]

THE SWORD'S TERRIBLE WEAPON

By shortwave radio, The Sword announces to his lieutenants that he is ready to use his new secret weapon against the town of Mashowgan. A first plane will drop a mysterious spray, like a gentle rain, on every major building in the city. A second plane will broadcast a shortwave radio beam over the city. The result will be fire springing up everywhere at once!

Captain Midnight knows that some awful blow is being planned against Mashowgan, but the nature of the coming attack is a mystery. He pleads with Major Steele to have the entire city evacuated at once. Major Steele consents, and the city officials and citizenry are immediately informed. The evacuation proceeds over just hours.

The Sword realizes that he must act as soon as possible. Even if Mashowgan is deserted, he will devastate the town. He has one of his planes blanket the city with the invisible spray. When a second plane broadcasts a secret shortwave beam, any spot where the spray has fallen will burst into flame!

Captain Midnight's Rockies-ambush enemy, The Rock, flies along to broadcast the shortwave beam that will bring destruction to Mashowgan. Captain Midnight has taken every known precaution to safeguard the city. It is completely evacuated, and he has planes flying overhead — but he doesn't know about the spray or shortwave signal. Neither does he know that the radio-transmitting plane does not have to fly directly over the city. But of course, The Sword in Death Valley knows all this too well — and cackles about it to his mother, in the safety and comfort of his underground retreat.

THE SECRET 4 ATTACK

By means of the secret spray and mysterious shortwave radio beam, The Rock starts a myriad of fires — as if by magic — all over the little city of Mashowgan! The inhabitants of the town have been evacuated — except that Captain Midnight, Chuck, Joyce, and Ikky standby at the lakefront. As countless fires spring up rapidly and eerily around them, they plunge into the lake to escape the rush of enveloping flames. Captain Midnight had also given orders that any suspicious looking airplanes which come near the city are to be followed. And now, only a short time later, Mashowgan has turned into a blazing inferno, and the members of the Secret Squadron tread water in horror!

TRAIL THE SECRET 4

A fighter plane, piloted by a young Air Force lieutenant, had spotted The Rock's airplane near Mashowgan and now follows The Rock all the way to Death Valley. But then the lieutenant is shot down! Parachuting out, he is quickly taken prisoner and sequestered in The Sword's sand-covered base. Here, he listens in frustration to search planes flying above, but he is powerless to do anything.

As night falls, the captured lieutenant gets an idea. If he could smash one of the low-protruding, heavily-draped and paint-blackened windows, he could send out a beam of light through the desert darkness and possibly attract attention. Waiting until he hears a plane flying not too high overhead — and taking advantage of the plane's noise and the muting qualities of his bunched up flight jacket — he boldly acts.

The circling plane belongs to Captain Midnight. He spots a sudden ray of light below, and flies toward it for a better look — and is then heavily fired upon! His craft is severely damaged, and he must parachute into Death Valley. His doomed airplane plunges to the ground in a fiery crash.

Midnight hopes the wrecked plane will at least serve as a blazing beacon to Chuck and Joyce, if and when their aircraft should fly over the area. As Midnight floats down, he is blown about by wind and flying sand, adding to his distress even before he hits the ground.

The howling wind ruffles Captain Midnight's parachute — causing a speedy, angled and jarring landing — and then drags him along the sand until he can disconnect the billowing chute. He then makes his way along the dark desert floor, suspecting that he must be near a well-camouflaged hideout.

Captain Midnight has no idea how near the hideout might be, until he hears — right under his feet — a heavy echoing THUMP. Lightly and noiselessly, he swiftly backtracks until he is sure he's no longer standing on the roof of the buried building. The wind kicks up further, and Midnight now finds himself enveloped in a sandstorm.

With planes having flown overhead, and at least one of them shot down, The Sword realizes some invader might be on the ground nearby. But the sandstorm rages violently, and his men refuse to go out and search until the wind has died down and the flying sand has subsided. The Rock, however, anxiously wants to redeem himself from the terrible disgrace of leading the Secret Squadron to the base. So he staggers out into the blinding curtain of whirling sand, determined to find and kill any stranger.

Chuck and Joyce search in their twin-seat P-40 for Captain Midnight, but the darkness and sandstorm below obscure ground visibility. To make matters worse, Ikky's plane has disappeared, and they have received no word from him.

The Rock's murderous quest results in a shock. Instead of finding and killing someone, a black-clad figure leaps at him out of the shrouding flurry of sand and knocks him out cold with a tremendous blow to the chin. How much more satisfying it would be for Captain Midnight to know the man he has flattened is the same one who shot him down over the Rockies!

Captain Midnight binds his captive, and the sandstorm gradually subsides later in the night. Soon after in the darkness, Midnight hears The Sword's henchmen hurrying out to look for him. But at that moment, a plane appears in the night sky, and the searching saboteurs stop and crouch in their tracks to avoid being spotted.

Inside the hideout, The Sword quickly decides not to pursue his enemies, but — together with his mother — to run away from them. He will hastily desert his followers and fly with his chief henchmen to a new rendezvous in South America. However, he first orders the water storage tanks poisoned, so that the men he leaves behind will either die of poison or thirst. The Sword and his mother then hurry along a tunnel that leads into a hangar with a few awaiting planes. The Sword is truly an underground, underhanded, underworld mamma's boy.

It is now November of 1948. The Sword, his mother, and his lieutenants — except for The Rock — have left the Death Valley hideout and now fly toward South America, where they have arranged to regroup.

Curtiss P-40 twin-seat aircraft. PHOTOGRAPH: STEPHEN A. KALLIS, JR., WITH SECRET SQUADRON INSIGNIA BY LEONARD ZANE

And while all this is happening, what has become of Secret Squadron Agent Ichabod Mudd? The answer is that he had suffered engine trouble, and had to land his plane some distance from the saboteurs' Death Valley hideout. With the sandstorm's passing, Ikky has finally been able to find and rejoin Captain Midnight.

CAPTAIN MIDNIGHT'S GAMBLE

Captain Midnight — with The Rock as his prisoner — tries to persuade the group of saboteurs who had been abandoned to surrender. Because of his supposed death that was reported some weeks ago, the gang members disbelieve his announcement that he *is* Captain Midnight. But The Rock is the first to believe, much to his chagrin, as Midnight describes details of the incident over the Rockies. And besides the humiliation of leading the Secret Squadron to the hideout of The Secret 4 — and then ruining their base — this revelation adds even more to The Rock's misery and self-disgust.

It is still dark, as Captain Midnight contacts Chuck and Joyce, telling them he and Ikky have reunited. He tells them to circle their plane over The Sword's Death Valley hideout, not far from the smoldering wreckage of his own crashed plane. After giving these instructions, he orders The Sword's henchmen to surrender, or they will shortly be bombed out of existence. As a matter of fact, Captain Midnight knows that Chuck and Joyce do not have a single bomb, but Midnight and Ikky then send The Rock — as Captain Midnight's prisoner and spokesman — to reason with The Sword's henchmen. Waiting tensely in the darkness, the Squadron agents hear a short volley of shots in the distance. Some reasoning.

Captain Midnight does not know what has happened, but expects a coming fight in which he and Ikky will be heavily outnumbered. However, the circling P-40 brings the two Secret Squadron members on the ground some hope. This is because in another fifteen minutes, it will be dawn. Chuck and Joyce will soon be able to see what's going on, and will be able to differentiate between friend and foe as Captain Midnight directs.

It turns out the gunshots Captain Midnight and Ikky heard were from a squabble between The Sword's men — loyalists versus rebels. And the rebels — led by The Rock — had won. In short order, the henchmen approach Captain Midnight and toss down their weapons.

The Sword has decided to make a second attack without delay. He will destroy a huge American military supply base, or if not, he tells himself, he will die in the attempt. But Captain Midnight's prisoner, The Rock, is willing to talk, and Captain Midnight and Ikky interrogate him, extracting every piece of information they can. As the questioning proceeds, Joyce guards the prisoners and Chuck remains waiting in the plane.

SOUTH AMERICA

The Sword, in the guise of one of his three remaining followers — The Blackjack, The Dagger, or The Needle — flees with them to South America. From there, they hope to launch a second devastating attack on a U.S. military supply base. While The Sword is either The Blackjack or The Dagger or The Needle, each of the three denies being The Sword. Another thing none of them knows is that the Secret Squadron is now hot on their trail. In fact, just as the Secret Squadron approaches one end of the little town of Paso del Carmona by automobile, the three saboteurs slip out the other end disguised as Indians.

Escaping into the jungle, The Secret 3 are now led by an old beggar woman who is The Sword's mother in disguise. But then The Sword receives an order from his own homeland. He has been sternly directed to return to his country and report to the leaders. He realizes this will probably mean his execution for failure; so he decides to disobey the orders and carry out his second attack on America several days earlier than he had planned.

Captain Midnight and Ikky drive on their way to a place named Rio del Barrio, to pick up a plane and search the jungle by air. On the way, they come to a spot where the dirt road is washed out. On one side of the washout looms a sharply rising shoulder of ground, on the other a precipitous drop of fifty feet.

The Sword also faces some challenges. His three lieutenants seem almost on the verge of rebellion, but fear keeps them from turning back, and so they continue their long ride to a secret rendezvous in the jungle. The Sword's mother, in beggar woman's disguise, still leads them.

Captain Midnight is almost blocked in his hurried drive back to Rio del Barrio. But by taking a successful risk on the road, he and Ikky are eventually able to reach their plane, and they take off to search for some trace of the fugitives. As their aircraft gains altitude, they also wonder how Chuck and Joyce are doing.

One by one, the three chief saboteurs obey orders from the radio voice of The Sword and take to the air from a clearing in the jungle. As the three planes take off, Chuck and Joyce reach the edge of the clearing on foot, and Joyce pulls out her Pocket Locator to inform Captain Midnight.

Meanwhile, Captain Midnight has been flying over the field where The Sword's secret base is now said to be located. Noticing no sign of human life, he flies a little farther on, and passes over a second field that's level enough to be used as a landing surface. Captain Midnight lands and walks along one side of the field, while Ikky checks out the other — when suddenly Midnight notices his Pocket Locator flashing. Captain Midnight receives Joyce's report about The Secret 3 airplanes taking off, and from where. So he and Ikky immediately scramble back into their plane to give pursuit.

CONFRONTATION AND ANSWERS

The Sword's three planes head northward to carry out a second, horrible incendiary attack on an American military supply base. Captain Midnight and Ikky fly their craft toward the scene, and Chuck and Joyce have to make their way back to their own twin-seat plane to try to regroup with Captain Midnight.

In the skies somewhat south of the U.S. border, Captain Midnight's aircraft catches up with the planes it pursues. A fierce dogfight soon breaks out between The Sword's three aircraft and Captain Midnight's lone plane.

In a ferocious air battle, Captain Midnight shoots down all three of The Sword's planes! All the sinister enemies smash to fiery deaths — except for one individual, who escapes by parachute. Joyce and Chuck arrive in their P-40. They spot the burning wreckages and the descending chute, and soon land.

Captain Midnight is not quite sure which plane carried which member of the criminal gang. However, the Secret Squadron is at least able to determine the identity of the group's leader: "The Sword That Hangs over America" was The Secret 4 member who called himself "The Needle."

The parachuting form floats down, and Chuck and Joyce rush to effect capture. Just as the figure's chute crumples to the ground, Captain Midnight also swoops down, and he and his agents soon discover that the sole survivor of the dogfight is The Sword's mother.

The Secret Squadron stays to enjoy two weeks of well-earned rest and relaxation in South America. Following that, Captain Midnight receives permission from Major Steele to resume the Squadron's pursuit of the evil Ivan Shark.

ENDNOTES

1 For example, note an "Arkansas Toothpick" type of broad two-edged blade, as described on Internet sites such as swords.com.

2 These are East versus West, Cold War times during the U.S. Red Scare era of 1947-1957.

3 At this point in the broadcasts, Ovaltine holds a contest for bicycle prizes. The question is: Who is The Sword? The correct answer, submitted by listeners on the backs of Ovaltine labels, will be drawn at random. Five bicycles a day will be awarded as prizes. The bicycles will be Monarch Super-Deluxe models with "twenty exclusive features you won't find in any bike in America: Racing-type chain and drive, streamlined airflow design," and so on.

15

The Return of Ivan Shark

(1948-1949)

THE LAND THAT TIME FORGOT

The Secret Squadron agents recall that actress Greta Hayden had overheard Ivan Shark declare to his daughter, Fury, that they would head for his base he called "The Land Which Time Forgot." Miss Hayden said Shark added that this base was near the "Island of the Lost People" (which had been devastated by a volcano).

Andrew Maxon delivers a fully stocked amphibian — including the adopted Great Dane dog — from Washington to his Secret Squadron comrades in South America. At a nod from Captain Midnight, he also covertly slips a small packet into Ikky's hand. Andy then remains there to arrange for possible use of a helicopter — while Captain Midnight, Chuck, Joyce, and Ikky fly off in the amphibian. They take the Great Dane with them, plus a parrot that Joyce has recently acquired as another pet.

Ivan Shark was last seen trapped by an earthquake in the remote "Land That Time Forgot." This Land is an oppressively hot and humid valley, ensconced in the crater of a dormant Antarctic volcano.[1]

Captain Midnight and his companions begin searching for traces of Ivan Shark in an area south of the South Shetland Islands, not far from the previously devastated "Island of the Lost People."

The crater of Ivan Shark's island refuge is cup-shaped, with high overhanging cliffs that foil scaling from the inside. At first, things looked as if Ivan Shark, Fury, and a handful of their followers would be trapped there permanently. The valley was safe enough during the daytime, but apparently a place of incredible terror at night.

Despite the night threats, the undaunted Ivan Shark had long before built himself a big fortress near the valley's edge. This retreat was enclosed by a tall heavy wall, within which a tower rose high for surveying the surroundings. Shark's followers could therefore safely retire to quarters inside the fort during the dark hours.

For untold ages, time and evolution seem to have stood still in this forgotten valley. Many strange animals live here from ancient geologic epochs — along with even Stone Age hominids! For Shark, the place affords what he had wanted for a superb hideout, and more. Besides seclusion and protection, the hidden valley provides him with a magnificent assortment of terrifying animals that he can watch, study, admire, and hide from the rest of the world with relish. To Shark, the place is a personal collection of animated art works — his own exclusive zoo of horrible creatures, unseen and unknown anywhere else on earth — even if he and his band also sweat day and night in this crater-sealed hothouse.

HOMINIDS

Low-forehead humanoid creatures thrive huge and apelike in the valley, with their primary weapons being enormous stone clubs which they can hurl with astonishing accuracy. By day, the island's many weird and terrifying creatures disappear into a thick tropical forest in the center of the valley. By night, they come out — and prey and shriek and roar and fight and devour.

Ivan Shark has managed to capture two of the apelike hominids. He has judged they are Stone Age Neanderthals and that their species had reached there, either in escaping *Homo sapiens* enemies from Southern Europe, or having migrated from some closer land long ago. Shark has trained his pair of ape-men by using electric prods. He has even given the two of them names — Mu and Arkon — and has made them his personal bodyguards.[2]

Of course, Ivan Shark is now miserable. Since his latest arrival and awful entrapment, he has been planning to escape somehow from what has become his far-flung prison. At first, it seemed that only an outside aircraft could rescue them. Then Shark had a brilliant idea. He decided to make use of an underground river that flows through the valley, surfacing briefly at its southernmost point, where the river flows through a circular tunnel down into the ground again.[3]

While Shark has been lost to the world for months, he and his remaining followers and his two Neanderthals have been working a scheme to block up the exit tunnel. Shark believes that once this is accomplished, it won't be terribly long before the crater fills up, forming a lake. He has already built a huge raft, which — as the water rises — will slowly float to the top. This is his great getaway plan.

SOUTH ATLANTIC SEARCH

While Ivan Shark's escape operation is underway, the Secret Squadron members fly their amphibian low over this general Antarctic area. Suddenly, they hear what sounds like an explosion coming from a cone-shaped island in the distance. The explosion is Shark's dynamiting to block the tunnel.

The Squadron agents fly their amphibian in the direction of the noise, and they soon hear a second explosion — apparently from inside the mountain isle ahead. Because of possible volcanic activity on the island below, Captain Midnight climbs the plane to higher altitude. But instead of fire and lava, the Secret Squadron sees a surprise: a green and tropical valley inside the mountainous cone! And so Shark's valley is discovered, though the Secret Squadron does not know it is the criminal mastermind's base. The plane, however, is getting somewhat low on fuel. So Captain Midnight decides to return to the South Shetlands to fuel up, and then come back to explore this strange green oasis in the frigid South Atlantic.

Meanwhile, Ivan Shark has seen the amphibian. He doesn't know it contains his greatest enemy, but he redoubles his efforts to block the river. He surmises that an exploring party may come, and he doesn't want to be discovered and captured. Even if he and Fury disguise themselves, he realizes that too many questions would likely be asked and that his identity would be discovered. He also still has a fortune in jewels from looting the Wisconsin city. A search of his effects — should he be rescued by the outside world — would also most likely uncover that whole exploit and reveal his plundering.

BEASTS

Later on, from the vantage point of Shark's fortress watchtower, some monstrous creatures of the past appear. A spectacular territorial battle develops between an enormous Iguanodon and an equally huge Stegosaurus armed with back plates and tail spikes. These two beasts had presumably been extinct since the Early Cretaceous and Late Jurassic periods of 125 million and 150 million years ago, respectively! Why are such prehistoric creatures in this place, which have been long dead everywhere else? The most important factors seem to be: (1) remarkably steady 90° to 95° F (32° to 35° C) temperatures; (2) over 50% humidity, for many millions of years; and (3) consistently clear skies that have sustained this

Iguanodon. PHOTO BY PERMISSION: © 2011 TODD MARSHALL. ALL RIGHTS RESERVED

sheltered valley ever since the Jurassic and Cretaceous geologic periods.

The next morning, the Secret Squadron amphibian flies back to the island — now called "The Land That Time Forgot" in the radio program. The amphibian lands on a narrow, shallow marsh ending by a small glade. It is daylight, and there is no sign of life. Not even a bird sings or a monkey chatters. The creatures of the past are holed up in the dense central forest and in caves in the overhanging cliffs. Captain Midnight is at once struck with the place's possibilities. What a site for some remote atomic bomb research plant. He is determined to explore the island extensively.

Midnight stays in touch with Major Steele by the amphibian's shortwave radio, which can also relay Pocket Locator messages, as can a radio repeater device in the cabin. He receives permission to stay as long as he thinks is necessary.

Meanwhile, Ivan Shark has spotted and recognized his old enemy! He is amazed, and at the same time overjoyed. Stealing Captain Midnight's amphibian offers a sure way out! Plus, Shark has an enormous advantage: He knows Captain Midnight and his crew are in the valley. But the Secret Squadron cannot know that he is hidden within only a few miles of their camp!

Stegosaurus. PHOTO BY PERMISSION: © 2011 TODD MARSHALL. ALL RIGHTS RESERVED

Captain Midnight makes a startling series of discoveries. He comes upon a recently killed skeleton of a prehistoric animal, and then upon a series of enormous footprints in the mud at the edge of the marsh. Also indented in the mud are footprints of what must be a huge man or woman. They could be from a large ape, but the outlines are so nearly human that Midnight believes they indicate some mighty savage. He warns his Secret Squadron comrades to stay on the lookout and stick together. Ikky replies that he already feels a whole lot too sticky in the awful heat and steamy air.

Meanwhile, Ivan Shark believes another large blast of dynamite will block the river effectively, and he also envisions a scenario of gratifying carnage. Night will fall in a few hours, and he spies on the Secret Squadron setting up camp. He knows in the hours of darkness that great beasts will emerge and will roam across the valley to forage for food and water. He believes it is unlikely that the Secret Squadron is armed with much more than small arms, which would have as little effect against the hides of the huge prehistoric animals as they would against a fifty-ton tank. He foresees a wonderfully terrible end for his enemies, and easy seizure of their plane!

Night falls. The Secret Squadron sits around, talking of the future and wondering what might have happened to Ivan Shark, who has been

Allosaurus. PHOTO BY PERMISSION: © 2011 TODD MARSHALL. ALL RIGHTS RESERVED

strangely dormant for some time. Suddenly, the night silence is broken by a shattering roar, and then by the largest lizard-like animal they have ever seen. The creature bounds out of the forest — some twenty-eight feet long and rearing up over eight feet tall — its huge chest and tail now revealed in the open. They don't know its name, but recognize the type. It's a dinosaur! In fact, it is an Allosaurus — thought to be extinct since the Late Jurassic — and the big lizard eyes them most fiercely and hungrily.

And there is more: Before the Secret Squadron's horrified gaze, another monstrous animal that might be some fabled dragon of the Arthurian legends races after a smaller reptile that bounds over the nose of the Squadron's amphibian! The chasing beast is a Megalosaurus from the Middle Jurassic of some 166 million years ago. Its prey, an Othnielia, is seven feet long and from the Late Jurassic. The Megalosaurus measures thirty-six feet long and twelve feet tall. The ferocious monster leaps high in hot pursuit of the Othnielia. Then shockingly: upon descending, the Megalosaurus's huge hind legs smash down onto the plane's cockpit — and crush it like tinfoil!

The Secret Squadron agents fire a volley of rifle shots to try to drive

Megalosaurus pursuing *Othnielia*. PHOTO BY PERMISSION: © 2011 TODD MARSHALL. ALL RIGHTS RESERVED

off the more nearby Allosaurus. (Shark may have slightly miscalculated the Secret Squadron's firepower.) But the twenty-eight foot creature is undeterred, and comes bounding after the agents, who desperately run for an enormous tree at the clearing's edge. In the nick of time, the Squadron members haul themselves up on the branches and climb safely out of the roaring predator's ravenous reach.

Ivan Shark hears the scattered rounds of gunfire, and will wait for dawn to learn more when Gardo, Mu, and Arkon can go out to investigate.

Meanwhile, the Secret Squadron members — their bodies sweaty and grimy — nestle high in the tree branches, and they come to witness sights that should have been buried in the past. They see men of the long dead Stone Age hunt and chase the Allosaurus. Later, they watch a lumbering, herbivorous Shunosaurus of the Middle Jurassic approach and browse on the foliage of the very tree in which they hide.

And then a monstrous winged creature — a pterodactyl of the Late Cretaceous — flies from out of the night to attack Joyce!

Shunosaurus — here attacked by a *Kaijiangosaurus* — and both discovered in China. PHOTO BY PERMISSION: © 2011 TODD MARSHALL. ALL RIGHTS RESERVED

A lucky shot from Captain Midnight breaks one of the pterodactyl's leathery wings, and the flying reptile crashes, flopping to the ground at the foot of a nearby tree. But in the darkness, what the Secret Squadron members do not notice is that Joyce's 1948 Code-O-Graph has been knocked from her pocket and has fallen to the ground.

Out of hiding from behind shrubbery, another Allosaurus pounces onto the downed pterosaur. The Allosaurus tears at the winged creature with its powerful jaws, and shortly drags it off — further disrupting the ground in the immediate area.

All this is of such extraordinary and terrifying interest! What any scientist would give to see the sights the Secret Squadron sees — as pages from prehistoric eras unfold before their eyes! Besides the amazing zoological discoveries, watching these prehistoric men and beasts excites Captain Midnight all the more about this place. This is because Ivan Shark had said he would escape to "The Land Which Time Forgot."

Dawn approaches, and the roars and crashes slowly die down. With the dawn, the Secret Squadron members warily climb down from the tree and survey the wreckage of their plane. While the cockpit is in shambles, Captain Midnight uses the shortwave repeater radio in the main cabin to relay a Pocket Locator message to Andy Maxon. Contacting Andy, Midnight asks him to bring a helicopter from his

Unnamed African pterosaur. PHOTO BY PERMISSION: © 2011 TODD MARSHALL. ALL RIGHTS RESERVED

location in South America to rescue them not later than Monday. Midnight advises refueling spots along the way, and hopes Andy will get there before even the next nightfall. Out of precaution, though, Captain Midnight and his marooned Squadron agents proceed to build a platform high in their big tree. This work preempts their exploring for a few morning hours.

Also during the early morning, Gardo cautiously works his way to the edge of the clearing. He spots the smashed amphibian cockpit, and realizes what has happened. Then he briefly watches the Squadron members working on their tree platform. Quickly, he returns to tell Ivan Shark the good news about the Secret Squadron's wrecked plane and their tree-platform work. Shark calls Gardo an idiot, yelling that this is bad news because they could've stolen the amphibian and escaped!

THE CAVEMEN THREATEN

Ivan Shark immediately wants to start the lake rising and drown out the Secret Squadron. But Fury has a more vengeful idea. Mu and Arkon's fellow tribesmen hate and fear the modern humans (the Sharks) who have captured two of their brothers. Apparently, the tribesmen missed smelling the Secret Squadron high up in the tree. But right where the cavemen were hunting the previous night, Fury suggests that just before dusk a scent trail be laid down from there to near the Secret Squadron's tree. Such an action can be done stealthily when the Squadron members will likely be away from the tree.

Fury explains to her father that sometime after dusk, the cavemen will pick up the trail and will most certainly swarm up the tree and attack. The Secret Squadron may kill some of them, but in the end, Captain Midnight and his agents will surely be wiped out. Fury sees them savagely beaten to death by the stone clubs of the Neanderthals! Even if the Secret Squadron could somehow manage to repulse the cavemen's attack, blocking the river and flooding the crater is still Shark's ultimate weapon. Her father consents. What is just one more night if his sworn enemy is terribly destroyed! *[This is another example of Fury Shark's intelligence and skillful manipulation of her father. She often hatches murderous and grisly ideas — but gets Dad to direct them or carry them out. This is a pattern throughout the Captain Midnight series. Ivan Shark murders people time and again. But Fury never does. In fact, in the rare cases where she ever even kills, she does so only in self-defense, or by accident, as happened with Professor Pitcairn/Sodman. She's an intelligent, creative, and diabolical strategist, nonetheless.]*

Meanwhile, Andy Maxon flies a helicopter toward the mountain isle — and develops engine trouble! He has to make an emergency landing on a tiny nearby atoll to effect repairs. It is almost dusk when he is ready to fly again; but Captain Midnight has given the strictest orders that whatever happens, under no circumstances is Andy to land the helicopter in the valley at night. Midnight has not explained the reason for this order. He has felt the story is so strange that it must be seen to be believed, and also for the terrible threats to be fully appreciated. Andy decides to settle down on the atoll for the night, and to take off first thing in the morning.

Meanwhile Gardo, Mu, and Arkon have scattered odd bits of recently worn clothing from the area where the cavemen had hunted, to the very edge of the clearing bordering Captain Midnight's arboreal shelter. Gardo places a final bit only a few yards from the huge tree in which the Secret Squadron has built its platform. In the fading daylight, Gardo spots something small, red, and golden that gleams on the ground under some shrubbery. He sneaks there and picks the object up. It is one of Captain Midnight's clearly-labeled 1948 Code-O-Graphs! With relish, he leads the two ape-men behind the shrubbery, and then turns to take a last peek back to see if anyone is coming. Just then, across the clearing about fifty yards away, a returning Ikky thinks he spots the face of a savage in the foliage near the tree. He fires his rifle a little wide of the figure as a warning. A sharp grunt indicates he has scored a hit. This is because the shot has wounded the ape-man Mu, who was unseen and near Gardo.

Gardo returns with the wounded Mu to Ivan Shark's fortress. Shark is so joyful and triumphant to get his hands on Captain Midnight's 1948 Code-O-Graph, that he completely ignores doing anything for the injured Mu — stirring more of the caveman's hatred.

While Fury and Gardo pack Shark's baggage and the huge fortune in jewels, the criminal mastermind exercises a new scheme. He hastily radios a Code-O-Graph enciphered message to Secret Squadron Headquarters in Washington, claiming he is Captain Midnight. The message requests an amphibian to be sent immediately, and gives exact directions on where to land in the hidden Antarctic valley (well away from the Secret Squadron's encampment). The message further asks for two leading atomic scientists to be brought along in the amphibian to evaluate the location for atomic weapons testing.

So Ivan Shark now has three different plots underway: (1) wipe out the Secret Squadron with attacking cavemen, (2) loose another blast of dynamite to drown the Secret Squadron out and create a lake for rafting to escape, (3) have Secret Squadron Headquarters unwittingly fly an amphibian directly to him. And besides these immediate schemes, Shark's active brain is already at work hatching a grand plan for the future, too!

At nightfall, the strange prehistoric noises start again. The Secret Squadron had managed to catch some sleep the previous night; and Midnight believes that with the possible attacks of airborne creatures, they must all take turns keeping watch throughout the dark hours.

Joyce suddenly notices her Code-O-Graph is missing. But Chuck consoles her: What difference will it make in this forgotten place? "That's the problem," Captain Midnight says. "This is evidently Ivan Shark's 'Land Which Time Forgot,' and Shark may be here."

Captain Midnight orders Ichabod Mudd to reveal a certain surprise. Nodding with a smile, Ikky pulls out a new *1949* model Code-O-Graph. He had designed the 1949 model during the summer. Headquarters had fabricated several prototype samples, and Ikky had received this one in the small packet that Andy Maxon had recently delivered. Midnight orders Ikky to encode a 1949 Code-O-Graph message to Major Steele to cancel the 1948 version immediately and to start using the 1949 model. By Pocket Locator, and with the signal relayed via the amphibian's radio repeater, Chuck transmits the coded message.

In the deepening night, the Secret Squadron agents wait impatiently for the moon to rise above the rim of the cliffs surrounding the valley. The darkness is dense. They hear beasts crashing in the distance and the occasional roars of Allosaurus dinosaurs. The waiting grows nerve-wracking. Even Ikky no longer wisecracks. Suddenly, almost as if a floodlight had been turned on, the moon starts up over the cliff's edge. Slowly, it climbs. The ground below is still shrouded in darkness, and an occasional pterosaur flaps by menacingly.

At last, the clearing below the Secret Squadron becomes illuminated in the moonlight. Peering down, they face a chilling sight: A small cluster of ape-men has surrounded their tree. The hominids gaze up, and point and shake their stone clubs. One of the ape-men — evidently the leader — hurls a club, apparently to judge the distance. It flies by, only a few feet below their platform. Captain Midnight doesn't wait a moment. Taking careful aim, he fires. The leader spins and falls. His followers quickly pick him up and carry him farther away, shouting, and waving their clubs. Midnight has Chuck and Ikky fire a few shots over the cavemen's heads to drive them deeper into the forest. "But if they ever attack *en masse*," warns Midnight, "we haven't a chance. We'll be overwhelmed."

Hearing the distant shots, Ivan Shark realizes his plan (really Fury's) is probably succeeding. It sounds like the Secret Squadron is at this moment being attacked by the ape-men. But Shark still harbors suspicions of Gardo's earlier actions:

GARDO:…When I lays a trail, Boss, I lays a trail!

IVAN SHARK: And almost give the whole plan away by sticking your stupid head up to get shot at.

GARDO: Oh, it wasn't me dat got shot, Boss, it was Mu! And dat was just a lucky one. They musta seen the branches movin' at the end o' the clearin' — or, or somp'n.

IVAN SHARK: It was you, blundering around like a dumb ox that attracted their attention, I'm sure of that…

GARDO: Aw, now, Boss why pick on me when I done right?

IVAN SHARK: To keep you from imagining — even for one instant, Gardo — that you have even *half* the brain of an imbecile![4]

Shark senses what he hears may not be a final Neanderthal attack. This is because the shots are few, rather than in heavy volleys that he expects during a final, massive assault.

1949 KEY-O-MATIC CODE-O-GRAPH

The 10 January 1949 Captain Midnight radio broadcast describes Ivan Shark's having secured the 1948 Code-O-Graph and sending a phony message to Secret Squadron Headquarters. Part of this broadcast also describes the new 1949 "Key-O-Matic" Code-O-Graph — plus a disturbing point that hints the Secret Squadron may again be on the brink of being disbanded! Below is a transcribed excerpt of the broadcast.

ANNOUNCER: And a short time later, Ikky decodes:

ICHABOD MUDD: "message arrived — old Code-O-Graph made obsolete — Key-O-Matic being sent out to all members — anything else I can do — signed Steele."

CHUCK RAMSAY: Boy, there certainly is, isn't there, sir?

CAPTAIN MIDNIGHT: Yes, Chuck. Ask Major Steele to have an amphibian flown down, right away.

ICHABOD MUDD: Oh boy, will I be glad to see that arrive!

CAPTAIN MIDNIGHT: Code the message, Joyce. Use Code B-8.

JOYCE RYAN: Just a minute, Chuck, while I fix this Code-O-Graph. Geemaney, is this little key a slick idea! Okay Chuck: 2-9-8-7 *[K-I-B-M, therefore super-enciphered by some memorized scheme]*...

ANNOUNCER: And in Washington, as Major Steele receives the message:

MAJOR STEELE: "send amphibian right away — urgent — important."

LIEUTENANT: That's what the first *phony* message asked, Major Steele. The one we're pretty sure was from Ivan Shark.

MAJOR STEELE: Afraid this one is a phony, too, Lieutenant?

LIEUTENANT: Well, sir, I — I can't help being suspicious…

MAJOR STEELE: Lieutenant, you're forgetting that this was decoded on the new Key-O-Matic Code-O-Graph, aren't you? This one *has* to be on the level.

LIEUTENANT: Ho, ho — of course, sir!

MAJOR STEELE: Also, this one makes no mention of the two atomic scientists. So, it's obviously been sent by a different person.

LIEUTENANT: Yes. Uh, Major, I wonder what made Captain Midnight suddenly decide to have the new Key-O-Matic flown down to him? It's certain lucky for us that he did.

MAJOR STEELE: One of the Captain's brilliant hunches, probably.

LIEUTENANT: Now I know why you never ignore them, sir.

MAJOR STEELE: I've found, Lieutenant, that Captain Midnight's hunches are usually based on something very tangible. So, Lieutenant, see that the amphibian leaves at once.

LIEUTENANT: Right away, sir.

MAJOR STEELE: One moment. Soon as you've seen about the amphibian, contact Captain Midnight and tell him it's on the way.

LIEUTENANT: Yes, sir.

ANNOUNCER: And a short time later, the Lieutenant returns.

LIEUTENANT: The amphibian is on its way, sir.

MAJOR STEELE: Good.

LIEUTENANT: Uh, Major Steele?

MAJOR STEELE: Yes, Lieutenant?

LIEUTENANT: Do you realize, sir, that the first message asking for an amphibian — the phony one — was an attempt on Shark's part to capture America's two leading atomic scientists?

MAJOR STEELE: Ha, I realized it only too well. I don't think the Secret Squadron ever came nearer to a real disaster.

LIEUTENANT: Oh, that's for sure, sir.

MAJOR STEELE: The misspelling of one word saved us.[5]

LIEUTENANT: That, and Ichabod Mudd's Key-O-Matic Code-O-Graph. If Ikky hadn't spent last summer working on it —

MAJOR STEELE: And if Captain Midnight had by chance postponed sending for it — well it — doesn't bear thinking about.

LIEUTENANT: The Secret Squadron would've been disgraced, sir.

MAJOR STEELE: Probably — or disbanded!

LIEUTENANT *(sighs):* Well, sir, with the new Key-O-Matic, we've double protection — if it should fall into enemy hands.

MAJOR STEELE: You mean they not only have to have the Code-O-Graph, but they have to have the key, too.

LIEUTENANT: Exactly, sir!

MAJOR STEELE: Yes.

LIEUTENANT: Our enemies can capture as many of the Code-O-Graphs as they like, but if they don't have the secret key, too, it's useless to 'em.

MAJOR STEELE: I know. Ikky should get a special citation for inventing it. Ha, ha — with a banquet. Nothing but hot dogs and hamburgers!

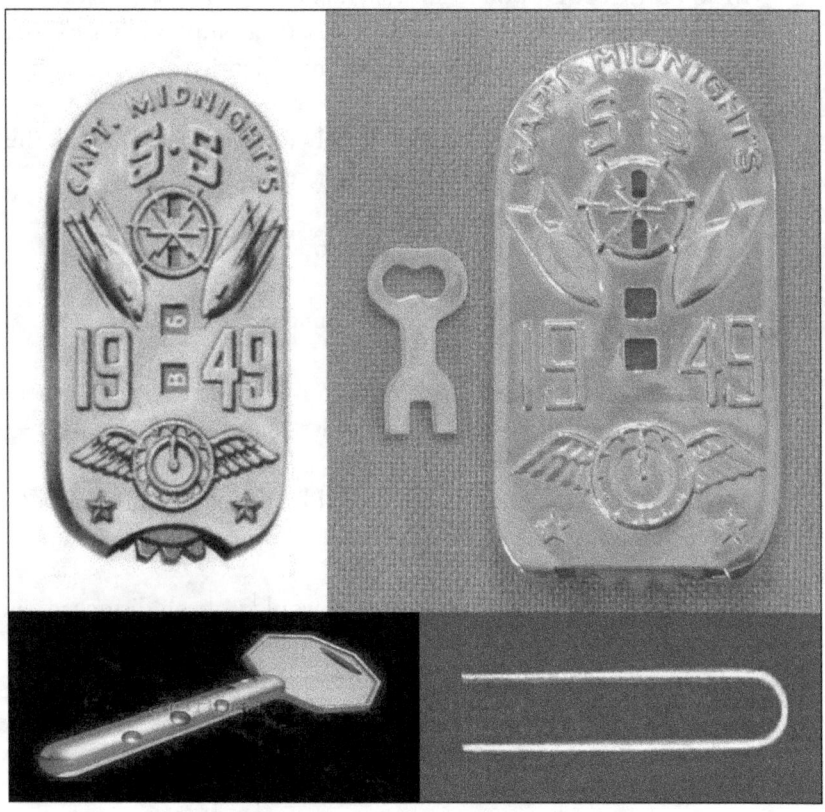

1949 "Key-O-Matic" Code-O-Graph. Its tiny, two-tined key sets the Master Code. The key is inserted into the slim rectangular slots, and pressed down to disengage the numbered top gear with a spring clutch, while the bottom gear is hand-rotated to the appropriate letter to set against the top number. The simplistic key provided no security at all in setting Master Codes, and a cross-cut paper clip *(bottom right)* could be used. A key much more like the one shown, for example *(bottom left)*, could have been inserted into a back vertical tube and set the gearing from there.
PHOTOGRAPH: LEONARD ZANE

Cover and Page 3 of the 1949 Secret Squadron Manual. Who is the mysterious man between the woman (Fury) and the bald man (Gardo)? Could it perhaps be the so-called "Professor Khala" of the later 1949 "The Devil on Ice" serial? He somewhat resembles Ivan Shark on the bottom right. PHOTOGRAPHS: LEONARD ZANE

SHARK'S GRAND DREAM

In his eternal and indefatigable optimism, Ivan Shark never strays from his dream of global empire. In order to achieve this, he wants to begin with conquest of a wealthy and obscure nation that is already conditioned and gripped by autocratic rule. A small, rich kingdom will be ideal, and he intends to gain control of such a kingdom that is far from the United States. So he decides on "Bartestan," which is situated in an isolated corner of Southern India, and whose Raja is reported to be an immensely rich and benevolent despot. Immediately upon their escape, Shark's group will therefore fly to Bartestan, and buy and intrigue their way into a position of power.

With boundless and energetic confidence, Shark also has in mind a fantastic secret weapon that he believes — with assistance by atomic scientists — can be brought into even mass production in just months. With this weapon, he feels sure that he can terrify the entire civilized world into submission! *[What could this weapon be? The answer must await Captain Midnight's later adventure called "The Devil on Ice."]*

THE CAVEMEN ATTACK

While Ivan Shark savors his world-dominion dream, Andy Maxon can't sleep. He's been given orders not to land in the valley at night, whatever happens. But the moonlight is out, and it is so intensely bright in the crystal-clear sky, that he decides to reconnoiter. He won't land, but he'll at least take a look. He starts up his engine and heads the helicopter toward the distant mountain isle.

For perhaps an hour, the ape-men keep their distance from Captain Midnight's tree. Some hide in the undergrowth; some collect at the clearing's far side. The alert Squadron members now watch a weird and exciting scene. A huge Iguanodon crashes out into the clearing! At once, the horde of Neanderthal men attack. With clubs and short spears, they swarm around the enraged beast. Before long, the cavemen drag the Iguanodon down and kill it. Then the women hack off huge pieces of meat with stone knives and carry off the booty, evidently for a coming feast.

Soon, however, the chief of the Neanderthals that Captain Midnight had wounded emerges from the forest. He stirs his tribesmen into attacking the Squadron agents who crouch on their tree platform. With growing frenzy, the cavemen charge and attack, and the Secret Squadron members have no choice but to start shooting in earnest and in heavy volleys!

Across the valley, Ivan Shark hears the continuous shooting. Maniacally, he rejoices at what is sure to spell the Secret Squadron's doom! His voice booms out:

IVAN SHARK: That's it! That *must* be it! They're attacking, Gardo! Oh, if I could only be there to lead and urge them on! Go to it, my brave cavemen! My primitive tribe of strong-arm gorillas! Swarm up the tree by tens, by twenties, by hundreds! Pour over them in an irresistible flood of mighty arms and strong hairy bodies! On! On, to victory! (Cackles fiendishly.)[6]

Then Captain Midnight hears the sound of an aircraft! Realizing at once that it must be Andy Maxon in the helicopter, he says, "If only I'd thought to get him to bring along a couple of bombs!"

As the helicopter approaches, the attacking cavemen take it for some monstrous, night-flying creature — and hastily retreat into the forest. The helicopter circles, and Captain Midnight waits until it is fairly close to the tree where they hide. Then he fires four shots — spacing them as the secret signal of the Squadron. Ikky climbs to the very top of the tree and waves a flashlight to attract Andy's attention.

Andy Maxon sees the light, quickly approaches the huge tree, and hovers over it. Ikky cries to Andy that they're surrounded by a bunch of cavemen killers who are scared of the helicopter. He warns never to land in the valley until daylight. He yells that Andy should land on the *rim* of the crater, where he can hear any gunfire. Three shots will mean to take off again and scare the cavemen away from the tree.

Twice during the night, the Neanderthal men attack, and twice Andy flies over and frightens them back into the jungle. Then at last, and exhausted from lack of sleep, the Secret Squadron sees a first crack of dawn. Andy Maxon flies down and takes his Squadron comrades back up to the rim of the crater, where they wearily plan a campaign. But before going ahead with the plan, Captain Midnight insists they all get some rest.

Ivan Shark realizes that for the time being, the Secret Squadron has once more eluded him. Nevertheless, and with Gardo's help, he sets the final charges that will bring hundreds of tons of rock crashing down into the river. Shortly after this, Shark's two ape-men — having borne ever-growing grudges — rebel and fiercely attack; but the master criminal and his daughter defend themselves with rifles. After slaying the Neanderthals, Shark still laments that it's a pity because they were such "magnificent instruments."

After a few hours of sleep, Captain Midnight and Andy leave their Squadron comrades and take off in the helicopter to circle the valley. They eventually see the river that causes its fertility. They see the caves, and then they spot the fort and watchtower — but absolutely no sign of life. They decide to land in another open glade that stretches toward a series of enormous caves. Midnight decides that under no circumstances will they leave the helicopter. They will slowly maneuver around to see if they can get any glimpse of the huge animals, and perhaps scare up any ape-like tribesmen. Midnight still has not discovered Ivan Shark's presence, and he also has not reckoned that the evil mastermind has had the Secret Squadron under surveillance.

SHARK'S DRASTIC ACTION

Ivan Shark, now hidden in ambush, is determined to put the helicopter out of commission for the time being, and later seize it. Just as Andy and Midnight prepare to take off again, Shark and his men pour gunfire at the craft, and a well-placed rifle shot disables it. As Captain Midnight and Andy sprint for cover, Midnight and the arch criminal finally and momentarily spot one another. And then Shark orders the last loads of dynamite to be set off.

A mighty roar echoes in the valley, and almost at once the rushing underground river starts to flood its banks. Midnight and Andy immediately make for the huge trees, and climb into some branches. After learning Ivan Shark is there, it is not long before Captain Midnight grasps his enemy's objective. Midnight knows the water will soon send the animals crashing out into the open, and the ape-men will certainly take to the treetops — perhaps even into the very tree in which they are hiding!

Meanwhile, the huge explosion — and Midnight's and Andy's failure to return to the crater's rim — make Chuck, Joyce, and Ikky realize something has gone dreadfully wrong. They see the water flooding fast over the valley. And as they watch from the rim, they witness the awesome sight of many prehistoric monsters rushing out to avoid the rising waters.

DESPERATION

The water rises quickly — and Shark, Fury, and Gardo busily load the large raft with their valued possessions. In his tree, Captain Midnight is shocked and distracted by the sudden flooding — dropping his Pocket

Locator into the spreading water, so he cannot contact the Squadron agents on the crater's rim.

Fury and Ivan Shark, carrying two small bags of jewels and half-mad with excitement, push out onto the rising water on a small raft. Gardo follows on the larger raft, with the baggage and big stores of loot securely lashed on.

"The Land That Time Forgot" poster for the 1975 adapted Edgar Rice Burroughs film of the same name. PHOTOGRAPH: AMICUS PRODUCTIONS, LTD.

The ape-men take to the trees. The big saurian animals flee to one rising section of land in the center of the valley. Too frightened by the flood to fight amongst themselves, the primeval beasts soon stand trembling and immobile, as the water rises up their great scaly flanks. The terrified pterosaurs fly up and out to escape their rock-ensconced world, which has protected and nurtured their species for scores of millions of years. But as soon as they emerge from the crater and begin to flap away, the harsh subzero weather brutally shocks their warm-blooded Aves systems, and they frantically retreat and dive back into the volcanic cone.

Ivan Shark, almost out of his mind, shouts that he is drowning a world! And at that moment, an Iguanodon plunges madly into the flood and makes for the large raft. Too late, Shark sees the danger. He and Fury have no choice but to paddle their small raft away as fast as they can. But the enormous thrashing beast overturns the large raft with Gardo and the lashed-on baggage and loot.

RESCUE AND DISAPPEARANCE

Not a moment too soon, a U.S. Navy amphibian arrives! Its crew first rescues Captain Midnight and Andy, and then the rest of the Secret Squadron agents.

The Navy crew and Secret Squadron agents soon capture Gardo and recover the loot. But there is no sign of Ivan Shark, or Fury, or the smaller raft.

Just one day later, the flooding water covers the tallest trees. Some surviving dinosaurs cower inside the higher caves, and bemused pterodactyls circle above the rapidly-filling crater lake. But the time remaining for all these prehistoric beasts is to be suddenly shorter than their rudimentary brains can imagine…

EPILOGUE

Did Ivan Shark and his daughter Fury escape and somehow ever make it to India? What happened to the flooded island? Did the crater simply fill up and overflow, drowning all the cavemen and animals in the lake and sea? What about the pterosaurs? Did they manage to fly out of the remote, frigid region and reach some tropical refuge? Or was the journey simply

Consolidated Vultee PBY-5 Catalina amphibian. PHOTOGRAPH: CONSOLIDATED VULTEE AIRCRAFT CORPORATION VIA STEPHEN A. KALLIS, JR.

too cold, too long, too shocking to their bodies — and too bewildering to primeval brains that had known only sweltering temperatures and high humidity over vast geologic epochs? Were conditions overwhelming to such primitive brains that — not unlike even the hominid race from The Land of Lost People — could not even conceive of a place to flee beyond their safe, ages-old greenhouse? And was there even something more that suddenly cut their time short?

From where had the Neanderthals emigrated, and how? Because of confused, ragged — or perhaps intentionally inadequate and even contradictory information — only certain speculations remain.

(1) Perhaps the dinosaurs were spared extinction in earlier ages by some volcanic, superheated steam rising high from fissures and small cones inside the otherwise long-stable crater. The extremely hot steam plumes kept the sky overhead clear, and also often condensed into clouds and rained down. Thus, the ground was warmed by substrate magma, and also kept wet enough to support and nourish flora and fauna. Perhaps Ivan Shark was right about Neanderthals that migrated there in the much later Stone Age. Or perhaps these hominids were some species from the South American mainland that only looked like Neanderthals. Or perhaps they were really a *Homo erectus* species from Africa. Or they could have come from another island in the area that was near "The Island of the Lost People." Or possibly even originally from "The Island of the Lost People," itself, and had been driven away by the more recently evolved, four-fingered species.

(2) Because even traces of Ivan Shark's "Land That Time Forgot" have remained undetected, it follows that the cratered mountain — together with its flora and fauna — were not only flooded, but were somehow utterly destroyed. Everything had to be obliterated to such an extent that not even corpses or skeletons or fossils from the place have been found.

(3) The "rising section of land" in the center of the valley is perhaps a clue. Was the ground simply at a higher elevation — or come to be floating on water? Or was some other phenomenon at work?

(4) Amid the icy Antarctic Circle, the conical mountain had continued to generate enough warmth to keep its inner valley tropical. This indicated hot underground strata, which in turn indicated magma at shallow

depth. This condition coincided with characteristic volcanism of the area in general — as was manifest at the Island of Lost People not a terribly long distance away.

(5) When the huge crater filled with water, the weight and strain on its underlying strata grew enormously. This was enough to crack the rock base. Magma began pushing up the crater's bed of strata, and the rising central strata thrust up a central section of land.

(6) The Secret Squadron — and perhaps Ivan Shark and Fury, too — escaped the island just in time, because the rest happened quickly. In the underground depths, the water and fiery magma mixed. Superheated steam brewed — and the ancient, dormant volcano once again blew — this time suddenly, hugely, and to smithereens! Before even the circling pterosaurs could sense what was happening, the flora and fauna were abruptly slammed by massive and shattering concussions; exterminated by sudden belching and churning of gigantic clouds of scorching poisonous gasses; bombarded by sprays of burning lava; and incinerated, instantly vaporized and destroyed forever by the sudden cataclysmic explosion.

(7) All traces of the tropical valley, its plants, and its animals were summarily blown to fiery, molten, and gaseous oblivion. What remained was gradually cooling lava — perhaps some above the ocean's surface, perhaps completely submerged. Who can say? The Secret Squadron decided to keep "The Land That Time Forgot" also "The Land That Humanity Forgot."

ENDNOTES

1 As both scripted and broadcast, this serial adventure exhibited considerable story confusion and blundering. First, its scripts were strangely split into two groups of months that overlapped the same broadcast dates of another serial story! No other Captain Midnight radio scripts are known to have done that. Second, the early broadcasts of this serial placed the volcano in the badlands of New Mexico! Third — and despite the embarrassing contradiction — the volcano's location was fortunately later changed to somewhere in or near South America. Fourth, the story was crudely and brazenly modeled after the Edgar Rice Burroughs *Caprona* or *Caspak* novels — beginning with material in common with Burroughs' first Caprona book entitled *The Land That Time Forgot* — and mixing many different animal species from greatly separated geological epochs, without any kind of explanation. The story was thus oddly clumsy and slipshod — highly uncharacteristic of Robert Burtt's normally skillful, well-researched work. Serious questions have therefore been raised about whether he authored or perhaps only partially authored the adventure. So the present account remedies inconsistencies, as part of forming a more coherent and plausible serial, and with far fewer imitations of the Burroughs novels. See also Appendix 5.

2 Also refer to the Neanderthal named, "Ahm," in Edgar Rice Burroughs' *The Land That Time Forgot*.

3 This is virtually identical to the river that flows through Burroughs' *Caprona* volcanic-crater island.

4 From the 4 January 1949 radio broadcast.

5 And Secret Squadron agents never misspell coded messages?

6 From the 10 January 1949 radio broadcast.

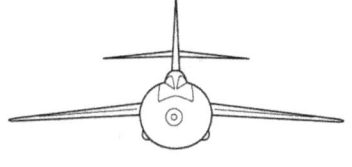

16

The Devil on Ice

(1949)

FLYING SAUCER

Major Steele tells Captain Midnight, Chuck, Joyce, and Ikky of an exotic new aircraft that was sighted flying over the Arctic. The plane seems to be completely safe from all known weapons, and it looks like a bulletproof, shell-proof, whirling ring of light — like a "flying saucer." This craft has been invented and flown by a certain mysterious and brilliant "Professor Khala," who has taken refuge in a secret Arctic base to escape a possible purge in his own country. He continues his experiments at his northern base. In Major Steele's office, Captain Midnight and his agents also meet Lieutenant John Hogarth — a fighter pilot who has seen the plane and has also attempted and failed to destroy it.

The mysterious Professor Khala feels completely safe from attack, even by forces allied with him or those sympathetic to his cause. He may even be recruiting followers, because Captain Midnight learns that a certain group of possibly involved malcontents in Chicago is suddenly and strangely excited and industrious. They are working in a new burst of activity that Midnight believes may be connected with the mysterious flying saucer's appearance. He decides someone should try to infiltrate the group. Joyce Ryan, now in her early twenties, volunteers. Captain Midnight accepts, and outlines an overall plan for her and other members of the Secret Squadron.

TRAPPED ON THE ARCTIC WASTE

In Washington, Major Steele receives a message from secret American Arctic Airbase X-V-1. It tersely reports that Captain Midnight's plane has crashed some distance from the base and that a blizzard is blowing!

Aboard the plane were Captain Midnight, Chuck Ramsay, Joyce Ryan, and Ichabod Mudd. Major Steele immediately tries to contact the Secret Squadron leader by Pocket Locator.

Inside the downed Squadron plane in the frozen Arctic waste, Captain Midnight decodes Major Steele's Pocket Locator message. Midnight answers, reporting the worsening blizzard made the airplane uncontrollable, and he ordered Joyce to parachute out. This was both to maximize her safety and to pursue her important new mission without delay. She bailed out while Midnight, Chuck, and Ikky stayed aboard — risking even greater odds of disaster. But Midnight was at least able to crash-land in the snow without injuries to the three remaining on board. Midnight counted on Joyce's successful landing and on her resourcefulness in soon finding her way to Base X-V-1.

A Secret Squadron member, identified as BJ, sends a coded message to Major Steele from Chicago. The message says it is important that Joyce Ryan come to Chicago immediately, to try to join a group of fanatic fifth columnists and find out what they are planning.

Joyce is unharmed in parachuting down to the frozen Arctic tundra, and she answers a Pocket Locator message from Major Steele, saying she will travel to Chicago to meet BJ as soon as she can. Major Steele then sends a message to Captain Midnight, directing him to stay with the crashed plane and await rescue. The rescue party will also come for Joyce.

Captain Midnight feels the potential threat to America's future is too important for him to remain idle. He answers Major Steele's Pocket Locator message, expressing his determination to abandon the comparative safety of the plane. Before Steele can object, Midnight breaks contact and soon heads out into the snowy tundra with Chuck and Ikky. Eventually, they gradually ascend to an outcropping of icy rock — and pause under it to catch their breath — as Ikky wheezes uncomfortably.

Through an intermediary named Boris, Professor Khala contacts the head of a fifth-column espionage organization. The fifth-column chief is named Harry Hooke, and he lives in a luxurious estate in a posh Chicago suburb. Khala is prepared to assist Hooke's operations with his aircraft, which has so far proven invulnerable to attack.

Before any rescue party can be sent out for them, Captain Midnight, Chuck, and Ikky make their way on the ground to Arctic Airbase X-V-1. Upon arriving, they learn Joyce made it there quite some time before and has already departed for Chicago.

After the snowstorm subsides, Captain Midnight quickly begins an airborne search for the mysterious "flying saucer." The hunt does not take long. Far within the Arctic Circle, he encounters this strange craft. And upon challenging it, and launching all the firepower he can against it, he learns first-hand that the "saucer" craft is indeed absolutely impregnable against all his forms of attack. Following the disturbing encounter, he pursues his possibly remaining lead: Joyce's potential infiltration of Chicago's fifth columnists.

JOYCE RYAN'S MASQUERADE

Carrying out Captain Midnight's concocted plot, Joyce Ryan arrives at Harry Hooke's estate in the outskirts of Chicago. In disguise, and presenting forged credentials and references, she impersonates a Southern girl named Cora Lee Mayfield.

Meanwhile, Professor Khala — the seemingly ruthless inventor of the mysterious flying saucer — has one particular soft spot: he loves exotic predator animals.[1] He very much wants a new keeper for his private zoo; and to Harry Hooke's amazement, the first thing Khala demands in return for the benefits of his invention is to be provided with a competent, obedient, and experienced zookeeper at once!

Joyce — playing the part of the young Southern girl Cora Lee Mayfield — is hired by Harry Hooke. His assistant, a hardboiled woman named Mrs. Magda Kredl, checks up on Joyce's story. In disappointment, she phones to tell Mr. Hooke that Cora Lee's story is true. Unbeknownst to Mrs. Kredl, what has happened is there really is a Cora Lee Mayfield, who does not know that her identity has been assumed by someone else. Joyce cleverly makes herself up to look like the real Cora Lee, and she behaves most skillfully in taking the young woman's place. There is, however, a way Joyce can be discovered: If Mrs. Mayfield — the real Cora Lee's mother — ever sees Joyce face-to-face…Captain Midnight hopes Magda Kredl will not think of that.

While Joyce has been accepted by Mr. Hooke, her freedoms and movements are so restricted that she is in fact a prisoner. Her confinement soon extends to being locked up in a room of Hooke's country home. When this happens, she sends Captain Midnight a Pocket Locator message.

Harry Hooke's personal assistant, Magda Kredl, is sure there is something phony about this Cora Lee Mayfield. So Mrs. Kredl persuades the real Cora Lee's *father* to travel to Chicago to visit Joyce, aka Cora Lee.

From Joyce's messaging, Captain Midnight learns what Mrs. Kredl is up to. When Magda Kredl drives old Mr. Mayfield on the way to Harry Hooke's estate, Captain Midnight has her picked up for speeding and held overnight for attempting to bribe a police officer! The police then take Mr. Mayfield to a small Chicago hotel.

Early the next day, Mr. Mayfield is sitting in the hotel lobby, when a tall broad-shouldered stranger approaches him.

Upon Magda Kredl's release from jail and return to Hooke's estate, she shows Mr. Mayfield in at the residence to see "Cora Lee." Joyce's stomach turns, as Mr. Hooke and Mrs. Kredl watch with anticipation. And then old Mr. Mayfield positively identifies Joyce as his daughter, Cora Lee! Suddenly, it is Magda Kredl who suffers defeat, while Joyce does her best to conceal her relief. Mr. Mayfield goes on to say that Cora Lee's former office supervisor (an undisclosed Captain Midnight, of course) telephoned him and is anxious to get in touch with her. Realizing that somehow Captain Midnight has managed to fix things, Joyce now breathes a visible sigh of relief.

Harry Hooke now more fully accepts Joyce, and he allows her the freedom to drive her "father" back to his hotel and to get some clothing. A half-hour later, Joyce is in Chicago — now ostensibly to get clothes — as she speaks on the telephone with Captain Midnight.

CAPTAIN MIDNIGHT'S MASQUERADE

Exciting events unfold for every active Secret Squadron agent. Chuck Ramsay is called hurriedly to Chicago. He is to fly an atom bomb from there to Arctic Base X-V-1. Ikky patrols in a jet plane over the Arctic Circle — when he meets and tries to follow the flying saucer to its base. However, Ikky must soon turn back because of foul weather. And Captain Midnight learns from Joyce that a mysterious scientist "somewhere in the North" is demanding — of all things — a competent and experienced zookeeper! The next morning, Joyce works in the library of Harry Hooke's house, waiting to talk with Hooke, and thinking of her latest conversation with Midnight.

Captain Midnight — now disguised and pretending to be a soft-spoken zookeeper named Marcus Cooley — visits Harry Hooke's mansion. He hopes to be abducted by Hooke and to be flown to Professor Khala's secret Arctic base. Ikky is determined that the next time the saucer appears, he will follow it, however bad the weather is. Chuck has been assigned the important mission of flying an atom bomb to Base X-V-1. The next morning, Harry Hooke talks with Joyce, alias Cora Lee Mayfield, about handling the seizure of the zookeeper and taking him to Professor Khala's northern base.

CAPTAIN MIDNIGHT'S RADIO EPISODE OF 4 FEBRUARY 1949

The radio transcript of 4 February 1949, below, portrays what happens at this point in "The Devil on Ice" adventure. It also describes Professor Khala's disintegration rays.

ANNOUNCER *[Pierre Andre]*: This is your last chance! Yes, this is your last chance to join the new 1949 Secret Squadron. This is the last day I can tell you about it. Supplies are almost gone, and *so* many fellows and girls are sending in, we must close this offer at midnight Sunday. So send in tonight, or tomorrow for sure. And now, on with the action packed adventure, "The Devil on Ice," with Captain Midnight and the Secret Squadron.

ANNOUNCER *(continuing):* Yesterday, Captain Midnight — disguising himself as a white-haired, black-browed old man, called Marcus Cooley chuckles and says:

CAPTAIN MIDNIGHT: Heh, heh, if Joyce didn't know I was coming to call on Hooke, she'd never recognize me. That'd be a fine test of this disguise of mine.

ANNOUNCER: And Hooke, the subtle evil-minded chief of a gang of fifth columnists, thinks of another test that he will put Joyce to. He will arrange for Joyce to meet the so-called "Marcus Cooley" unexpectedly in his study. He will watch the meeting from a hidden alcove.

ANNOUNCER: Meanwhile, at a heavily guarded atomic plant, Chuck Ramsay is saying goodbye to Major Steele, who's flown down from Washington to be sure that Chuck realizes the tremendous importance of his assignment. Listen, as Major Steele says:

MAJOR BARRY STEELE: Chuck, I'm only going to say one more thing — beginning to think I'm an awful old fussbudget.

CHUCK RAMSAY: Well, Major, your neck is out a mile. You can say anything you want to, sir. You've certainly earned the right.

MAJOR BARRY STEELE: Thanks, Chuck. In that plane of yours is the most tremendous secret yet discovered by mankind. The most heavily guarded super-secret in the world. As far is America is concerned, it may mean for her either life or death.

CHUCK RAMSAY: I know that, sir.

MAJOR BARRY STEELE: In case of any unforeseen accident, you — know what your orders are, don't you?

CHUCK RAMSAY: Blow the ship up immediately, sir. Everything is set so I can do it in a flash.

MAJOR BARRY STEELE: Good. Goodbye, Chuck, and good luck.

ANNOUNCER: Chuck grips Major Steele's hand and then turns, and as he does so, he thinks to himself:

CHUCK RAMSAY'S THOUGHTS *(via filter microphone):* If there's any danger of a slipup, I'll destroy that plane if it means destroying myself, too.

ANNOUNCER: And back in Chicago, Captain Midnight — disguised as a white-haired, vigorous old man with a heavy accent — is just ringing the bell to the front door of Hooke's country home. *(pause)* An elder butler, George, opens the door.

CAPTAIN MIDNIGHT: I have an appointment with Mr. Hooke.

GEORGE: Your name, please?

CAPTAIN MIDNIGHT: Marcus Cooley.

GEORGE: Oh, yes, Mr. Hooke is expecting you. Come in.

MRS. MAGDA KREDL: *(coming on)* Who is it, George?

GEORGE: Someone to see Mr. Hooke.

MRS. MAGDA KREDL: Who is it? What does he want?

GEORGE: It is a private matter, Mrs. Kredl.

MRS. MAGDA KREDL: Oh, don't be absurd, George. Not for me, I'm sure.

GEORGE: I have the strictest orders that no one — I'm afraid that included you, Mrs. Kredl — was to see or talk to, uh — to Mr. Hooke's visitor.

MRS. MAGDA KREDL: Oh, what nonsense! George, are you deliberately standing in front of that man so I can't see him?

GEORGE: Yes, Mrs. Kredl, those were my orders.

MRS. MAGDA KREDL: Did Mr. Hooke mention me by name?

GEORGE: No, Mrs. Kredl.

MRS. MAGDA KREDL: Oh. Then he must have meant Cora Lee. Well, never mind, I'll ask Mr. Hooke myself what this is all about. Co — Cora Lee wants not to see this man.

SFX: *Footsteps fading. Two footstep sets coming on.*

GEORGE: This way, sir. Mr. Hooke will see you in his private study.

ANNOUNCER: And as George leads the way, Captain Midnight's brilliant brain is working furiously. He thinks:

CAPTAIN MIDNIGHT'S THOUGHTS *(via filter microphone):* Now — what did that mean? Why shouldn't Hooke want Cora Lee to see me? He's suspicious.

ANNOUNCER: As George opens the door to Hooke's study, he says:

GEORGE: Mr. Hooke will be with you shortly, sir. Will you take *this* chair?

ANNOUNCER: As Captain Midnight sits down, he thinks:

CAPTAIN MIDNIGHT'S THOUGHTS *(via filter microphone):* "Will you take *this* chair?" This chair is right under a strong light. I'm going to look for some hidden peephole or alcove or something.

ANNOUNCER: Slowly, Captain Midnight lets his eyes drift around the room. Then he thinks:

CAPTAIN MIDNIGHT'S THOUGHTS *(via filter microphone):* That heavy drape. That looks as if it covers a small doorway. I'll bet Hooke is behind it, watching me. I've got to figure this out. Why didn't he want Joyce to see me when I came in? Think, Midnight, think fast! Ah — I've got it! He wants to see the meeting between Joyce and myself — and, Holy Smokes, I'm disguised! She may not recognize me. I was boasting to myself only a few moments ago that she wouldn't recognize me. If I don't act fast, she may come bursting in here and not know who I am!

ANNOUNCER: Meanwhile, far within the Arctic Circle, Professor Khala talks to a man obviously of some importance who has flown in from his country.

PROFESOR KHALA: Yes, in a week — less, perhaps — my plane, so lightly called the "Flying Saucer," will not only be completely safe from any known weapons — but *armed* with any known weapons, it will be able to attack and shoot down its adversaries.

FOREIGN VIP: You have at last found a way to shoot them with the disintegrating ray?

PROFESOR KHALA: Better, still. I have found a way to drop bombs through the protective shield of my disintegrating rays. Can you imagine what that means?

FOREIGN VIP: Yes, yes!

PROFESOR KHALA: I could take a bomb load over any city in the world — Washington, if need be!

FOREIGN VIP: Yes, Washington, if need be.

PROFESOR KHALA: And all the might of the American air fleets, *combined*, could not harm one bolt in my plane. They would be helpless, while I slowly cruise around, wiping it off the map!

FOREIGN VIP: And now, it is essential that you return home. Honors beyond your imagination would be heaped on you. Riches, anything you want. I swear it. Our chief swears it!

PROFESOR KHALA: And of course, the commander of the firing squad that liquidated my friends — my fellow scientists — he swears it, too, no?

FOREIGN VIP: Oh, who have you invented this weapon for — our country — or yourself?

PROFESOR KHALA: Ha, ha! That is the question you should have asked me long ago! The answer is the answer to all your hopes and fears.

FOREIGN VIP: I have asked it, now. Tell me.

PROFESOR KHALA: I have invented it for my country *and* myself.

FOREIGN VIP: But — but, what are you going to do with it?

PROFESOR KHALA: First, I am going to destroy the air fleets of America. Then, if that has not brought this rich and boastful country to its knees, I will pulverize Washington till it is a heap of rubble!

FOREIGN VIP: But for that you will need bombs, and yet more bombs.

PROFESOR KHALA: And for that, you will *provide* me with bombs and yet more bombs!

FOREIGN VIP: Only on our terms.

PROFESOR KHALA: Only on my terms!

FOREIGN VIP: This is treason!

PROFESOR KHALA: I plan for our country well ruled. World dominion. That's treason? Or haven't you have it in your guts? Heh, heh, heh. And you had better decide to throw in your lot with mine. Look, this is the edge of science! Men of science should rule the destiny they have created.

FOREIGN VIP: When the world is rocked by the news — Washington a shambles — I will throw in my lot with yours.

PROFESOR KHALA: Then you had better make your plans quickly. For that day will not be long delayed.

FOREIGN VIP: Tell me, Khala, is your Flying Saucer safe from every form of attack?

PROFESOR KHALA *(slyly):* What form of attack are you thinking of?

FOREIGN VIP: An atomic weapon. You must not forget that the accursed Americans have that. And they alone have it — so far.

PROFESOR KHALA: Because they alone have it, I cannot test my plane against its deadly force. That question I cannot answer, because — the answer is one I do not know. It is the one thing I am afraid of.

FOREIGN VIP: It is the one thing that we are all afraid of! It is the one thing that holds us back.

ANNOUNCER: While Khala dreams his evil dream of world dominion, and seems to be so close to achieving it, the Secret Squadron works desperately to circumvent him. It is now an hour later, and Khala is taking the very important person from this country on a short flight — to show him the wonders of the so-called, "Flying Saucer."

SFX: *Furious winds.*

ANNOUNCER: A storm is coming up. Suddenly, the very important person says:

FOREIGN VIP: Khala! A plane much faster than ours is following us!

PROFESOR KHALA: Ha, ha, ha! It will turn back soon, don't worry. It is not storm-proof, blizzard-proof like my plane. This weather will force it to return to its base.

FOREIGN VIP: Do you know, I suppose? But it seems to be sticking very doggedly on our trail.

PROFESOR KHALA: So let it. Its end, then, is certain. A quick crash in the frozen tundra — and obliteration!

ANNOUNCER: Well! Who is in the plane that's following Professor Khala? Is it Ikky, who has sworn blizzard or no blizzard to track the flying saucer to its base? And will it mean for him a quick crash and obliteration? What of Chuck? Has he reached Base X-V-1 safely with the atom bomb? And has Captain Midnight found a way to warn Joyce? Don't miss Monday's thrill packed adventure, "The Secret Signal!"

It is indeed Ikky who is "sticking very doggedly on *[Khala's]* trail."
Later on, with Joyce's help, Captain Midnight allows himself to be drugged at Harry Hooke's mansion. This is because he is sure of being flown to the secret base from which the flying saucer operates. Chuck — flying a new B-47 jet bomber towards the Arctic Circle and carrying a tactical-size atom bomb to Base X-V-1 — is not heard from. Ikky, having followed the flying saucer into a raging blizzard with his F-86, is forced to crash-land near the very base that Captain Midnight thinks is all-important to discover! Even as Ikky's plane careens earthward, he sings at the top of his voice in sheer bravado. After his forced landing, and without suffering injury, Ikky carefully disguises himself and treks off toward the base.

Joyce Ryan (aka Cora Lee Mayfield) flies Harry Hooke and Captain Midnight (aka Marcus Cooley and now recovering consciousness) to a rendezvous with Professor Khala. When approaching Khala's icy landing strip, Joyce silently decides she will deliberately crack up the plane upon landing. In an effort to force Professor Khala's hand, she judges that if he is given the choice of leaving her far in the wilds of Canada — to die of cold and starvation — or taking her back with him to his secret base, he will choose the latter alternative. A few seconds later, when Joyce's plane begins to settle on the ice, she subtly executes a maneuver that causes the plane to slide broadside. The plane slides and smashes into a

Boeing B-47 bomber. PHOTOGRAPH: NATIONAL MUSEUM OF THE USAF

structure, with just enough impact to damage the craft so as to require repairs before it can be flown again. Joyce is indeed a resourceful and plucky young woman!

FLYING SAUCER REVEALED

Captain Midnight understands what Joyce's scheme must be. Hooke, Joyce, and Midnight exit the damaged aircraft, and are finally introduced to the sinister Professor Khala — the Squadron agents as Cora Lee Mayfield and Marcus Cooley.

In a nearby open hangar, Captain Midnight sees for the first time what the "flying saucer" is. It appears to be of an advanced airfoil design — but still only a jet and rocket-powered plane with conventional wings and tail structures. The craft's sleek profile might be interpreted to look saucer-like, but Midnight soon learns the side-view is not the fundamental secret of the plane's illusion while flying.

Professor Khala wants to show off his brilliant invention, and so he takes Harry Hooke, "Cora Lee" and "Marcus Cooley" up for a brief flight. Captain Midnight now gets to learn how this plane works.

Khala's plane is not a fast aircraft, and it usually operates as a *conventional jet plane when not using energy shielding.* Activating the energy shield creates a surrounding, rather flattened bubble of protective energy around the craft.

When flying in the energy-shielded mode, though, there are a couple of disadvantages: First, molecules and atoms of air are dispersed around the plane, and the airfoil can no longer keep the plane aloft. So switching to rocket power is necessary, with multidirectional nozzles whose thrusts keep the plane up and moving through the skies, by action-reaction propulsion alone. Second, rocket fuel is too limited to fly in energy-shielded mode continuously, even though the plane's power-generating apparatus can deliver continuous power for the energy bubble. While a side-view of the craft can be somewhat deceptive, it is primarily the energy aura that makes the plane appear from the *outside* as saucer-shaped, and only in the energy-shielded mode.

A very potent on-board energy source is required to generate such a great amount of power for the protective ray aura, and Khala's craft does contain such a powerful generator: a compact, sealed nuclear reactor. As Midnight learns these things, he realizes how much he would like to overpower Professor Khala right now on the plane. But he restrains himself. He doesn't dare risk it during this flight, because so many unknown things could go wrong — including perhaps destroying the unfamiliar craft and all of them along with it. So he has to accept that too much is at stake, and bides his time as the simple and soft-spoken animal keeper, Marcus Cooley.

PROFESSOR KHALA'S DISINTEGRATION RAY TECHNOLOGY

In Captain Midnight's earlier "Ray of Revenge" adventure of late 1945 to early 1946: One disintegration ray tower was blown up by the crash of Ivan Shark's "rocket plane" on a plateau in Bhutan. The other tower was situated on a high Zanskar mountain peak in Northern India, until Captain Midnight had flown his amphibian into the tower and toppled it deep into a mountain gorge, and had bailed out to save himself before the crash. That collapsed tower had contained an atomic-powered particle-beam weapon that was capable of transmitting its destructive energy over vast intercontinental distances.

Only three parties knew of the spot where the Zanskar, Indian tower weapon had fallen: (1) Ivan Shark and his chief lieutenants; (2) ex-Nazi scientist Manfred Mueller; and (3) Captain Midnight and four of his Secret Squadron agents — i.e., Chuck Ramsay, Joyce Ryan, Ichabod Mudd, and Harry Sykes.

As with the Zanskar rays, Professor Khala also has a particle-beam

Professor Khala's mystery aircraft can look somewhat like a saucer from the side. But during the energy-shielded mode, it can also project a rather flattened aura of energy around itself that makes it appear saucer-shaped from any angle. In reality the plane is a conventional, combination jet and rocket aircraft. It is usually propelled by jets, and by adjustable-attitude rockets only in energy-shielded mode. PHOTOGRAPH: LEONARD ZANE

ray apparatus that requires atomic power for the enormous disintegration energy it emanates. The name "Khala" is also a fitting one. It originates from Tibet and is Sanskrit for "ferocious."[2] So Professor Khala might come from a Soviet-block satellite nation of Tajikistan or Kyrgyzstan, for example, with each not far from Northern India and Tibet.

Tesla Globe or Dome or Shield. As mentioned earlier in the "Ray of Revenge" adventure: Nikola Tesla's electromagnetic disintegration-ray concepts had been published in 1937 and 1940. Such concepts included purported protection of an object or craft by a particle-beam ray shield known as a "Tesla Globe" or hemispherical "Tesla Dome" or "Tesla Shield."[3]

Professor Khala has evidently found a way to convert Manfred Mueller's long-range particle beam weapon — or at least its type of technology — into a self-contained Tesla Shield. But if Khala also has the necessary, on-board nuclear reactor to power the Shield, why doesn't he also have an atomic bomb? The indication is that while utilizing atomic energy, Khala has not developed the technology for an explosive device.

Perhaps more interestingly, Professor Khala may have in fact recovered Manfred Mueller's actual weapon that was nuclear-powered. And Mueller could have sealed and booby-trapped the atomic reactor from opening by anyone who did not possess the secret of safely opening it that he alone knew. So Khala would thus not have mastered nuclear fission technology, at all. He would not be able to create an atomic bomb to test his plane's ray-shield and shock-absorption capabilities against such enormous energy.

PROFESSOR KHALA'S ARCTIC BASE

Professor Khala lands his exotic aircraft and welcomes his "guests" Harry Hooke, Captain Midnight (alias Marcus Cooley), and Joyce Ryan (alias Cora Lee Mayfield) into one of his base living facilities. He introduces them to his wife, Sara, who seems rather youthful and also looks somewhat familiar to Captain Midnight. Khala then gives "Marcus Cooley" a first glance at various penned and ferocious animals in his private zoo. Of course, the three visitors are actually Khala's prisoners, under guard by his henchmen. He can always determine the fate of any or all of them at his whim.

Inside a lavish drawing room at his Arctic base, Professor Khala decides to exercise what proves to be his fiendish sense of humor. He announces that Cora Lee Mayfield and Harry Hooke shall play chess. Whoever wins shall stay at the base. The other shall be killed! Khala then exits the facility, to return once more to the skies in his mysterious aircraft — perhaps for another rendezvous with the Foreign VIP, or with some other insidious agent.

PLOT TANGLES

A surprise is in store for the Secret Squadron. Neither Joyce nor Captain Midnight knows that Khala's men have captured Ikky. He is also now a *formally* designated prisoner at the base, who is being held incommunicado until the professor comes back. Several hours later, the so-called "flying saucer" safely returns to the base, and Professor Khala and Sara enjoy a cozy fireside chat.

Even though they are shut up in Professor Khala's secret Arctic base, things soon begin to look surprisingly favorable for members of the Secret Squadron. The disguised Ikky has been introduced to the other disguised Secret Squadron agents and has secretly identified himself. Moreover, Joyce seems to receive Sara Khala's approval and encouragement. And Sara follows "Cora Lee's" urging to save Harry Hooke (whom Joyce has defeated at chess), and intervenes with the professor. Captain Midnight is also now in the good graces of the professor himself! But then, Madame

Khala suddenly seems to sense something. Something that she keeps to herself, for the time being...

Captain Midnight continues plotting an atomic bomb attack on Professor Khala's secret airbase. But he first has to determine the exact location. He also has to be quite sure that when the atom bomb is dropped on the base — that it works not only on the base, but on the flying saucer and the professor as well. He cannot take a chance of a slipup, so he proceeds slowly.

Professor Khala doesn't yet know that events may make it possible for America to learn the exact location of his airbase and destroy it. Nor does he know that three of America's most brilliant secret agents are themselves prisoners at his base! Nor does he know one more thing: that two of his own personnel are scheming to kill him! In a whispered conversation with Harry Hooke, Joyce is the first to get an inkling of the assassination plot.

Secret Squadron Headquarters receives orders that to avoid an international incident, only a member of the Secret Squadron is to drop the atom bomb on Professor Khala's hidden base. Chuck Ramsay is now the only Secret Squadron member at Base X-V-1, so he learns that when the time comes to drop the bomb, he would have to be the one to do it. He knows that Captain Midnight and Joyce are probably prisoners at Khala's base, and perhaps even Ikky. He confers anxiously about this by shortwave radio with Major Steele in Washington.

FOREIGN STRIKE

The dictator of a certain powerful nation (an unnamed Joseph Stalin of the USSR) sends a mighty fleet of bombing planes winging across the Atlantic. Acting on information supplied by the previously seen "Foreign VIP," their mission is to wipe out the secret base where Professor Khala is working on the world's latest and extremely ominous invention — his so-called "flying saucer." Because this invention will make Khala master of the skies over *any* country, the dictator is rightly anxious. He fears that Professor Khala intends to use the awesome craft to seize power over the nation that the dictator himself has wielded for so long.

Captain Midnight, Joyce, and Ikky remain prisoners at the secret base. Professor Khala's private quarters and other key buildings are surrounded by his protective disintegrating rays. But the question is, will the facilities stand up under the enormous weight of bombs sent against them? And in Captain Midnight's mind, is he safe in his own quarters at the zoo, even though shielded by the rays? Not only that, where are Joyce and Ikky at this moment?

An unpredictable whim of Professor Khala's seems to save Joyce, Ikky, and "Mack" (Captain Midnight, aka Marcus Cooley) from certain death. But Professor Khala has decided to leave Harry Hooke and some of his disloyal men *unprotected*, confining them in a security building outside his protective ray shield.

The foreign bombers soon strike, and huge bombs rain down relentlessly on and on! As the massive attack rages on the professor's base, Madame Khala suspects this raid might be only a prelude to one by an American air fleet carrying the atom bomb! She convinces the professor that the risks are too high, and to take off for parts undisclosed. The two soon hurry down a long passageway leading to Khala's private hangar. This private hangar is, of course, one of the most important buildings protected by the disintegrating ray.

ATOMIC WEAPON

Major Steele is suddenly called back to Washington and ordered not to use the atom bomb that Chuck has flown to Base X-V-1. This change of orders is due to a message received from a certain country (the USSR). The communication identifies the location of Professor Khala's base and states that an attack has been carried out. The message explains that the purpose of the attack was "to wipe out a menace to world peace," and that the attack has been successful! Actually, the commander of the foreign country's air fleet did not dare admit even partial failure.

Immediately after the foreign bombers had departed, Professor Khala and Sara had also left in their invulnerable craft with the disintegrating apparatus. And at the surviving facilities of the now-abandoned base, Joyce and Ikky stock up with various supplies. While they do this, Captain Midnight searches the rest of the complex for other items of potential value or interest. Upon examining Professor Khala's study, Midnight finds a map of Canada, which shows markings in a Saskatchewan area. Taking the map, Midnight rejoins his colleagues.

After packing their provisions and outfitting themselves in the finest Arctic wear, the three Secret Squadron agents step out into the tundra. Captain Midnight hopes the one atom bomb the Secret Squadron has been allowed will not be wasted on the abandoned base. So the first thing he and his comrades do is write a huge message in the snow that reads:

BASE DESERTED TRY ORDINARY BOMBS FIRST

Captain Midnight and his two agents then head away from the base as fast as they can.

An American reconnaissance plane from Arctic Base X-V-1 flies low over Professor Khala's secret base, as had been identified by the foreign country's communiqué. The plane photographs both the devastated and curiously undamaged structures, with an unscathed one being an aircraft hangar. The plane also flies above the message written in the snow, and turns back for Arctic Base X-V-1.

As Captain Midnight, Ikky and Joyce head in the direction of faraway Arctic Base X-V-1, the Secret Squadron leader soberly weighs hopes of reaching it. But at least the weather is presently clear. It is then that they spot the low-flying U.S. reconnaissance plane, and Joyce flashes at it urgently with a signal mirror.

The three Secret Squadron agents are soon rescued and taken to Base X-V-1. There, they reunite with Chuck, who had flown the atomic bomb there in his B-47. This bomb is a much smaller, tactical-type than the large strategic ones that were used to destroy huge areas of Hiroshima and Nagasaki in Japan.

At Base X-V-1, Captain Midnight radios Major Steele that the atom bomb is the only remaining weapon that might possibly overcome Professor Khala's disintegrating ray. And although the professor has fled, Midnight thinks he might have a clue to his destination. Captain Midnight also requests Steele's permission for the four Squadron agents to fly the B-47 and its atom bomb to Toronto. This is questioned by Major Steele, because the B-47 is designed for a crew of three. But Midnight assures the Major that young Chuck and Joyce can squeeze into the navigator's nose compartment, so Steele consents.

American warplanes soon drop conventional bombs on Professor Khala's secret Arctic airbase, destroying all the remaining buildings after the foreign country's mostly failed attack. But the professor has fled to another hideout that he had previously built in the wilds of Northern Canada, "just in case."

Now at his new northern retreat, Professor Khala promises Sara that within a week he will bomb Fort Knox and destroy the United States gold supply![4] Khala also sends a message to the dictator of the nation that first bombed his Arctic Circle base. He warns the dictator that his next move — after a certain spectacular coup — will be a trip back to the country to exact his revenge!

After delivering the atom bomb to Toronto, Captain Midnight and his three chief agents board an express train for Saskatchewan.

Professor Khala has been waiting for a snowstorm. He knows that a blizzard, which will ground any other plane, doesn't affect the flying ability of his "flying saucer." He wants to carry out a bombing test during the next turn of foul weather — or possibly even sooner, if his patience runs out.

It is early morning in southeastern Saskatchewan, as Captain Midnight and his three chief agents arrive in their train at the Calder rail station. Midnight stares out the window, deep in thought. Although not yet certain, the Secret Squadron leader believes they may have tracked down Professor Khala's hideout at a lake in this northern Canadian locale.

Some two hours after reaching Calder, the four Secret Squadron members creep through snow-laden undergrowth that borders a lake. It is the lake at which Professor Khala's suspected cottage hideout is purportedly built.

Captain Midnight receives a Pocket Locator message from Major Steele. The message warns that permission to use the atom bomb will be canceled at nine o'clock the following morning. Midnight turns to his colleagues, and in a low voice, says they must immediately confirm whether or not this is truly Professor Khala's hideout.

Captain Midnight and his Secret Squadron comrades discover a camouflaged, lakeside hangar that houses Professor Khala's remarkable aircraft. From Joyce's very risky eavesdropping, they also learn the professor has something terrible and dramatic planned for the next day! Following these discoveries, they stealthily retreat back to Calder.

In Calder, Captain Midnight radios Major Steele. He requests that Steele send a supersonic fighter-bomber to Toronto and also meet him and his three agents there. Major Steele acknowledges the request, saying simply that the code directive is "ZERO HOUR."

Captain Midnight's request is not an easy one to fill. The 1949 B-47 jet bomber's top speed is only a little over 600 mph, and even the F-86 fighter can do only 685 mph. The only choice is again the "Silver Dart" model of the Douglas Skyrocket plane that Midnight had flown against Ito Gobi's supersonic jet in South America, and the Douglas plane is barely big enough to carry even the tactical-size atomic bomb.

Major Steele flies the Dart/Skyrocket to Toronto — where he, Captain Midnight, Chuck, Joyce, and Ikky meet at the airport. The atom bomb is loaded onto the supersonic craft, and everything is ready for Midnight to take off at the appointed Zero Hour. Steele, Chuck, Joyce, and Ikky will follow in Chuck's B-47 (with the two youthful agents once more squeezed in). They will try to witness the outcome of this ultra-deadly battle, and to be available to offer any possible aid.

The 1949 Key-O-Matic Code-O-Graph features two symbolic atom bombs, as shown in the detailed photo below. Note also the photograph of the U.S. "Fat Man"-type atomic bomb, dropped on Nagasaki, on 9 August 1945. The Fat Man had a blast yield equal to 21,000 tons of TNT.

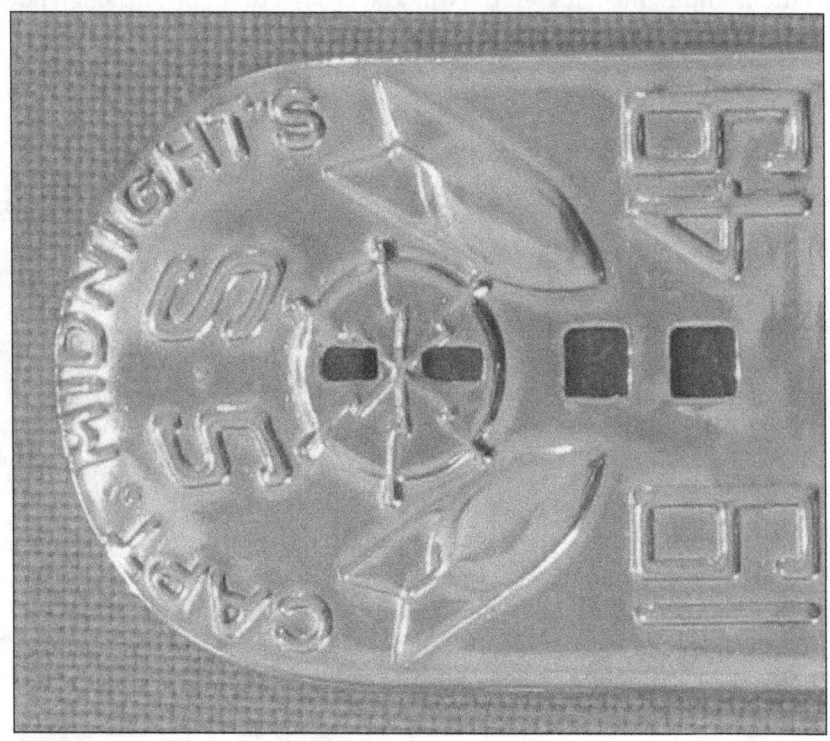

Above: 1949 Code-O-Graph detail with bombs. *Left:* U.S. "Fat Man"-type atomic bomb dropped on Nagasaki, Japan on 9 August 1945.
PHOTOGRAPHS: LEONARD ZANE, NNSA

FINAL ENCOUNTER

Captain Midnight flies away from civilization, over the desolate Arctic waste, with the Secret Squadron's B-47 lagging far behind. When Midnight reaches the remote Saskatchewan hideout, he at last drops the atom bomb on Professor Khala's hitherto invulnerable plane!

Despite its protective ray shielding, Professor Khala's plane is utterly destroyed by the atomic blast, and the professor along with it!

After taking this awesome step, Captain Midnight reflects on an ancient Hindu scripture: "Now I am become Death, the destroyer of worlds." And he reminds himself what Professor Khala would have become.

PROFESSOR KHALA'S IDENTITY

The oldest etymology of the word "Khala" comes from Sanskrit, meaning "Ferocious." From this, it can be deduced that Professor Khala's roots reflect the Middle East, or perhaps a Middle Eastern or Russian satellite nation such as Tajikistan or Kyrgyzstan. Who was Professor Khala, really? What was his background? Where did he come from? More specifically, might he perhaps have come from anywhere near India's "Bartestan?"

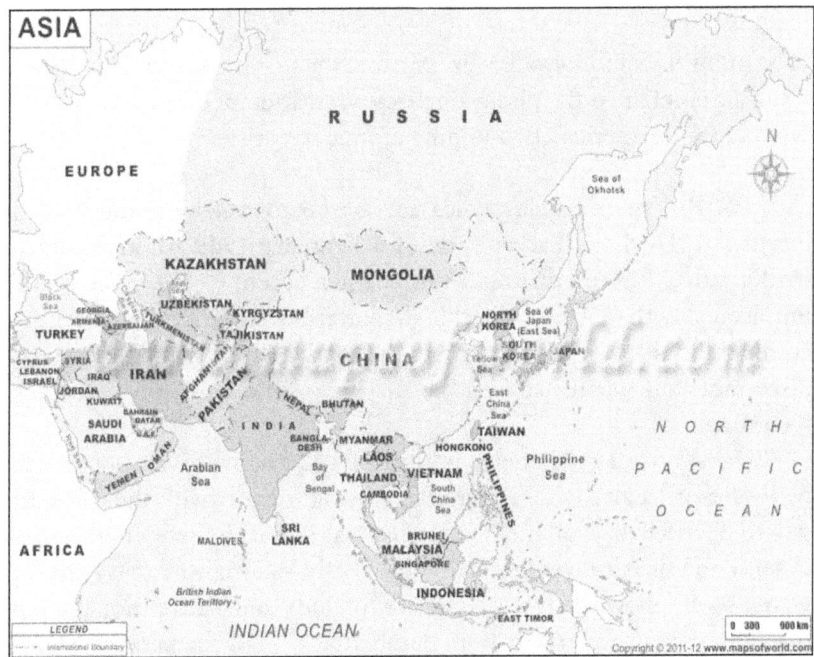

Asia map. PHOTOGRAPH: MAPXL COMPARE INFOBASE LIMITED

POINTS TO CONSIDER

First: How would Professor Khala have known where to recover Manfred Mueller's lost disintegration weapon (from the "Ray of Revenge" adventure)? Only Ivan Shark's gang members who were present at the time — and Manfred Mueller, himself, and the Secret Squadron — knew the precise location of the chasm where the weapon had fallen.

Second: Manfred Mueller was last known to be in Ivan Shark's "rocket plane" over Bhutan, and he presumably bailed out. It would seem he would have been Professor Khala's and/or Ivan Shark's first and perhaps only choice to adapt the particle-beam apparatus into the disintegrating weapon and shield for Professor Khala's combination jet airplane and rocket craft.

Third: In "The Return of Ivan Shark" adventure during January of 1949, the master criminal made a significant remark. He said that "after gaining control of a kingdom," he had in mind "a fantastic secret weapon" with which he could "terrify the civilized world into submission."

Fourth: Atomic energy was necessary for Professor Khala's power supply and disintegrating rays, and in early January 1949, Ivan Shark was planning to capture two leading American atomic scientists. Recall that in the 10 January 1949 radio episode of "The Return of Ivan Shark," a Secret Squadron Lieutenant remarked to Major Steele:

> LIEUTENANT: Do you realize, sir, that the first message asking for an amphibian — the phony one — was an attempt on Shark's part to capture America's two leading atomic scientists?

Fifth: Professor Khala's voice can be heard on the audio recording of the "Devil on Ice" episode of 4 February 1949. Though tinged with a rather Eastern-European or Russian accent — the voice is still unmistakably that of Ivan Shark! No matter how Shark tries, he cannot completely disguise his extremely distinctive voice, which is clearly discernible and identifiable in the surviving "The Devil on Ice" audio recording.

Sixth: Who was the rather youthful "Sara Khala," who was supposed to be Professor Khala's wife? After at first being friendly with the three disguised Secret Squadron members, what was it that she suddenly seemed to sense and then keep to herself? Why was she so insightful that America would soon follow the foreign power's "prelude" of a conventional weapons raid with an American atom bomb attack? Had she penetrated one or more of the Secret Squadron agents' disguises, and so decided that she and the "professor" should make a run for it and "take off for parts undisclosed"?

Seventh: Who is the man shown on page 3 of the 1949 Secret Squadron Manual — seen between Fury and Gardo — who bears a resemblance to Ivan Shark in the same picture? Is this mysterious man Ivan Shark disguised as Professor Khala?

Was Professor Khala therefore really Ivan Shark in disguise? Was his revolutionary aircraft Shark's last bid to take over a very powerful foreign nation — so he could then use its resources and his invincible aircraft to subdue every country, and thus at last achieve his grandiose dream of "world dominion?" Even Khala himself proclaimed those very words in the 4 February 1949 episode:

"I plan for our country well ruled. World dominion."

Was Sara Khala actually Fury Shark, and were both she and her father disguised beyond visual recognition? A good deal of evidence points to these conclusions.[5] If true, when Professor Khala was destroyed by the atom bomb, so did Ivan Shark finally meet his end. If "Sara" was with "Professor Khala" — as she so often was — her end came as well.

CAPTAIN MIDNIGHT AND HIS SECRET SQUADRON'S DESTINY

What about Captain Midnight, his commanding officer, and the active agents of the Secret Squadron? What happened to Major Barry Steele, to Chuck Ramsay, to Joyce Ryan, to Ichabod Mudd, and to other active agents? Did the adventures of radio's Captain Midnight simply fade into oblivion? The present writer has worked to continue and revitalize the saga of radio's Captain Midnight and his Secret Squadron, via the original screenplay described in the final chapter of this book

ENDNOTES

1 As does someone else we know.

2 Refer to Internet sites such as vedabase.net for a translation of "Khala."

3 Captain Midnight's author, Robert M. Burtt, had apparently investigated disintegration-ray concepts of the time — again doing his research.

4   This of course is long before the James Bond *Goldfinger* story, and so is another Robert Burtt prophecy.

5   This may even indicate that Shark's *real name* could have been Khala. This would also fit his apparently Eurasian roots, and perhaps even suggest that his true first name could have been Ivan.

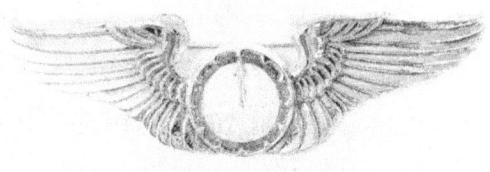

17

The Return of Captain Midnight

A VISIONARY SAGA

The 1940 to 1949 years saw radio's Captain Midnight journey through World War II, and progress from piston-engine planes to jets to jet/rocket aircraft. The exciting radio program also explored thrills of science fiction, archaeology, and paleontology — all the while portraying role models of moral strength, courage, and optimism for youths and adults alike. Captain Midnight embodied a nobility and adventurous spirit that became too scarce in later decades. There's every reason to recover that inspiration, to nurture it now and in the future.

FEATURE FILM PORTRAYAL

The Return of Captain Midnight is Leonard Zane's original screenplay, as described below.

> CAPTAIN MIDNIGHT: World War II flying ace and commander of the Secret Squadron counterespionage group.
> IVAN SHARK: 1940s evil mastermind and espionage leader.
> LOREN RAMSAY: Present-day pilot and adventurer who flies top-secret aircraft.
> ARTIS MATTHEWS: African-American tech and colleague of Loren Ramsay.

ALONSO SCHRECKER: Sinister Brazilian industrialist and Nazi-heir, "Conda," in the present day.

CARLA SAYAO: Brazilian descendant of Ivan Shark, and Conda's cohort.

SYNOPSIS: Captain Midnight saves America's Pacific Fleet in World War II. He continues his airborne counterespionage work until his mysterious disappearance over Brazil in 1970. **Action leaps to the present day,** where young Loren Ramsay matches wits in air and ground contests against Nazi-heir, Conda, who aims to take over Brazil's timber industry and deforestation. Thrills and chills abound, as Loren leaves the USAF for private adventure and high-tech discoveries with hypersonic aircraft. What is the purpose of the sunken, hexagonal pyramid in the depths of the Brazilian jungle? What happened to Captain Midnight? Will Loren and his team survive attacks by some of the most dangerous people on earth? Climb aboard, join in the adventure — and happy landings!

WRITER-PRODUCER, LEONARD ZANE created material produced in *Star Trek® III, IV,* and *The Next Generation.* He is screenwriter of *Concerto* (an epic on the life of composer Sergei Rachmaninoff), *The Greatest Gamble* (the last Raymond Chandler/Philip Marlowe story), *Black Panther®* (co-written with Donald Cook), *Intraverse* (adapted from Zane's novel), and *Only The Super-Rich Can Save Us!* (adapted from Ralph Nader's 2009 novel). In 2000, Zane adapted and produced Edmond Hamilton's classic *The Inn Outside The World.* He also produces and hosts television programs on social issues, and is represented by Character Talent & Associates: *Mark@CTATalent.com.*

Leonard Zane. PHOTO: JIM HARMON

Opposite page: Captain Midnight's P-38 nearing Howland Island; Unnamed General, Major Steele, Captain Midnight; Captain Midnight's XP-51 in December 1941. PHOTOGRAPHS: LEONARD ZANE

Top: Northrop YB-49 Flying Wing in 1948. *Bottom:* Captain Midnight's current mystery craft. PHOTOGRAPHS: NORTHROP CORPORATION, ADRIAN MANN VIA BILL SWEETMAN, WITH SECRET SQUADRON INSIGNIA BY LEONARD ZANE

APPENDIX 1

Robert M. Burtt and Jim Harmon

ROBERT MORRIS BURTT

Beginning shortly after Charles A. Lindbergh flew over the Atlantic, and continuing for twenty years, Robert Morris Burtt regaled America's radio listeners, young and old, with thrilling tales of adventure in the skies. Air heroes like Jimmie Allen, Captain Midnight, and Sky King kept millions glued to their radios from coast to coast in the United States and even in Australia. Many World War II pilots testified these exciting air serials first awakened their interest in flying.

Like the characters he created, Burtt lived an exciting and dangerous life. He spent six boyhood years with his missionary family in the interior of China, where he became fluent in the native language, and where he and his family were captured for a time by bandits. Later in France, he learned to fly and graduated as a fighter pilot. He fought in WWI with the 28th Pursuit Squadron of the famous 3rd Pursuit Group, whose top officers came from the Lafayette Escadrille. Shot down by a German plane fifty kilometers behind the German lines, he escaped to safety. And he was again shot down after dog-fighting over German lines, escaping only after feigning death in a shell hole.

Following the war, Burtt worked his way through Columbia University by giving aerobatic exhibitions at state and county fairs throughout North America. At Columbia, he held the javelin record and also played varsity football. After airplane barnstorming and working in over thirty jobs, he became western sales manager of Curtiss-Wright Flying Service. Confessing to the president that he really wanted to be a writer, he got an involuntary career boost. After the 1929 stock market crash, Burtt received a telegram: "Now you're a writer. The company is broke and you're fired."

Bob Burtt's love of dogs dated from the day in China, when a pet mongrel saved him from drowning in the turbulent waters of the Si Kiang River. While writing his radio serials, he also raised and trained

Robert Burtt in January, 1962. PHOTO: EXPOSITION PRESS INC.

greyhounds, at one time owning 135. Later, he became editor of the authoritative *Greyhound Racing Record*.

The Captain Midnight radio producers required Burtt's scripts to stay at least five weeks ahead of the broadcasts. With shows broadcast five days a week, this meant a minimum of twenty-five shows ahead. By October 1941, Burtt had written many episodes where Captain Midnight was countering Japanese intrigue in the Pacific. Burtt had conceived the idea of having the Japanese attempt to capture the Hawaiian Islands as their first base for invading the United States, and had built a half-year series on this theme. His work was far ahead, with fifty episodes written, when Pearl Harbor was bombed on 7 December 1941. Two important things immediately impacted him from that event. First, the FBI interrogated him in connection with the Pearl Harbor attack — wherein he even had the villainous Barracuda stealing plans for Pearl Harbor in advance of the actual attack! Second, his whole story line had to be scrapped and a new series developed on a rush basis. That incident was only one prominent example out of many prophetic things that Robert Burtt originated.

Robert M. Burtt wrote an enormous amount of material, which often came from far more than daydreaming. He read and researched voraciously — then contemplated and analyzed that information, exercising his imagination and visions from there. In those 1940s days, it took many hours in Chicago's public libraries, plus borrowed books and maps that he took home and studied. Even once in a while, when his schedule was too overwhelming in writing for two shows plus raising greyhounds, he evidently borrowed story material from some other authors, too. In that respect, our war and writing hero may not have been a saint; but he still created his own greatly original work that so inspired both youths and adults, and gave all his listeners such a lift.

JIM HARMON

The present author was privileged to have known and worked with Old Time Radio's (OTR's) great champion and writer, Jim Harmon, ever since he provided audio tapes of Captain Midnight radio programs to me in the 1970s. Jim's groundbreaking OTR books, such as *Jim Harmon's Nostalgia Catalogue* and *The Great Radio Heroes*, are definitive introductions to OTR adventure programs and their radio premiums.

While there were some 1,851 Ovaltine-sponsored Captain Midnight radio broadcasts,[1] Appendix 4 of the present book shows there are only eleven surviving postwar recordings. In an effort to locate more Ovaltine-sponsored recordings from 1940-1949, Jim Harmon (in his capacity as a director of SPERDVAC) wrote a letter to Nestlé Beverages (the owner of the Ovaltine brand) in 2009. While overstating the number of Ovaltine Captain Midnight radio programs, the letter mentioned the present author's work to discover more of those recordings, and the letter read as follows:

July 20, 2009

Mr. Charlie Poesch
Finance Officer
Nestlé Beverage Division
Nestlé USA
70 6th Ave NW
Waverly, IA 50677-1601

Re: Captain Midnight Radio Program Disks/Tapes; Nestlé Case ID 16727241

Dear Mr. Poesch:
   The Society to Preserve and Encourage Radio Drama, Variety and Comedy (SPERDVAC) is the world's leading organization that conserves Old Time Radio (OTR) and encourages today's radio theatre.
   OTR researchers have recently determined Nestlé Beverages likely has received up to 2,600 OTR "Captain Midnight" programs on audio disks/tapes. Ovaltine of Villa Park, IL was the sponsor and broadcaster of the programs from Chicago during 1940-1949.
   In 2000, the Customer Service Group of Himmel Nutrition Inc. confirmed to Stephen A. Kallis, Jr. (author in 2000 of Radio's Captain Midnight — The Wartime Biography) *that Himmel had received the Captain Midnight audio disks and tapes from the Ovaltine Foods Division of Sandoz Corp., upon Himmel's acquisition of Ovaltine. There were reportedly hundreds of disks and tapes containing the original, 1940s 15-minute radio episodes.*
   On May 15, 2007, Himmel Nutrition sold its Ovaltine license to Novartis, which included the Ovaltine brand. Nestlé S.A. acquired Novartis Medical Nutrition in late 2007, which included the Ovaltine brand, and U.S. Nestlé took over Ovaltine in April 2008.

American folklore historian, Leonard Zane, contacted your Glendale, California offices and made inquiries about only tapes under the subject Case ID. But your contact knew nothing.

In the 1940s, the daytime "Captain Midnight" radio program was as popular in America as "The Lone Ranger" was at night. Since we know Himmel had the recordings, and Nestlé bought everything associated with the Ovaltine product line, SPERDVAC now respectfully requests the Nestlé group that handled the Ovaltine acquisition do a thorough search to locate these radio treasures. The recordings were apparently still at Himmel just two years ago.

Please contact me about how you might help recover these programs that remain "lost."

Sincerely,

(signed) Jim Harmon

With Jim's sharply declining health, in November of 2009, he asked me to carry on the search for the Ovaltine Captain Midnight radio recordings in his behalf, and I have since done so for SPERDVAC. The search for such recordings with Himmel, Nestlé, Novartis, and Sandoz regrettably came to naught. The search cases and investigations were closed, and so if any additional Ovaltine recordings are ever found, it appears that private collectors would be the only hope.

ENDNOTES

1 Refer to *radiopremiumexchange.com* for this tally.

1948 Secret Squadron Manual cover. Why so happy, with a Squadron P-40 going down in flames and aviators parachuting? Is the smiling aviator glad that another of his colleagues has also bailed out safely? Are the two other parachutists possibly downed aviators from enemy aircraft? PHOTOGRAPH: LEONARD ZANE

APPENDIX 2

1946-1949 Code-O-Graph Details

Captain Midnight's mechanical cipher devices, or "Code-O-Graphs," are signatures of the entire Ovaltine-sponsored series from 1940-1949. The basics of the postwar Code-O-Graphs appear during the adventures portrayed in this book.

The Code-O-Graphs were all based on Alberti Cipher Disks. Code transmission to General Reserve Squadron members was monoalphabetic substitution cipher. For longer messages, this would make the messages fairly insecure, particularly with word division. For broadcast messages, their brevity helped their security, though, because most were too short for meaningful statistical analysis.

1946 "MIRRO-FLASH" CODE-O-GRAPH AND MANUAL

The 1946 model Code-O-Graph and Secret Squadron Manual are shown in Chapter 1. As a cipher device, the 1946 model has the same tolerance problem as the 1945 "Magni-Magic" Code-O-Graph: the play in the rotor makes it possible to misalign numbers or letters, making the message a bit more difficult to decipher.

The 1946 letter-number setting key has one advantage over single-setting windows. Any letter can be set next to any number. This means there are 26 x 26 possible combinations of letters and numbers, which — as pointed out in the handbooks — equals 676 possible key combinations. However, the advantage is offset by a disadvantage: one of the letters is compromised. For instance, a ciphered message with a Master Code setting of R-13 means that whenever number 13 appears in a message, it stands for R.

The mirror in the center of the rotor is some 0.66 inches in diameter and behind about 0.04 inches of clear plastic. Such a design degrades the optical quality of the mirror. As the name "Mirro-Flash" suggests, one use of the unit is to send messages using reflected sunlight.

The 1946 Secret Squadron Manual that came with the Code-O-Graph measures 8-3/4" x 6" and is printed in vivid color. Its sixteen pages contain such displays as secret signs and signals of "The Secret Wing of the Secret Squadron"; pictures of Secret Squadron heroes and villains; and of course, displays of the Code-O-Graph and detailed instructions on how to operate it. The 1946 Code-O-Graph is the last of the badges, and the 1946 Manual is the last large-sized one. The 1947-1949 Manuals were still printed in color, but measured a pocket-size 6" x 4-3/8".

1945 and 1946 Code-O-Graph Comparison. PHOTOGRAPHS: LEONARD ZANE

1947 "WHISTLING" CODE-O-GRAPH

As seen in Chapter 3, the 1947 "Whistling" Code-O-Graph is a cipher disk mounted on the side of a police-style whistle. The rotor has a protrusion on its back that fits into a socket on the whistle's body. The circular portion of the whistle is about 1.25 inches in diameter; the rotor is about 0.94 inches, and the knob is 0.43 inches across. Side-to-side slippage is practically nonexistent, but the rotor can pop out of its socket fairly easily. Fortunately, it can also be popped back in.

1948 "MIRRO-MAGIC" CODE-O-GRAPH AND MANUAL

As with all other Code-O-Graphs since 1942, the 1948 model had been conceived by Ichabod Mudd. Unlike the cheap plastic 1947 device, this new model was to have been made completely of brass and steel. It was to be the finest, most multifunctional Code-O-Graph in *Captain Midnight's* history. Mudd's ciphering inspiration for this unit commemorated Ovaltine's Little Orphan Annie decoder of ten years before. But the 1948 "Mirro-Magic" Code-O-Graph would go well beyond that, with a big steel signal mirror (uncovered by dimming plastic) and a large secret compartment accessed by removing the back. Unfortunately, though, both Ikky and his 1947 Code-O-Graph had been captured by Ivan Shark in late 1947. So Secret Squadron Headquarters was forced to rush the new 1948 model before Ikky could oversee final engineering and construction — and there were some regrettable consequences of this.

1938 Radio Orphan Annie Decoder. PHOTOGRAPH: LEONARD ZANE

Ikky's 1948 mechanical-engineering enhancements of the Radio Orphan Annie decoder of exactly a decade earlier were excellent. But the 1948 Code-O-Graph suffered from the materials used. While the hefty aluminum control knob is very serviceable, the working innards are also made of aluminum instead of sturdy and far more reliable brass. And the back of the Code-O-Graph is made of vinyl instead of stamped

Left: Metal wheel cap with rubber O-ring. *Right:* Brass compact
PHOTOGRAPHS: FOOSE WHEELS, JTV

brass. A brass back could have had a thin, recessed rubber O-ring for friction fitting the back inside the Code-O-Graph's main body, like a metal wheel cap. Or the whole metal case could simply have been a hinged and polished brass compact. Either way, the *whole* back could have been a polished brass mirror. Even with the vinyl back, however, the secret compartment it conceals is many times the volume of that in any other Captain Midnight radio premium.

The 1948 model is the only postwar Code-O-Graph to use a single-number Master Code setting key. The two metal disks are kept in alignment by using a circle of dimples in both, to create a friction coupling. Because of the less sturdy aluminum, this proved not completely effective, and sometimes there would be slippage between the two disks. This meant that sometimes in the middle of trying to decipher a message, the setting might change, making the rest of the message unreadable. This problem never happened with the Radio Orphan Annie 1938 decoder, with its strong brass disks.

Regrettably, the red plastic back has been prone to warping and shrinkage with time, making it an increasingly poor fit over the years. As a result, many surviving 1948 Code-O-Graphs have no backs, or are sometimes even minus their mirrors. The 1948 Mirro-Magic Code-O-Graph is the last one to incorporate all metal moving parts — an ambitious but ultimately and regrettably flawed attempt to recover from the cheap 1947 model. The 1948 Secret Squadron Manual, however, once more measures 6" x 4-3/8" and has sixteen color pages, as does the 1947 Manual.

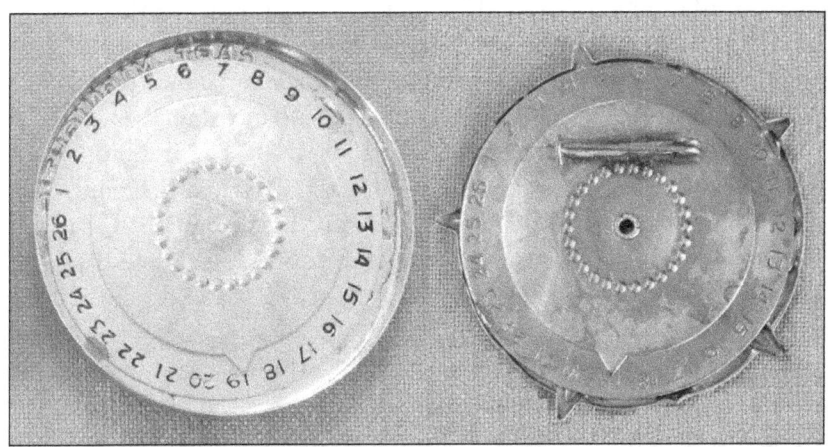

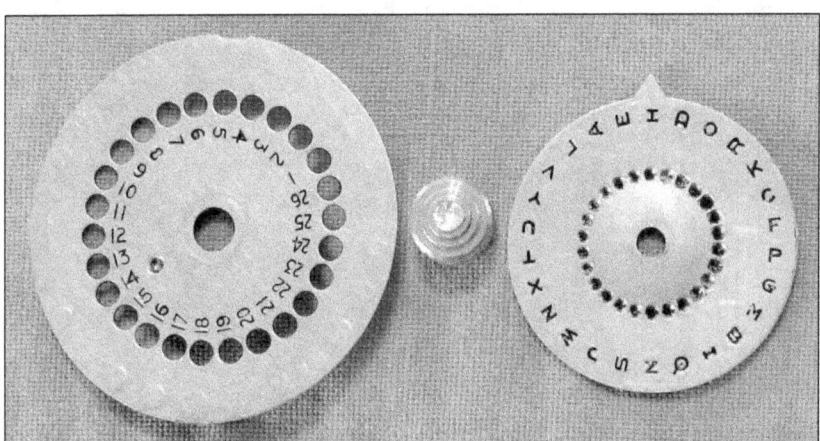

Top: Comparison between innards of Captain Midnight's 1948 Code-O-Graph and the Radio Orphan Annie 1938 Decoder. The Code-O-Graph's ample secret compartment, shown here, is the largest one ever made for any Captain Midnight radio premium. But due to Ivan Shark's capture of Ichabod Mudd in late 1947, not even the stamping dies were changed in rushing the 1948 models out. So the two ciphers are exactly the same! *Below:* 1948 Code-O-Graph numbers and letters disks. PHOTOGRAPHS: LEONARD ZANE

1949 "KEY-O-MATIC" CODE-O-GRAPH AND MANUAL

The last of the Captain Midnight Code-O-Graphs was the 1949 "Key-O-Matic." It was a compact package, some 2.125 inches long, 1.125 inches wide, and 0.217 inches thick at its main body, and 0.35 inches thick including bearing extensions. Its case was stamped brass in two snap-together pieces (as the 1948 model should have been). The 1949 model had two interlocking red plastic gears, one with a number scale, and the other with a cipher alphabet. As with its immediate predecessor, the 1949 Code-O-Graph revealed only one letter and number at a time.

As shown in Chapter 15, the built 1949 Code-O-Graph does not exactly match the design that was shown in the Manual. The mis-coordination might have indicated that Ichabod Mudd (as in 1948) had not been able to oversee final engineering and fabrication; and perhaps also because the radio program was being phased-down and prepared for cancellation.

The 1949 Master Code setting reverted to the letter-number scheme, used in all but one of the dated Code-O-Graphs. Setting the Master Code was achieved through use of a clutch mechanism at the gear with the number scale. A small, two-tined key was designed to fit into tiny rectangular openings above the number-scale gear. Inserting the key depressed the gear, disengaging it so the cipher-alphabet gear could be repositioned. For instance, in choosing Master Code B-17, the gears

1949 "Key-O-Matic" innards. PHOTOGRAPH: LEONARD ZANE

would be turned so that the 17 appeared in the number window. Then the key would disengage the gear, so the cipher alphabet gear could be moved. This gear would be adjusted so the letter B would appear in the window. The key would then be withdrawn so the gears could engage in the new setting. Because of the way Master Code settings were achieved, the unit was named the "Key-O-Matic" Code-O-Graph.

The 1949 Code-O-Graph's clutch mechanism consisted of a small, brass spring-plate that fit under the number gear. Because of the interlocking gears, setting slippages or alignment ambiguities were designed to be prevented. Once again, however — as had been problematical with the 1948 Code-O-Graph — the problem was materials. The metal clutch plate was made of brass, rather than more sturdy and reliable spring-steel. So the brass clutch sometimes lost its curvature, and stayed too flat from pressing the key against the flat plastic gear on top of it. When that happened, the clutch plate failed to keep the two gears engaged. Fixing this failure required popping open the Code-O-Graph, which had been intended to remain sealed. But opening the Code-O-Graph, and then re-bending the brass plate and resealing the device could be done simply enough, even if a recurring nuisance with repeated Code-O-Graph usage. Really dedicated Secret Squadron members could also perform more permanent field maintenance, by replacing the brass plate with one made of appropriately bent spring-steel or stainless steel.

The Key-O-Matic was intended to be the most thoroughly engineered of the Code-O-Graph family, and yet it still suffered from design problems in addition to materials used. First of all, the tiny key was very easy to lose, and so designers didn't want the Code-O-Graph to be so secure that nothing else could be substituted for a lost key. This presented a dilemma, because a simplistic key design defeated security altogether. The Manual that came with the Key-O-Matic suggested the owner should put the key on a loop of string as a measure for keeping it secure. In fact, more than half the Code-O-Graph owners lost their keys within a couple of months, and less than twenty percent of the surviving units have their keys.

Another security issue was the snap-together brass case. It could not only be snapped apart for field maintenance, it could also be opened to set the Master Code without a key. A cross-cut paper clip, or other stiff two-pronged metal probe that could fit in the key slots, could also be easily substituted for a key. This remedied the lost key problem, but once again completely defeated security. So the whole key approach that was used was itself a major design flaw. Based on that particular approach, for which there was no easy cure, the key became an object of ridicule even among young kids. Perhaps some entirely different method of Code-O-Graph design should have been engineered for setting the Master Code. Perhaps even a combination lock, with the sequence shown in the Manual, and also easily remembered, could have been engineered rather than using a key at all. Again — as in 1948 — perhaps Ichabod Mudd was not able to complete the engineering as he had with other Code-O-Graphs. Another possibility is that Ikky had engineered the key and clutch approach simply to prevent slippage of disk alignment — which had been so problematical with the 1948 Code-O-Graph — *and not as a security device at all.* Therefore, broadcasts may have wrongly promoted the security idea that had never been Ikky's original intent.

The size of the 1949 Code-O-Graph made it an excellent pocket item, with nothing sharp and protruding to catch on fabric. Finally, two more disturbing portents about the Secret Squadron's future were indicated when the 1949 Code-O-Graph was issued. First, the Manual that came with the Code-O-Graph had been reduced to eight pages. This was only half the number that always came in years before (regardless of booklet dimensions), and this time the pages weren't even numbered, as had always been done before. Second, page 3 of the manual quoted Ivan Shark as saying, "We must capture a Code-O-Graph or all is lost." *Enthusiasts never expected Ivan Shark to declare the end of his dreams upon simply lacking a new Code-O-Graph!* Of course, as Jim Harmon had pointed out, all Ivan Shark ever had to do to get a Code-O-Graph was to send in his Ovaltine label like everybody else.

At any rate, these various portents gave Secret Squadron listeners strong suspicions that the days of radio's Captain Midnight were coming to an end, which did happen by year-end.

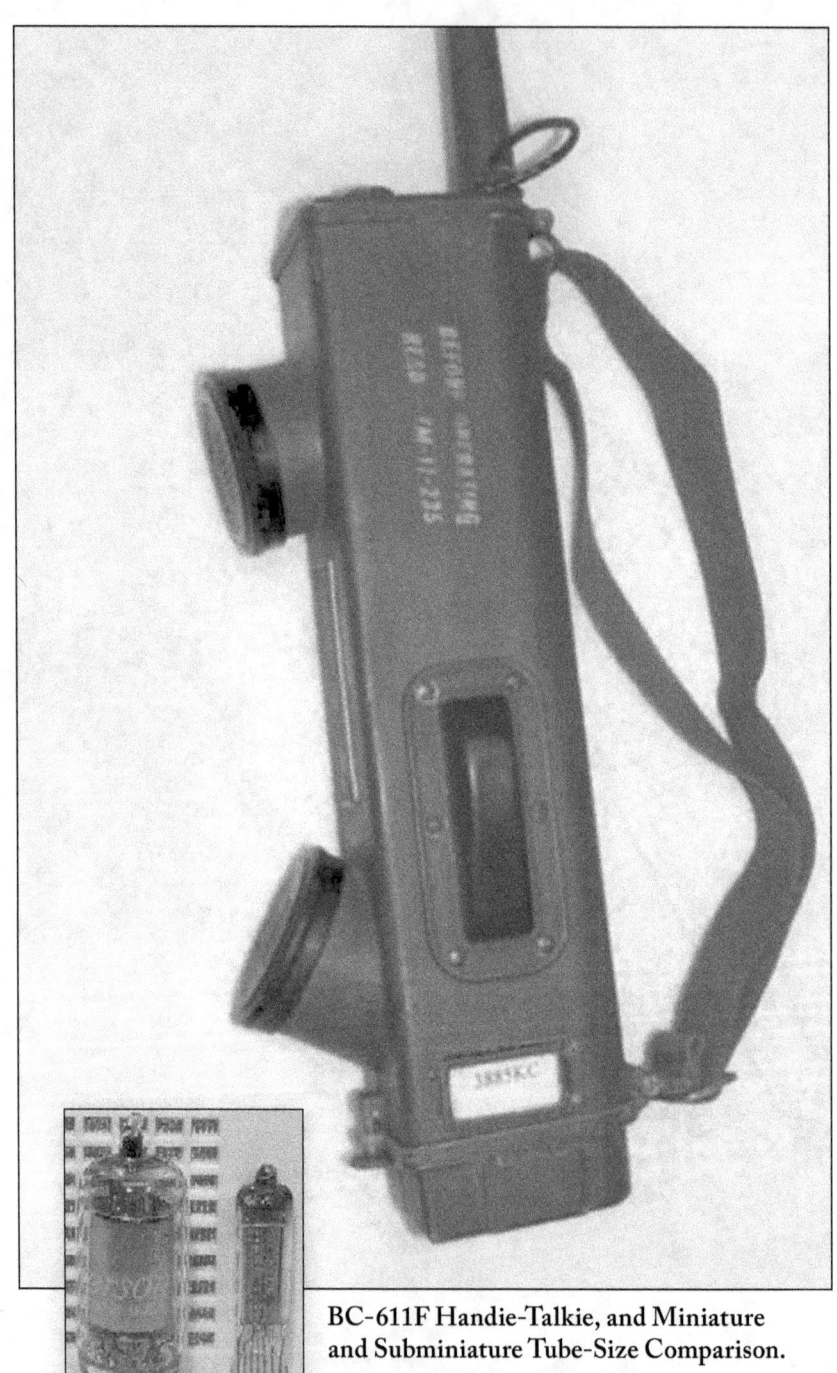

BC-611F Handie-Talkie, and Miniature and Subminiature Tube-Size Comparison.
PHOTOGRAPH: LEONARD ZANE

APPENDIX 3

Captain Midnight's Pocket Locators

1942 MODEL POCKET LOCATOR

Captain Midnight's first Pocket Locator (PL) was introduced in 1942, in collaboration with Sir Allen Brundage of the British Secret Service. (See Pages 187-188 of *Radio's Captain Midnight — The Wartime Biography*, by Stephen A. Kallis, Jr.)

The PL was an extremely miniaturized two-way radio used throughout the rest of the radio show's years. The device was designed to send and receive flashing-light signals, and was a daydream of many of the millions of radio listeners. The Pocket Locator was a conceptual, perhaps theoretically achievable, ultra-miniature AM transceiver that functioned like a 1940s Handie-Talkie. (See photo on the facing page.)

ENGINEERING AND COMPONENTS

A retro-designed, vacuum-tube Pocket Locator has been developed that for the first time satisfies the vintage criteria of the radio program. Research into this technology was done by Leonard Zane and the late 1940s radio engineer Bob Kelley (W6TCE). Data and components of the most miniaturized 1940s radio technology were provided to electronics engineer Tooru Kawabata, who engineered and built both working 1942- and 1946-model Pocket Locators. See the circuit diagram. To also accommodate dot-dash audio capability, an optional audio circuit was added for plugging in a high-impedance ceramic earphone. (At least the *Captain Midnight* radio program had not ruled out such private audio capability as another possible PL feature.)

Operating at 1/4 Watt output-power like the BC-611, the ultra-miniature Pocket Locator nonetheless outperforms the Handie-Talkie—having a range of 4.4 miles on level ground, and 50-100 miles from atop a 3,000-foot mountain. This is compared to a BC-611 range of one mile over level ground, three miles over ocean, and considerably more from a mountaintop. As with the BC-611, the PL is turned on and off by extending and collapsing its 30-inch, completely self-contained and telescoping antenna. Contrasted with the 7-tube Pocket Locator, the 1940s BC-611 has five miniature-size tubes, a considerably shorter range, measures 15-3/4" x 5-3/8" x 3-5/8", and weighs 5.45 pounds (3.85 lbs + 0.5 lbs for a 1.5 V filament battery + 1.1 lbs for a 103.5 V plate battery). The PL weighs 13.2 oz, or 15% of the BC-611, and the BC-611's physical volume of 306.88 cubic inches is over *twenty times* the Pocket Locator's case volume of 15.07 cubic inches!

A small winged-clock emblem (the Secret Squadron insignia) is affixed on the Pocket Locator's front. An internal, green indicating light (tube V5) shines through the emblem's clear center portion for dot-dash flashing in receiver mode. Most of the case insides are taken up by two 1.5 V "A" (size AA) batteries and two 45 V "B" batteries (Eveready No. 415).

Advanced Circuitry. The most advanced, top-secret communications electronics were necessary for 1940s Pocket Locators. This enabled Secret Squadron and other engineers to achieve the smallest miniaturization ever of vacuum-tube transceivers, by utilizing *subminiature* vacuum tubes and very finely wound miniature coils and transformers.

For comprehensive engineering details on reconstructing the 1942 Pocket Locator, **see the article,** "Building Captain Midnight's 1942 'Pocket Locator,'" in the October 2010 issue of *CQ* Magazine. The article, by Leonard Zane and Tooru Kawabata, starts on Page 22.

CAPTAIN MIDNIGHT'S POCKET LOCATORS

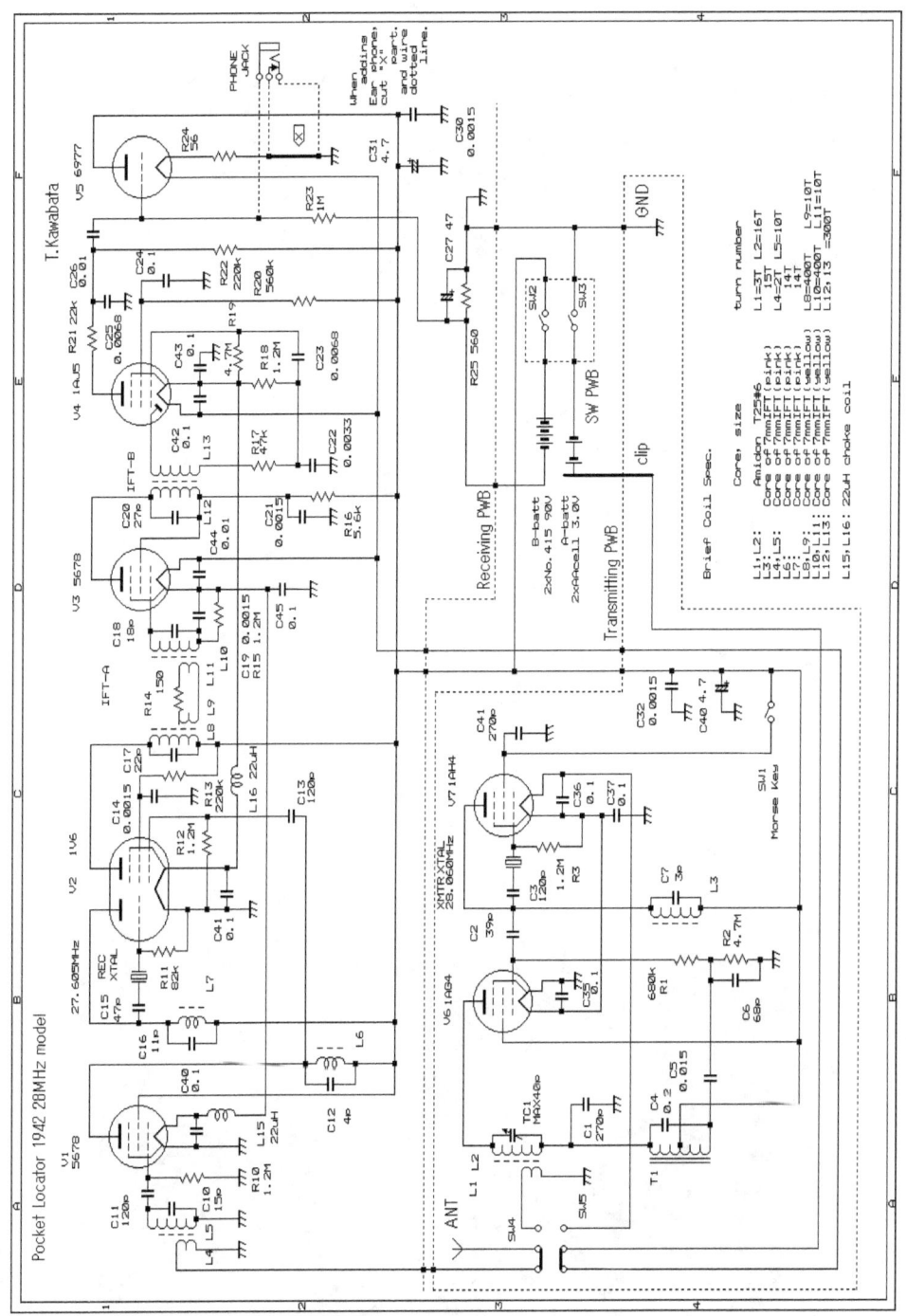

1942 Pocket Locator Circuit. PHOTOGRAPH: TOORU KAWABATA

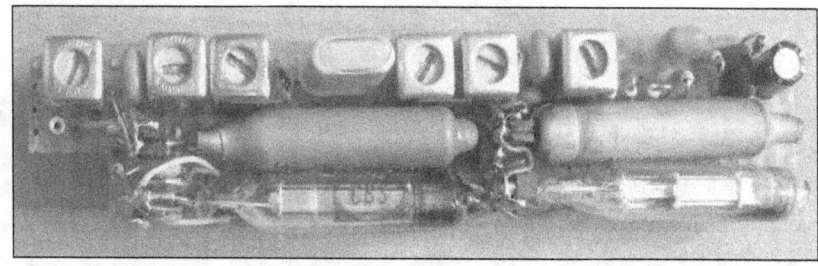

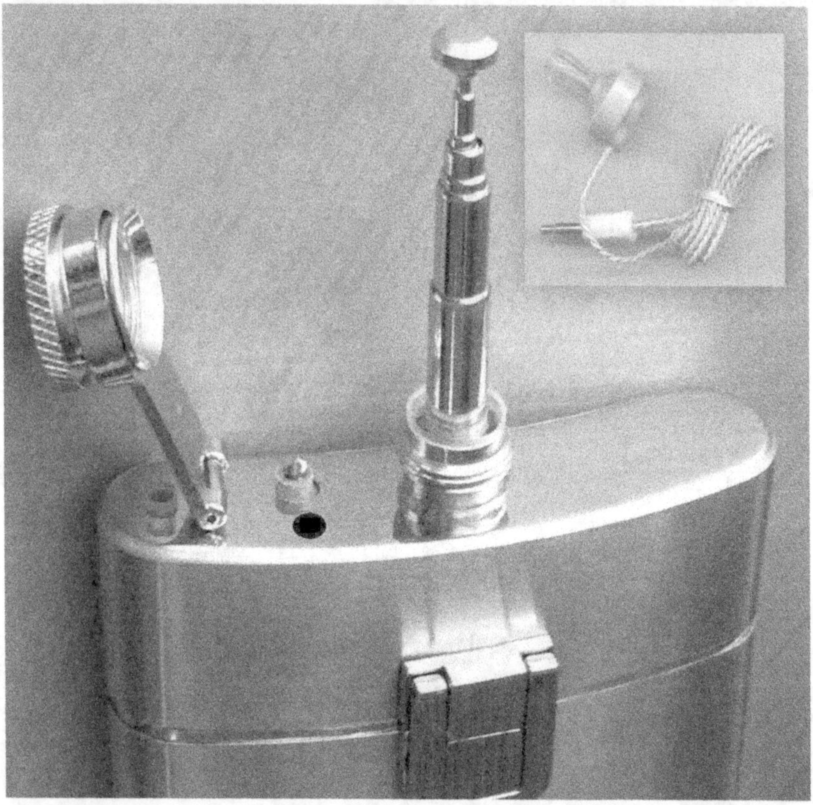

CAPTAIN MIDNIGHT'S POCKET LOCATORS 309

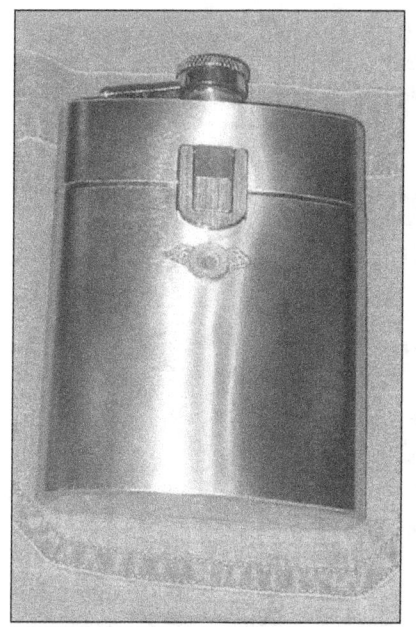
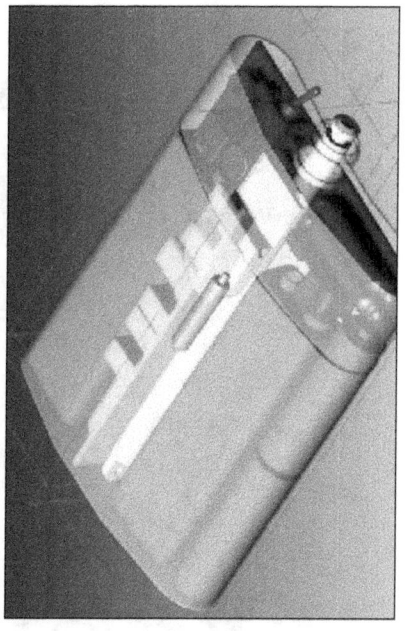
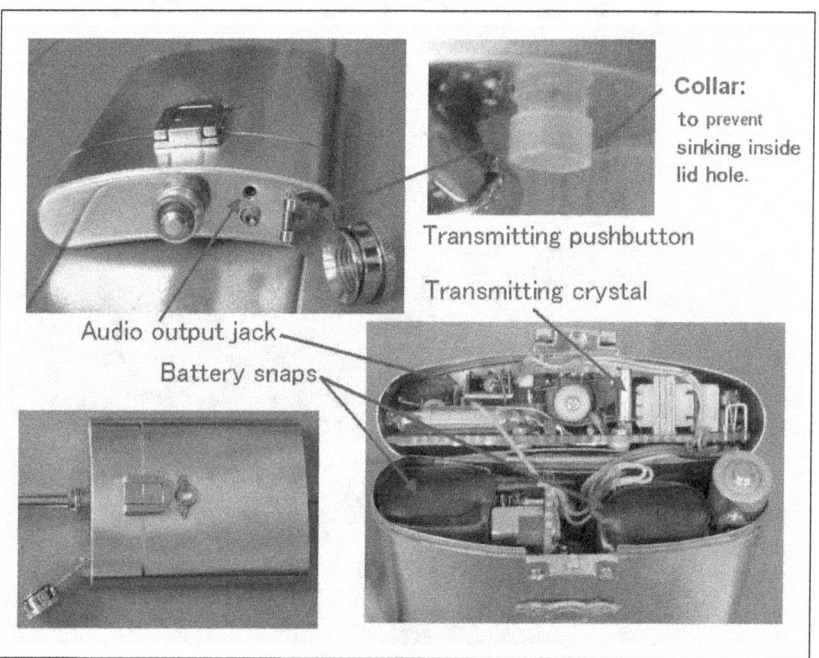

Above: 1942 Pocket Locator. Bottom: 1942 Pocket Locator details, including optional audio output jack. *Opposite:* 1942 PL Transmitter and PL Receiver Electronics. 1942 PL cap-strap key, transmitter button, transfer switch, and 30-inch telescoping antenna. PHOTOGRAPHS: LEONARD ZANE, TOORU KAWABATA

Above: Front cover of a specially created, 16-page 1942 Pocket Locator Manual for users, and measures 4-3/8" x 6". *Below:* 1942 Pocket Locator and Jeff Kirk P-51. CREATION AND PHOTOGRAPH: LEONARD ZANE; PHOTOGRAPH: LEONARD ZANE AND JEFF KIRK

1946 MODEL POCKET LOCATOR

Electronic engineering of the 1946 Pocket Locator is similar to the 1942 model, with:

1940s-vintage subminiature tubes, including a green indicating-light tube.
Ferrite-core and hand-wound coils.
90V tube-plate voltage and 1.5V tube-filament voltage.
4.4 mile minimum range over land.

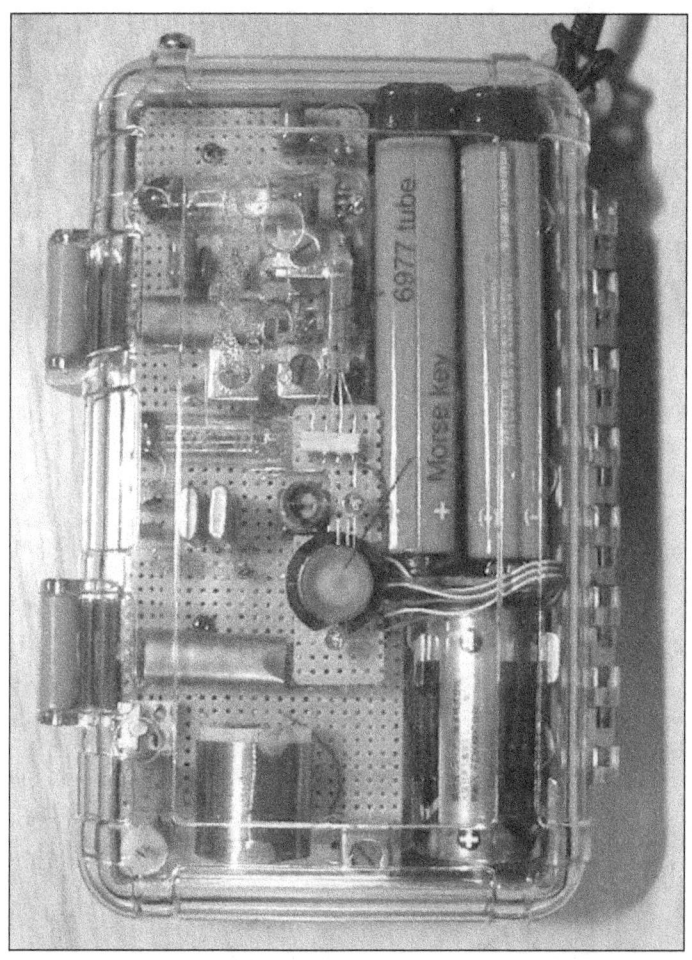

1946 Pocket Locator Electronics. PHOTOGRAPH: TOORU KAWABATA

APPENDIX 4

Surviving Post-War Recordings

As of this writing, audio recordings of *Captain Midnight* post-war radio programs that are known to survive are listed below.

PROGRAM	DATE
The Double Cross	*46.08.14*
The Man with the Missing Finger	*47.02.11*
The Slave Smugglers	*47.03.12*
The Map of Mystery	*47.04.07*
The Stolen Star	*47.05.14*
The Jewels of the Queen of Sheba	*48.03.26*
The Return of Ivan Shark / The Cave Men Attack	*49.01.04*
The Return of Ivan Shark	*49.01.10*
The Devil on Ice	*49.02.04*
The Phantom Rustlers	*May 1949*
The Flying Ruby (30 minutes)	*49.09.20*

APPENDIX 5

"The Land That Time Forgot"

(1) The original *Captain Midnight* scripting for "The Return of Ivan Shark" adventure serial had the villainous Shark go to what he called "The Land Which (or That) Time Forgot." The scripting also described creatures on that Land which included: dinosaurs, ichthyosaurs, horses, pterodactyls, saber-tooth tigers, mammoths, and also a small tribe of immensely strong and brutish Neanderthal people! Such disparate species mixtures were blatant emulations of the Edgar Rice Burroughs *Caprona* or *Caspak* series of novels. In order to avoid copying, and also to simplify the hodge-podge of animal species throughout numerous geological epochs, the present book's account of "The Return of Ivan Shark" serial confines exotic species to dinosaurs and Neanderthals (or perhaps hominid species similar to Neanderthals or *Homo erectus*). The described isolated and long-stable environmental conditions account for the survival of at least some types of dinosaurs. Neanderthals — or some species that physically resembled them — would somehow have reached "The Land That Time Forgot," during the much later Stone Age, and then remained isolated there.

(2) The 1918 novel, *The Land That Time Forgot*, by Edgar Rice Burroughs portrayed the mythical South Atlantic isle of "Caprona," and also called "Caspak" by the hominid natives there. In or near Antarctica, this large island was ringed all around by steep cliffs that sheltered a warm lake and tropical valley — the inside of a huge and ancient volcanic crater. Over countless ages, the massive crater had maintained warmth in which life could flourish amid the frozen Antarctic. The same was true of the Captain Midnight adventure.

(3) Edgar Rice Burroughs named his Caprona from an island ostensibly reported in 1721 by a fictitious Italian explorer named "Caproni." The island is somewhere in or near Antarctica (its precise location was never identified), and over time Caproni's report slipped into obscurity and neglect.

(4) Caprona contained a huge crater lake, fed by streams as well as a subterranean river flowing into the sea. This is also true of the Captain Midnight adventure.

(5) Burroughs called the isle "The Land That Time Forgot" ("B-TLTTF"). This was because within its sheltered valley and lake throve dinosaurs and fierce mammals, and even Neanderthal and *Homo sapiens* hominids. All fauna were of widely disparate geologic epochs, compared to those found elsewhere on earth, and yet all lived together at the same time in Caprona. The human castaways in Caprona were attacked by a horde of beast men, and the humans took one as prisoner: Ahm, a Neanderthal.

(6) Burroughs offered his own evolutionary speculations of how such an amalgam of species and epochs could exist side by side.

(7) In Burroughs's B-TLTTF: the farther south and west were the habitats of reptiles of different epochs than experienced on the rest of the planet.

CAPRONA / CASPAK — *The People That Time Forgot*, by Edgar Rice Burroughs — published in 1924, Chapters 4-7:

(1) "Coming up from the beginning, the Caspakian passes, during a single existence, through the various stages of evolution, or at least many of them, through which the human race has passed during the countless ages…as we traveled northward…the land had gradually risen until we were now several hundred feet above the level of the inland sea…the Galus [humans] country was still higher and considerably colder, which accounted for the scarcity of reptiles.

"The change in form and kinds of the lower animals was even more marked than the evolutionary stages of man. The diminutive ecca, or small horse, became a rough-coated and sturdy little pony in the Kro-lu country. I saw a greater number of small lions and tigers, though many of the huge ones still persisted, while the woolly mammoth was more in evidence…

Out of Time's Abyss, by Edgar Rice Burroughs, 1924 (last Caspak novel) Chapter 2 passages:

(1) "...why he had seen no babes or children among the Caspakian tribes with which he had come in contact; why each more northerly tribe evinced a higher state of development than those south of them; why each tribe included individuals ranging in physical and mental characteristics from the highest of the next lower race to the lowest of the next higher, and why the women of each tribe immersed themselves in the morning for an hour or more in the warm pools near which the habitations of their people always were located; and, too, he discovered why those pools were almost immune from the attacks of carnivorous animals and reptiles.

(2) Non-Galu or Non-*Homo sapiens* female hominids deposit eggs in warm-water pools.

"The egg from which [fauna] first developed into tadpole form was deposited, with millions of others, in one of the warm pools and with it a poisonous serum that the carnivora instinctively shunned. Down the warm stream from the pool floated the countless billions of eggs and tadpoles, developing as they drifted slowly toward the sea. Some became tadpoles in the pool, some in the sluggish stream and some not until they reached the great inland sea. In the next stage they became fishes or reptiles...and in this form, always developing, they swam far to the south, where, amid the rank and teeming jungles, some of them evolved into amphibians. Always there were those whose development stopped at the first stage, others whose development ceased when they became reptiles, while by far the greater proportion formed the food supply of the ravenous creatures of the deep.

(3) "Few indeed were those that eventually developed into baboons and then apes, which was considered by Caspakians the real beginning of evolution. From the egg, then, the individual developed slowly into a higher form, just as the frog's egg develops through various stages from a fish with gills to a frog with lungs. With that thought in mind Bradley discovered that it was not difficult to believe in the possibility of such a scheme — there was nothing new in it.

(4) "From the ape the individual, if it survived, slowly developed into the lowest order of man — the Alu — and then by degrees to Bo-lu, Sto-lu, Band-lu, Kro-lu and finally Galu. And in each stage countless millions of other eggs were deposited in the warm pools of the various races and floated down to the great sea to go through a similar process of evolution outside the womb as develops our own young within; but in Caspak the scheme is much more inclusive, for it combines not only individual development but the evolution of species and genera. If an egg survives it goes through all the stages of development that man has passed through during the unthinkable eons since life first moved upon the earth's face.

(5) "The final stage — that which the Galus have almost attained and for which all hope — is cos-ata-lu, which literally, means no-egg-man, or one who is born directly as are the young of the outer world of mammals. Some of the Galus produce cos-ata-lu and cos-ata-lo both; the Weiroos only cos-ata-lu — in other words all Wieroos are born male, and so they prey upon the Galus for their women and sometimes capture and torture the Galu men who are cos-ata-lu in an endeavor to learn the secret which they believe will give them unlimited power over all other denizens of Caspak.

(6) "No Wieroos come up from the beginning — all are born of the Wieroo fathers and Galu mothers who are cos-ata-lo, and there are very few of the latter owing to the long and precarious stages of development. Seven generations of the same ancestor must come up from the beginning before a cos-ata-lu child may be born; and when one considers the frightful dangers that surround the vital spark from the moment it leaves the warm pool where it has been deposited to float down to the sea amid the voracious creatures that swarm the surface and the deeps and the almost equally unthinkable trials of its effort to survive after it once becomes a land animal and starts northward through the horrors of the Caspakian jungles and forests, it is plainly a wonder that even a single babe has ever been born to a Galu woman.

(7) "Seven cycles it requires before the seventh Galu can complete the seventh danger-infested circle since its first Galu ancestor achieved the state of Galu. For ages before, the ancestors of this first

Galu may have developed from a Band-lu or Bo-lu egg without ever once completing the whole circle — that is from a Galu egg, back to a fully developed Galu.

(8) *Chapter 3:* "Do the reptiles come up the river into the city?" asked Bradley.

"The water is too cold — they never leave the warm water of the great pool," replied An-Tak.

The 1947 Captain Midnight adventure "Death Deals a Diamond" explains that Ivan Shark's discovered "'Island of the Lost People' is located somewhere in Antarctica." This Island is somewhere south of the South Shetland Islands. A volcano eruption eventually devastates the Island, destroying all the Lost People with it. Shark and Fury flee in a helicopter, escaping from Captain Midnight and the Secret Squadron. As with Burroughs's Caprona, this remote South Atlantic part of the world is a likely location for Captain Midnight's identically-named adventure of "The Land That Time Forgot." Ivan Shark already had extensive operations in the area, and could be expected to have a hide-out on another nearby island that also contained prehistoric or exotic species.

Perhaps the Captain Midnight broadcasts could not risk emulating the Burroughs *Caspak* series too closely, for possible legal infringement reasons, so the Secret Squadron events were first set in the patently incredible location of New Mexico. This stark absurdity, alone (later changed), arouses strong suspicions on the legal aspects.

An analytical surmise is that the *Captain Midnight* radio program experienced considerable story confusion, as explained earlier in Chapter 15. Did author Robert M. Burtt take a hiatus from work in late 1948 — or even threaten to quit — and thus leave the show's producers with a shortage of material? Did the producers and other writers therefore hurriedly and chaotically cobble a story together? There appears to be no record or way of telling. But the story did clearly draw upon the Burroughs Caprona/Caspak model, as the basis for the crater world in the "The Return of Ivan Shark" adventure. The present book attempts to resolve much of the chaos, and also to minimize the imitation and make the adventure more tractable and credible.

Index

Numbers in italics refer to photographs

A-26, Douglas Bomber 138, 139, 158, 217-218
Abyssinia 163-164, 166, 170-173, 175, 188, 190-192
Addis Ababa 163-164, 166, 169, 172-173, 182
Adirondack(s) 126, 128, 130
Albright, Stuart James 15, 19
Allosaurus 236, 236-238, 242
Ape-men (or Cavemen or Neanderthal) 232-233, 240-243, 248-253, 255, 315-316
Arctic Airbase X-V-1 257-258, 260, 267, 272-274
Arkon 232, 237, 240
Arnold, Mayor 65-66
Atom Bomb 20, 234, 270-279
Aztec Sun-God Ring 56-57, *57-58*, 61-63, *62-63*
B-1 bomber *158*
B-36 bomber 150-151, *151*
Ballard, Sheriff 21
Barko, Peter 214-215, 220
Bartestan 248, 277
Bascombe 22-23
Bearden, Thomas E. 36
Bell X-1 *148*, 161
Bergmann, Lyle G. 11, 17
Bhutan 30, 269, 278
Bicycle Contest 228
Birch, Paul, as a Major Steele type 35, *35*
Black Gulch 20, 22
Black Opal 14

Blackjack, The 217-219, 222, 226
Blattoff, Gregory 90-93
Boka-Yin 34
Boris 258
Bottle of Ink, The 214-215, 219-220
Bubastis, Asar 163-166, 169-176, 182-184, 187
Bueno Nuevo Ranch 208
Buenos Aires 25, 27
Burroughs, Edgar Rice 13, 161, 251, 255, 315-317, 319
Burtt, Robert 9, 11-13, 16-17, 40, 158, 185, 189, 255, 279-280, 289-291, 319
Butterfield, Brock 152-153
Cairo 166, 169, 172, 174
Calder, Saskatchewan 275
Calla Lilies 165, 170, 184, 186, 189
Canon, Captain Midnight Radio 14
Captain Midnight's Identity 15
Captain Midnight's Mystery Craft 286
Caraguela, Kingdom of 198-200, 202-203
Carrier, Baby Flattop or Jeep 40-42, *41*, 44-45
Castellani 53-55
Chandrapore, Prince of 110
Chinatown, Los Angeles 218, *218*, 219
Circleville 205
Code-O-Graph 9, 12, 19, 30-34, *33*, 75-77, *77-78*, 86, 90, 107, 128, 141-143, 145, 149, *149*, 183-184, 217, 238, 241-246, *246, 247*, 276, *276, 294, 299, 300*, 295-302
Code-O-Graph 1945 *21*, 30, 33, 295-296, *296*

321

Code-O-Graph 1946 9, *13*, 32-34, *33*, 76, 295-296, *296*
Code-O-Graph 1947 77-78, *77-78*, 86, 107, 142, 145, 296-297, 299
Code-O-Graph 1948 *149*, 217, 238, 241-243, 286, 297-302, *294, 299*
Code-O-Graph 1949 241-247, *246-247*, 276, *276*, 295, 300-302, *300*
Colt, Dr. 116-117
Compact and wheel cap 298, *298*
Congo 39-42, 44-45
Cooley, Marcus 260-262, 267-269, 271, 273
Coster, "Pop" 115-117
Countess of Hertel 73-74, 77-78
Crossfield, Scott 160
D'Arcy, Robert 104-108
Dagger, The 216-217, 222, 226
Daniels, Dick 67-70
Death Valley 215, 223, 225-226
Dent, Lester 13
Dinosaur(s) *234-235*, 236, *236-237, 239*, 242, 252-253, 315-316
Disintegration ray 22, 24-32, 34, 36, 39, 261, 264, 269-274, 277-278
Doc Savage 13
Eagle's Nest 126-129
East African Rift 164, 185
Epsilon ray 80-82, 85
Ethiopia 185, *185*
Everglades 75
F-86 fighter *148*, 150, 267, 275
Fabian 39
Fang 20, *26*
Fat Man bomb (also Atom bomb) 276, *276*
Fingers 58-61
Fletcher 105, 108-109
Floating Pleasure Palace 68
Florida Straits 79, 82, 85
Flying Ruby 14, 313
Flying Saucer 257-260, 264, 266-272, *270*, 275
Fog Bombs 201-202
Fordham, Commissioner 66-70
Foreign VIP 264-267, 272
Fu Manchu's daughter 20
Fuchs, Colonel 20
Garcia, Colonel 23
Gardo 20-21, 23-24, *26*, 28, 101, 107-109, 118-119, 122-124, 127-128, 136-138, 140, 143-144, 150, 237, 239-243, 247, 249-252, 279, *279*

Gas, coma producing 118, 120-130
General John Hubbard 56-58, 60-62, 65-70
General Percival Drake Cromwell 196, 198-200, 202
George (butler) 262-263
Georgetown 103
Gibbs 60
Gibson, Walter B. 11
Glaser, Dr. 20-22, 24-27, 30-31
Gleason 105
Gobi, Ito 152, 155-157, 159, 161, 275
Gobi Jet (B-1 bomber-type) *158*
Gonzales 47-48, 50
Gorilla, White 164-165, 184
Grainger, Sharon *49*
Grant City 22
Grant, Maxwell 11
Gray Coat 124
Gray Eagle 39
Great Dane, "Lightning" 124-125, 130, 231
Habib, Dr. 50-51
Harmon, Barbara 5
Harmon, Jim 3, 5, 9, 16, *16*, 284, 289, 291-293, 302
Helicopter, Jet 195-197, 200
Hodges, Professor 75-77, 80
Hogarth, Lieutenant John 257
Holiday Beach 7, 73-74, 76-77
Hollywood 138, 140, 142-144, 214-215, 219-220
Holmes, Sherlock 130
Hooda-Wijis 168, 170, 176
Hooke, Harry 258-264, 267-269, 271-273
Hyena 45
Iguanodon 233-234, *234*, 248, 251
Jet Jackson 15
Kallis, Stephen A., Jr. 5, 12-13, 15, 17, 26, 33, 37, 225, 252, 292, 305
Kebra Nagast 191
Kelly, Lyle William 17. 19, 21, 24, 44-45, 101, 103
Kent, Eleanor 104-105, 108-109
Khala, Professor 247, 257-261, 264-275, 277-280
Khala, Sara 271-273, 278-280
Knife, The 28, 32
Kramer, Fritz 124
Kredl, Magda 259-260, 262-263

INDEX

Land That (Which) Time Forgot 150, 231, 234, 238, 241, 251, *251*, 253-255, 315-316, 319
Laser 31
Lone Ranger 11, 293
Los Angeles 30, 142, 218-220
Lu Sing 125
Madagascar 195
Madero, Juan 47
Malloy, Jimmy 65
Malone 56-57
Manhattan 87, 109-110, 124, 220
Marchula Province 27-33
Marchula Temple 32-33
Mark, Chief 168-171, 176
Marks, Sherman *159*
Martin PBM-3D Flying Boat *112*
Mashowgan 222-223
Masterling, Carl 215, 218-219
Matthews, Professor 47-48, 50-55
Maxon, Andrew 166-167, 169, 172-174, 177-182, 184-187, 231, 239-241, 248-249
Mayfield, Cora Lee 259-260, 263, 267-269, 271
Mayfield, Mr. 259-260
Megalosaurus and Othnielia 236, *237*
Mendoza 47-48
Middleton, Fort 121-124, 128
Middleton, Lake 121
Miguel, Señor 197-202
Monko 39
Moon Gardens 105
Moore, Tom 173, *183*, 184
Moore, Wilfred 11
Moriarty, Professor 130
Mu 232, 237, 240-242
Mudd, Ichabod "Ikky" 19-20, 22-23, 25-26, 28-29, 32-34, 40, 42, 44-45, 49-51, 54-55, 57-61, 66-70, 74-77, 79-82, 86-90, 92-96, 99, 104-106, 108-111, 116- 122, 124-128, 130, 133-144, 147, 151, 153-159, *159*, 161, 163, 166, 169-170, 173-174, 177-182, 184-187, 197-201, 208, 213, 216-217, 219-220, 223-227, 231, 235, 241, 243, 245-246, 249-250, 257-258, 260, 267, 270-275, 279, 297-300, 302
Mueller, Manfred 24, 27-32, 270, 278
Muroc 147, 161

Neanderthals 232-233, 240, 243, 248-249, 253, 255, 315-316
Needle, The 216-220, 222, 226, 228
Neutron beam 31
New Orleans 66, 104-109
New York City 126-128, 135-136, 214-215, 219-220
Nosterium 77, 80-81
Orphan Annie Decoder 297-299, *297*
Orr, Angeline, as Joyce Ryan *81*
Ovaltine 5, 11-12, 14-15, 17, 19, *115-116*, 126, 184, 228, 291-293, 295, 297, 302
P-38 fighter 139, *139*, 158, 284
P-40 two-seat *78*, 224, *225*, 226, 228, *294*
P-46 fighter 216-218, *217*
P-80 fighter *21*, 24
Pacific City 7, 57-58, 62, 65, 67-70
Paloff 124
Panka 30-31, 34, 47
Particle Beam technology 24, 30, 36, 270, 278
Partridge, Richard 216
Paso del Carmona 226
Patagonia 22, 24
Patro 151, 155, 159
Consolidated PBY-5 Amphibian *252*
Peg-legged doctor 206-207, 209-210
Phantom Rustlers 14, 313
Pharaoh, The See Bubastis, Asar
Pit of the Reptiles 28
Pitcairn, Professor (aka Sodman) 116-122, 124-126, 128, 130, 240
Plateau, Hidden 164-166, 170, 176, 182-186, *185*, 188-191
Plutonia, S.S. 196-197
Pocket Locator 9, 21-22, 30-32, 42-43, *43*, 45, 51, 54, 60-61, 67-68, 75-76, 86, 90, 106, 118, 120, 128, 136-137, 141-143, 155-158, 166, 172-174, 186, 198, 216-217, 221, 227, 234, 239, 242, 251, 258-259, 275, 305-307, *307*, *309-311*
Polinoff, Peter 151-155
Port Flemington 213-215
Poseidon Undersea Resort 79
Prentiss, Ed *100*
Preston, Andrew H. 22-23
Printing Initial Ring 192-193, *192, 193*
Pterodactyl or Pterosaur 238-239, *239*, 242, 251-252, 254, 315
Pyramid 163, 165, 184-188, 190-191

Queen Anne liner 195, 200
Ramsay, Chuck 19-23, 25-26, 28-34, 37, 40, 44-45, 48, 51-54, 57-61, 66-70, 75-77, 79-82, 86-90, 93-97, 99, 104-106, 109-111, 116-129, 133, 136-137, 139, 140-144, 147, 151, 153-155, 157-159, 167, 169-170, 173-182, 184-187, 196-201, 208, 213, 216-220, 223-224, 226-228, 231, 241-243, 250, 257-258, 260-262, 267, 270, 272-275, 279
Ray, Disintegration See Disintegration ray
Ray, Epsilon See Epsilon ray
Reynolds, Ann 48-51
Riggs 110
Rio Del Barrio 227
"Rocket Plane" 21-22, 25, 27, 34-35, 89, 94, 269, 278
Rock, The 214-217, 219, 222-226
Ryan, Joyce 19-20, 22-23, 25-26, 28-29, 31-34, 39-40, 42, 44-45, 48, 51-54, 57-61, 65-70, 74-82, 86-88, 90, 93-96, 99-100, 104-106, 109-111, 116-130, 133, 136-137, 139, 141-144, 147, 151, 153-159, 161, 166-167, 169-170, 173-174, 177-179, 184-188, 190, 197-199, 201, 213, 215-220, 223-224, 226-228, 231, 238, 241, 243, 250, 257-261, 264, 267-268, 270-275, 279
Salvin, Dr. 74-82, 85
San Luis 24
Satan's Cay 78-81
Secret 4 214-216, 218-220, 222-223, 225, 228
Shadow, The 11
Shake-Up Mug 115, *116*
Shark, Fury 20, 26, *26*, 48-51, *49*, 53-56, 58-59, 88-89, 97, 99, 101, 109-112, 115-119, 121-124, 127-129, 135-138, 140-142, 144, 150, 231, 233, 240-242, 247, *247*, 250-252, 254, 279, 319
Shark, Ivan 9, 16, 20-30, *26*, 32-34, 47-56, 58-62, 87-91, 93-94, 96-97, 99, 101, 103-104, 106-112, 115, 117-125, 127-130, 133-144, 150, 158, 228, 231-233, 235-245, 247-255, *247*, 269-270, 278-280, 297, 299
Shah Tanz 28, 34
Sheba 9, 163, 165-167, 169, 171, 173, 175-177, 179-181, 183-185, 187-193, 313
Sheba Ring 165-166, 170-171, *171*, 175-176, 180-183, 188-189, *189*, 190-192
Shunosaurus and *Kaijiangosaurus* 238, *238*

Silver Streak Rollercoaster 73
Simien Mountain Range *185*
Sing Lo 215, 218-221
Skyrocket, Douglas D-558-II 160-161, *160*, 196, 275
Sodman, Professor (aka Pitcairn) 119-122, 124-126, 128, 130, 240
Solomon, King 165, 175, 188-191
South Shetland Islands 96, 231, 233, 319
Spy-Scope 126-127, *126*, 129
Stalin, Joseph 272
Star of Mazaruni 104-106, 108-109, 111-112
Steele, Major Barry 19, 22, 35, *35*, 37, 39, 48-49, 73, 80, 93, 95-96, 101, 115, 117-119, 121, 125, 128, 130, 140, 144, 147, 158, 160, 163, 196-197, 200, 213, 221-222, 228, 234, 242-246, 257-258, 261-262, 272-275, 278-279
Stegosaurus 233, *235*
Stormy Petrel 111
Strategic Defense Initiative (SDI) 31
Striker, Fran 11
Sword, The 213-217, 219-228
Sykes, Harry 22-25, 32-33, 270
Tanz 27-28, 31-32
Tesla Dome 270
Tesla Globe 36, 270
Tesla Shield 270
Tesla, Nikola 30, 36, 270
Tivoli Hotel 74, 76
Torpedo (henchman) 65, 67-68, 70
Tseday 164
Tumbusch, Tom 15
Tuttle, Joe 104-105
Uncle Ben 74-77
Uranium 127-128, 133-134, 147, 149-151
Valencia, S.S. 110
Vizcay 52-54, 56
Wander Company 5, 11, 35, 49, 100
Westmont Hotel 109-110
Whisper 51-53, 56
Wister, Pete 205-207
Wolfgang 173, 179
Y-64 22-24
YB-49 Flying Wing 286
Yates 101, 103, 105
Yeager, Chuck 161
Yellow Spider 14
Yucatan 103-105

Zane, Leonard 15-16, 21, 33, 35, 44, 57-58,
  62, 63, 77, 78, 107, 112, 116, 149, 160, 171,
  189, 192, 193, 218, 225, 246, 247, 270, 276,
  283, *284*, 286, 293, 294, 296, 297, 299, 300,
  304-306, 309, 310
Zanskar Mountains 27, 30-32, 34, 269-270
Zawata 40-42, 44

Bear Manor Media

Classic Cinema.
Timeless TV.
Retro Radio.

WWW.BEARMANORMEDIA.COM

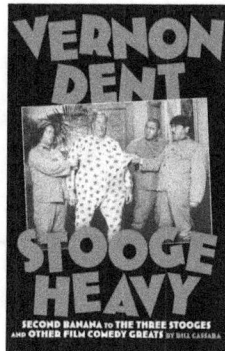

www.ingramcontent.com/pod-product-compliance
Lightning Source LLC
Chambersburg PA
CBHW050335230426
43663CB00010B/1866